The Atlanta Youth Murders and the Politics of Race

The Elmer H. Johnson and Carol Holmes Johnson
Series in Criminology

The Atlanta Youth Murders and the Politics of Race /

Bernard D. Headley

Southern Illinois University Press

Carbondale and Edwardsville

"I Hear the Children Singing" by Forrest Hairston © 1981 Bertam Music
Company and Forgen Music Co. All rights controlled and administered by
EMI April Music Inc. (ASCAP) on behalf of Jobete Music Co., Inc. All rights
reserved. International copyright secured. Used by permission.

Library of Congress Cataloging-in-Publication Data

Headley, Bernard D.
The Atlanta youth murders and the politics of race / Bernard Headley.
    p.   cm.   — (The Elmer H. Johnson and Carol Holmes Johnson series
in criminology)
Includes bibliographical references (p.   ) and index.
1. Serial murders—Georgia—Atlanta. 2. Afro-American youth—Crimes
against—Georgia—Atlanta. 3. Murder—Investigation—Georgia—Atlanta.
4. Trials (Murder)—Georgia—Atlanta. 5. Williams, Wayne Bertram.
6. Racism—Georgia—Atlanta. 7. Atlanta (Ga.)—Race relations.
I. Title. II. Series.
HV6534.A7H43 1998
364.15'23'09758231—dc21   97-52169
ISBN 0-8093-2214-5 (cloth : alk. paper)   CIP

For sons Bernie, Julian, and Zachary

and mother and father, Eleanor and Allan,

who completely understand the endless pain

of suddenly losing to tragic death a young child

Is there a playground up in Heaven for shorties?

I hear the children singing
But amidst the melody
I hear a tiny voice cry . . .

Why did we grow up
What were we thinking of
Why didn't we stay young
So in love
I hear the children singing
But I hear a tiny voice cry

Why can't I find love
Like we knew
When we were young at play
Will I ever hear the music
Will my sadness stay
I'm only a child
A tiny voice cries

I long to hear the melody
The one we danced to yesterday
When we used to laugh sadness away
I hear the children singing
But amidst the melody
I hear a tiny voice cry
My love remains young
And memories linger on
So a grown-up like me
Is forever a child

I hear the children singing
But amidst the melody
I hear a tiny voice cry.

> —Forrest Hairston,
> "I Hear the Children Singing"

The murders keep us apart. And slowly, with implacable repetition, the deaths of children like a corrosive acid eat away at the connections that bind our community. The city that marched and wept and sang together when Martin Luther King was slain . . . is threatened with a loss of hope.

> —Theodore W. Jennings Jr.,
> *Christian Century*

Contents

Illustrations

Tables

Photographs

Preface

Between late 1980 and early 1982, Atlanta, Georgia, was the focus of much national and international attention. Being the center of attention was, of course, nothing new to Atlanta. The city always seemed bent on finding ways to mesmerize the nation with its spirited stubbornness, its exuberant triumphalism. A case in point was the determination with which Atlantans undertook the arduous chore of rebuilding their city after General William Tecumseh Sherman and his Union army set fire to it in 1864, as part of Sherman's merciless Union offensive to bring a seditious South to its knees. So daunting had seemed the task of a city literally having to rise from its ashes after the Civil War that a good part of the Atlanta story has been likened to the flight of the mythical phoenix.

More recent episodes in that story were more flamboyant. In 1990, under the command of its business elite, upstart Atlanta, city of Bubba, stealthily edged out arguably better situated, more "world-class" locales to host the Centennial Olympics in 1996. And back in 1961, after weeks of holding the nation in beguiling suspense, the city, again under the firm hand of an economic center regime, peacefully integrated its all-white public schools—a feat city fathers had managed to accomplish amidst widespread fears of anarchy, which racist hotheads, who were then quite numerous and rather well worked up over the whole doggone issue of Negro rights, had planned to massively carry out.

But Atlanta's being the center of attention between 1980 and 1982 scarcely had anything to do with a war. Nor with athletic competition. Nor with civil or racial unrest—not in the conventional sense, anyway. What brought Atlanta to the forefront this time around did, however, have everything to do with race—although not because of the usual struggle over racial rights. Issues of that sort had reached a kind of understood, if not altogether quiet, *modus vivendi* with the election in 1973 of the city's first black mayor and the appointment four years earlier of three blacks to the city's board of education.

Race, nonetheless, was the dominant theme in this latest saga. A string of mysterious slayings and disappearances of black city youngsters had once again brought Atlanta into the spotlight. All told, between summer 1979 and spring

1981, twenty-eight males and two females were reported missing. Twenty-nine murdered bodies were eventually found in various locations in and around the city. The seemingly shameless slaughter of mostly children would become seared in the nation's consciousness as the "Atlanta tragedy."

Many in the black community contended that the Atlanta murders were racially motivated and that perhaps the Ku Klux Klan or some other dreaded white hate group was directly responsible. But the arrest, trial, and conviction of a young black man for the murder of two adult males—whose names had appeared on a special police task force list of the missing and the dead—brought an abrupt end to this latest Atlanta story.

This book relates some of the complex political and ideological issues of race and class that dominated the story of the Atlanta youth murders. Necessary space is given to various law enforcement, criminalistic, and legal details. The aim is not, however, to remake or to refute the case against Wayne B. Williams, the black man who state authorities said was responsible for most, if not all, the Atlanta murders—although I do believe that Williams was guilty.

No startling new information, or information not in the public record, is presented here. The objective instead is to give context to interweaving details, to chronologically recall (with C. Wright Mills's "sociological imagination") a set of dynamic events, and to describe what happened when the legitimate social constructions, collective fears, and conventional wisdoms of ordinary people came up against larger political, economic, and legal realities—and the world of science and scientific orthodoxies.

This book has been some seventeen years in the making. It has therefore undergone numerous respites and surges, rethinking and rewrites. Throughout the entire painstaking process, however, one underlying item has remained constant: the work's methodological frame of reference.

In my attempt to put into perspective a story about terrible incidents and the diverse reactions they evoked, I tried to follow an approach that the German sociologist Max Weber called *verstehen*. The term, as used by Weber and by social philosophers of the neo-Kantian school, means understanding from within by means of empathy, intuition, imagination. As formulated by Weber and developed by later theorists (e.g., Adler and Adler 1987; Outhwaite 1976; Truzzi 1974), *verstehen* "denotes a process of subjective interpretation on the part of the social researcher, a degree of sympathetic understanding between researcher and subjects . . . , whereby the researcher comes in part to share in the situated meanings and experiences of those under scrutiny" (Ferrell 1997, 10).

In the spring of 1980, research assistants and I were conducting the standard survey-type study of respondent opinions, attitudes, and assessments of crime in their Atlanta neighborhoods. Funded by the National Institute of Justice (NIJ) and conducted out of Atlanta University, the study was of representative samples of residents living on the city's poor black south side. It wasn't long before we learned that folks there were less interested in responding to our survey items than in talking about the disappearances and killings of several poor black neighborhood children, which they sensed had been taking place with some regularity over the previous seven or more months.

City authorities weren't listening, folks complained. Instead, the mayor and Atlanta police higher-ups seemed bent on treating the crimes in a routine manner. Some in the black political authority structure, folks were saying, had even chastised them for insinuating that there might be something dreadfully different and perhaps racially ominous in the mysterious occurrences.

I soon realized two things. First, if we as a research team expected to complete our well-designed (at least so we thought) survey instruments, we had better plan to spend a lot more time listening to the alarming concern that folks "out there" were voicing in the street, around dinner tables, and on their verandahs regarding the safety of their children. Second, as social scientists we needed to understand and record an unfolding complex social drama—one that could not be deciphered by sophisticated quantitative research designs.

I therefore vowed not only to listen to what folks most wanted to discuss but also to actively seek out the opinions of grassroots people who were beginning to organize various oppositionist struggles around the murders and disappearances.

I attended neighborhood meetings (tape recorder always close by), participated in various panel discussions and workshops, and chatted at length with people who were particularly close to the unfolding tragedy—among them Grace Davis, of Atlanta Women Against Crime, and Camille Bell, mother of murdered Yusef Bell and a founder of the Committee to Stop Children's Murders. This all culminated with my attending court most days during the trial of Wayne Williams. Twice, when his courtroom was packed beyond seating capacity, Judge Clarence Cooper kindly allowed me to view the proceedings from his chambers on his closed-circuit television.

But I also wanted to take into account, and perhaps try to place within a broader dialectic, the divergent view of what was happening in Atlanta as expressed by (a) black representatives of the Atlanta racial state and (b) Atlanta's white power structure. Mayor Maynard Jackson refused my request for an interview, stating flatly that "anything" he would "possibly have to say to me on the subject [was] already on the public record." And although Commissioner Lee Brown initially seemed favorably disposed to whatever it was he thought I was trying to do—and to my work generally as a sociologist of crime—he later became unsupportive. Willing to talk to me, however, were Fulton County commissioner (and former Atlanta commissioner of public safety) A. Reginald Eaves, former city councilman and United Youth Adult Conference founder Arthur Langford, and state legislator and longtime civil rights gadfly Hosea Williams—who, at the time we spoke, had nothing but time on his hands, since he was serving a stint in the DeKalb County jail for a traffic conviction.

Not quite as accessible were members of the city's white power guard—although the venerated Ivan Allen Jr., a former mayor and scion of the Ivan Allen Company, could have gone on for days bragging to me about his "city on the hill," whose racial success story he helped create. I also did find, in great abundance, readings of local white elite orthodoxies on things like crime—and on the string of slayings—in the local corporate media and in documents graciously made available to me by the Atlanta Historical Society.

In-depth, detailed information relative to the official investigation I retrieved by examining more than 10,000 pages of documentation in the FBI's files on the Atlanta youth murders and disappearances—files I obtained under Congress's Freedom of Information Act. A passing interview with John Glover, FBI Special Agent in Charge for Atlanta, gave added insights. My objective in all this was to use a combination of disparate sources to gain a better (and perhaps "critical") understanding of a set of occurrences that were as variegated as they were terrifying.

Acknowledgments

Along the tedious road to completing an unwieldy project, one invariably accumulates untold debts. So in using this space to thank folks who encouraged and assisted me over the years it has taken me to complete this book, I'm fully aware that I'm running the risk of failing to name others.

Julius Debro, then with Atlanta University, and Winifred Reed of the National Institute of Justice were directly responsible for bringing me to Atlanta in early 1980 to work on an unrelated NIJ-funded project. Research assistants Nancy Brown and Cindy Spence critiqued and challenged some of my early and clouded ideas about what at the time I thought was happening in Atlanta. Attorney Harold Spence generously gave me talking time he could have spent lucratively.

A Senior Fulbright Scholar award gave me a year off from regular teaching obligations at Northeastern Illinois University (NEIU) in Chicago so I could haul my many boxes of documents off to Jamaica, where I was able to devote needed blocks of time to prolonged thought and writing. And grants from the Atlanta Historical Society and NEIU's Committee on Organized Research made possible the extensive—and expensive—travels that a research project like this normally entails.

Several of my NEIU criminal justice students worked long and hard doing necessary library research. They summarized newspaper and journal articles, and checked and doublechecked references, dates, names, places, and countless other details. I thank them all: Loretta Hawkins, Daniel Jasinski, Eneida Garcia, John Oliver, Marko Urukalo, Bonnie Vesely, Arika Foster, and Kevin Jackson.

Colleague Dan Stern was always passing on serviceable stories and articles. Three technically accomplished people, Allison Forker, Shirley Trude, and Tim Karczewski, were immensely helpful with a variety of final-production tasks. Connie Woods of the photo department of the *Atlanta Journal and Constitution* was forbearing with my insistent requests. My wife, Althea, picked up on endnote and bibliographic information that was incomplete or didn't correspond with text. And copy editor Elaine Otto made sure I was achieving clarity and precision.

I also thank the outside readers of the book while it was in manuscript form for their generous reviews—as well as for their helpful criticisms, which I believe improved the quality of the work. I especially appreciated suggestions and technical corrections by Clark Atlanta University's Richard Allen Morton.

Finally, I thank Southern Illinois University Press and Editorial Director James Simmons for deciding to publish a work that others resisted because it defied easy classification, and for the honor bestowed on me by the inclusion of this book in the Press's Elmer H. Johnson and Carol Holmes Johnson Series in Criminology.

The Atlanta Youth Murders
and the Politics of Race

Prologue

The question was inevitable. If you lived or worked anywhere in or near Atlanta, Georgia, between summer 1980 and early 1982, as I did, and you happened to have ventured out somewhere beyond the vicinity, sooner or later someone was bound to ask, "Just what's that I hear happening in your city?" Somehow you got the feeling that the question had nothing to do with mundane, day-to-day goings on. Neither did it have anything to do with political shenanigans, or with some public official's peccadillo, or with the state of the city's much-heralded economy. Right away you knew the subject to which you were being (sometimes abruptly) directed.

When asked by someone living in America who happened to be black, the question would take on a special kind of urgency that was typically filled with righteous indignation, revealing even more directly an unspoken substance. Hence you were likely to get, "Just what in God's name is happening *down there* in Atlanta?" The explicit reference to "down there," you just knew, had everything to do with a certain political and cultural construction of place. Only when traveling outside the United States were you likely to get a more definitive framing of the same essential question: "What's happening with *those kids* in Atlanta?"

Simply put, "those kids in Atlanta," fourteen of them, ages seven through fourteen, all from the city's black poor and working class, their families in various stages of economic and familial distress, had disappeared between July 1979 and September 1980. Most had disappeared while running errands for a parent or neighbor or while engaged in sundry activities they thought would improve their impoverished circumstances—activities the mainstream media would disparagingly call "hustling."[1]

Days, weeks, and even months had passed before nine bodies were found, dumped at various locations, often at considerable distance from the victims' homes or where they were last seen alive. The police were saying they had no good leads in any of the cases, and with the whereabouts of the remaining five still unknown, hope had given way to fear—fear that more bodies would soon be turning up. Still more frightening was the dreadful possibility that other black children would be snatched.

More disappearances and more killings did, indeed, follow. Between October 1980 and May 1981, sixteen additional black males were reported missing. Their bodies turned up all over metropolitan Atlanta. Altogether, by May 1981 law enforcement authorities were investigating twenty-nine apparent serial slayings and searching for one missing boy. Atlanta was struck by an ongoing tragedy.

Twenty-seven of the dead were males ranging in ages from nine to their late twenties. The other two were girls, eight and twelve years old. Victims had been strangled, shot, stabbed, or clubbed. For other cases the authorities couldn't agree on cause of death, so they listed it as "unknown" or "undetermined." The killer or killers left no "calling card," nothing to indicate his or her twisted motive, nothing to reveal, even vaguely, his or her identity.

A special investigative task force was formed in the summer of 1980. Although under the control and command of Atlanta police, the task force's work was multijurisdictional. Its only function was to investigate the string of mysterious killings and disappearances. More than 100 local law enforcement officers were assigned to the task force during one heightened period. Its work, which ended up being directed in a major and politically problematic way by the FBI, centered on the lengthening list of missing and murdered Atlanta youngsters (see appendix A). In nearly all reflexive conversations about the Atlanta tragedy, it was this list to which folks kept referring.

Some discussions of the Atlanta murders inexorably would lead to inflated discourses on race in America.[2] Many feared the resurgence of a virulent brand of white racism, saying that the murders were part of a bigger organized plot to "kill off" black youngsters, if not all black people. Some believed, for instance, that the murders were the handiwork of white supremacist groups like the Ku Klux Klan. Others held that an agency of the federal government was carrying out the killings. Or that one government agency, like the FBI, had been in conspiracy with another—say, the Central Intelligence Agency (CIA) or the Atlanta-based Centers for Disease Control (CDC)—to commit mass murder. Or worst of all, the FBI and CIA were in diabolical cahoots *with* the Klan to murder black male children, whose bodies the CDC needed for penile experimentation.[3] Such "urban legends" were never confirmed, of course. But they became staples of the Atlanta story (Turner 1993; Best 1987).

Other conversations about what was happening in Atlanta took on grander themes. Segments of the Far Left saw the murders as tied to forces of institutionalized international oppression. The disappearance and killing of black American children—and a spate of juxtapositional killings of immigrant black West Indian youth in Great Britain, allegedly by the British police—could be linked in broader historical dialectic to, and were consequences of, the right-wing, reactionary politics of the Ronald Reagan/Margaret Thatcher era. The Atlanta murders were therefore manifestations of racial oppression everywhere: from "tiny villages in rural Mexico," where Atlanta came to "symbolize the vicious, imperialist system," to New York City and apartheid Johannesburg (Revolutionary Communist Party n.d.).

All these varied and "loose-cannon" charges prompted *Washington Post* columnist Carl Rowan (1981) to plead for blacks[4] in Atlanta and around the nation to "cool it." "Those deaths in Atlanta," he wrote, "may have nothing—or everything—to do with racism, but it is foolish to prejudge." These are times of "economic and political gloom" in America, he went on, "so feelings of racial paranoia come easily."

Rowan's plea must have fallen on a collective deaf ear. By early 1981, with the strange disappearances and killings in Atlanta continuing, the discourse on what was happening there widened. Elements of Atlanta's respectable black middle class—the city's acclaimed black bourgeoisie—had valiantly struggled in the early stages of the ordeal to deflect a particular cultural and ideological construction of the terrible incidents. They, along with others in Atlanta's liberal white ruling class, saw as simply dangerous to Atlanta's thirty-odd years of racial progress any attempt to attach racial meanings to mysteriously slain youngsters who happened to be black (Headley 1986). So in March 1981 local civil rights leaders began calling on *all* Atlantans, but particularly Atlantans who valued progress, to unite behind a black city administration and a longtime ally in times of racial trouble: the U.S. Department of Justice. Working together, they proclaimed, "We can solve this thing."

But, at the other end of the city's black social-class divide, a rallying of a different sort persisted. Poor black Atlantans—especially those whose children were murdered—insisted on framing the slayings as crimes of ominous origins, to which black officialdom had turned a naive, if not blind, eye. Thus, under the aegis of a grassroots organization, the Committee to Stop Children's Murders, formed by mothers of the slain and missing children, the city's black poor amassed in street demonstrations *against* Atlanta's black-run city hall.

Some within the city's black poor and working class were saying they had little faith in official law enforcement; they didn't think the Atlanta police would ever be able to apprehend the Atlanta killer or killers. So neighborhood men began patrolling their streets with homemade weapons—mostly baseball bats, bricks, sticks, and occasionally licensed firearms.

Atlanta authorities were, of course, not amused. Bats and bricks did not exactly fit into their conception of community policing. Rather, the patrols, city officials adamantly insisted, were under the control of "troublemakers," whose activities were pure vigilantism.

At its peak, the Atlanta tragedy was given prime coverage in all the national news media, led by the *Atlanta Journal* and the *Atlanta Constitution*. But the publishers of prominent outside newspapers, including the *New York Times* and the *Washington Post*, also assigned reporters full-time to the Atlanta story. So, too, did the national news magazines *Time* and *Newsweek*. United Press International assigned three reporters to cover the story. The *Wall Street Journal*, the *Christian Science Monitor*, and the *Catholic Reporter* offered regular updates. And *McCall's, Us, People, Esquire*, and the *New York Times Sunday Magazine* ran human-interest pieces. An article in the journal *Science* briefed readers on some of the tragedy's more recondite details. And renowned author James Baldwin wrote a feature for *Playboy*—a piece he would essentially reproduce as a thin volume, which turned out to be not much more than a far-flung, disassociated polemic (Baldwin 1985).

The nation's three major commercial television networks devoted prime news time to what was happening in Atlanta. On days when there was a particularly dramatic development, or "turn," in the case, all three networks' evening news programs would lead with the item. Twice the tragedy was featured on ABC's *20/20*. And serious, in-depth news programs like PBS's *MacNeil/Lehrer Report* and ABC's *Nightline* devoted considerable air time to the deepening mystery in Atlanta. (CBS later would give the nation, in an all-important May 1985 rating sweeps, *Atlanta Child Murders*, a two-part "docudrama"—which, because of its factual inaccuracies and feckless piety, would bring down the unrelenting wrath of the Atlanta establishment.)

Journalists from Canada, Africa, Latin America, and Europe came to cover what was happening in Atlanta. One Brazilian Sunday TV documentary, shown in March 1981 on the nation's most popular program, was called *Terror in Atlanta*. The program showed Atlanta police cruisers racing around the city, shrouded bodies on stretchers, and empty swings in a city park. And in March 1981, the country's largest news weekly, *Veja*, devoted a full page to Atlanta's "Terror in the Ghetto."

In May 1981, an unlikely series of events began unfolding. Weeks earlier, the bodies of five black Atlanta males had been fished out of the muddy Chattahoochee River, over which the Jackson Parkway bridge crossed. A FBI-initiated stakeout had been positioned under the bridge and on the roadway leading to it. In the predawn hours of Friday, May 22, 1981, an Atlanta police cadet heard a "loud splash." Glancing up at the bridge, he saw a slowly moving car. He radioed others in the surveillance team, who stopped the driver. This led to the arrest of Wayne Bertram Williams, a twenty-three-year-old self-proclaimed talent scout, for the murder of twenty-seven-year-old Nathaniel Cater.

In February 1982, a mostly black jury convicted Williams for the murder of Cater and one other young black man. The jury had heard expert testimony linking Williams in a chain of circumstantial evidence to the murder of the two men and that of several other Atlanta victims. Almost immediately after Williams was pronounced guilty, Atlanta's commissioner of public safety announced that Atlanta police were "closing the books" on the string of youth murders. Wayne Williams was thus officially declared Atlanta's mystery killer, the feared "black heart man"[5] who had haunted the city's streets for almost two years. There was much more to the story, however.

1

A City Too Busy to Hate?

Atlanta—"the city too busy to hate"—opened up racially before the rest of the South, and the move paid off in prosperity. It was good business to be the good guy. National corporations, convinced that Atlanta would avoid the ugly confrontations that have scarred so many Southern cities, flocked in. Restaurants thrived, hotels and office buildings sprang up, artists quit going North, big-time entertainers paid visits and major league sports came to stay.

     —*Nation*, December 23, 1968

Atlanta's economic success story reached its high-water mark in the 1960s, a decade that brought the city unprecedented growth. Less than a generation or so earlier, Atlanta would have been considered just another backwater Deep South town. That perception would no longer hold true by the late 1950s, when, after implementation of a "Plan of Improvement," the population of the greater Atlanta metropolitan area reached one million. The plan, moreover, allowed Atlanta to annex some one hundred thousand new citizens and expand from 37 to 118 square miles.

So impressive was Atlanta's economic growth in the 1960s that an irritating smugness prevailed within white elite circles, the depth of which was revealed in an October 1965 special Sunday supplement in the *Atlanta Journal and Constitution*, entitled "What Atlanta's Prosperity Means to You." The piece described Atlanta as "a city on the move, the capital of Dixie, envied by outsiders, cherished by insiders."

> The one unmistakable imprint that Atlanta leaves with visitors is her vibrant personality with an unemployment level unmatched anywhere in the nation. Indeed, the number of unemployed in the thriving metropolis is so few that it would be actually impossible to lower the percentage.
>
> The business pulse of the sprawling metropolitan area throbs at a healthy rhythm as new firms re-locate or open branches and a new permanent resident is added to the population at the rate of one every 16 minutes—24 hours a day, 365 days a year (*AJ&C* 1965, 1).

Playing the role of city booster was, of course, nothing new to the *Atlanta Journal and Constitution*. It was a responsibility given by founding publisher and post–Civil War "New South" advocate Henry Woodfin Grady. But, schmaltz aside, Atlanta was the economic envy of the nation. Some 26,000 jobs were created there each year between 1962 and 1966. The number of people engaged in nonagricultural wage and salary employment at the end of 1967 was 533,800, the highest of any city in the entire Southeast. Atlanta's unemployment rate stood between 1.7 and 2.3 percent, well below the national rate of 4 percent (*AJ&C* 1965, 1). In fact, the city's unemployment rate was consistently the lowest in the nation. Because unemployment was low, wages were high.

Atlanta's commercial and business elite had, in the 1960s, glowingly built on a tradition of civicism and an aggressive pro-business ideology. That tradition went all the way back to the city's hosting of the region's three "great" industrial expositions in the late 1800s.[1] The same themes of "systematic and organized promotion" which had brought the expositions to Atlanta would explain the city's modern growth and development, according to Atlanta chroniclers Dana White and Timothy Crimmins (1978).

By the mid-1960s Atlanta had become the economic giant and cultural-entertainment capital of the Southeast. The city also was the regional center for finance, transportation (Atlanta's original claim to fame),[2] manufacturing, commerce, tourism, and conventioneering—all of which city fathers had accomplished by urban renewal and redevelopment, which involved demolishing old buildings and entire neighborhoods.

Architect-developer John Portman opened the giant Peachtree Center, a megastructure covering dozens of acres that formed Atlanta's downtown spine. Architectural observers would refer to structures like Peachtree Center—with their complex of offices, hotels, and shopping malls—as mini cities, or "mixed-use developments" (MXDs). The seven-story lobby of the Peachtree Plaza Hotel (inside Peachtree Center), with its mirrored tower and gigantic circle of columns plunging into the lake below, was hailed by critics on opening day as a "Star Wars of a place." Also opened for business in the 1960s were a $13 million Memorial Arts Center (the only one in the nation housing all the visual and performing arts under one roof), a $10 million Civic Center with a 4,600-seat auditorium and 70,000 square feet of exhibition hall, and an $18 million professional sports stadium seating 57,000 for football and 51,400 for baseball. Acquisition of the Atlanta Braves, a baseball team, and of the Atlanta Falcons, a National Football League expansion team, added to the city's stature as a major league sports city.

Permits granted for new construction in 1967 exceeded $1 billion, $187 million of which was for nonresidential construction. Between 1961 and 1967, 101 office buildings and 36 hotels and motels were either built or expanded, and 144 manufacturing plants and 176 warehouses had relocated to the Atlanta metropolitan area. Retail sales reached $2.3 billion. Bank clearings totaled $42.6 billion, and per capita annual income stood at an all-time high of $3,500, a figure that was significantly greater than the national average of $2,900 (Driskell 1964; *National Geographic* 1969).

Atlanta's economic success story continued into the early years of the 1970s, despite a nationwide recession starting in 1973. But federal employment helped sustain economic growth. In addition to being home to two major military bases, the Centers for Disease Control, and a federal penitentiary, Atlanta and its immediate environs became Washington's principal regional headquarters metropole. Forty thousand federal government employees and a payroll in excess of $305 million circulated in and around the city in 1970. At the end of the 1970s Atlanta had "the largest concentration of federal agencies outside of Washington, D.C., of any city in the country" (Rice 1983, 42).

A promotional piece by the Adair Mortgage Company (1976) boasted that Atlanta "surged into the decade of the 1970s riding a wave of expansion, filled with a sense of movement and growth and life, seeking in a way its own identity, its own character, as the powerful new urban giant of the Southeast."

Opened for business in the early 1970s was another MXD, the Omni International Atlanta, which was erected on air rights above railroad switching yards. And built right next to the Omni were the city's 18,000-seat coliseum and the World Congress Center. Management of both the Omni and Peachtree Center wanted to establish "beachheads" of a renovated society within the chaos of the older city. When the Omni opened, for instance, the *New York Times* gushed that the suburban couple could "ice skate, dine, go to a movie, meditate, get chased by a witch, shop, get their hair done, and drink on a lily pad without once going out of doors where the undesirables might be" (Schlefer 1982, 38).

In their efforts to keep "undesirables" out of their safe and ordered world, management of both the Omni and Peachtree Center erected walls, physical and legal. Inside the sole pedestrian entrance to the Omni, discreet signs warned, "Persons under eighteen years old must be accompanied by an adult." That, management figured, would stop a few black teenagers trying to get in from the adjacent Vine City ghetto area.

In 1972 Atlanta was rated among the eleven most prosperous cities in the nation (Rice 1983). And before the end of the decade, the city would be home to seven Fortune 500 manufacturing companies, including Coca-Cola. Eight Fortune 500 service firms also would set up headquarters in Atlanta: Cox Communications, Genuine Parts, Citizens and Southern Georgia, First Atlanta, Trust Company of Georgia, Delta Airlines, Continental Telecom, and Southern Company.

The city also would reap abundantly from the transactions of

- 434 of the top 500 industrial firms,
- 74 of the 100 largest diversified service companies,
- 29 of the 100 largest commercial banking companies,
- 43 of the 100 largest diversified financial companies,
- 46 of the 50 largest life insurance companies,
- 36 of the 50 largest retailing companies,
- 36 of the 50 largest transportation companies, and
- 10 of the 50 largest utility companies. (Atlanta Chamber of Commerce 1981, 1984)

Twenty-five percent of these firms were internationally owned, reflecting, in the ever-glowing words of the Atlanta Chamber of Commerce, "Atlanta's growing importance as a worldwide marketplace" and the "next great international city."

Atlanta's tourism and convention business also increased during most of the 1970s. In 1965 convention delegates spent $26 million in the city; in 1975 they spent more than $400 million. The sales figure for eating and drinking places in 1970 was $577 million; five years later it climbed to $2 billion (Rice 1983, 39). By the late 1970s, according to a story in the *Wall Street Journal*, the city, although about the size of Cleveland, had "made itself the nation's No. 3 convention city," outranked only by Chicago and New York, despite Atlanta's "lack of any cultural or entertainment attractions of national reputation" (*WSJ* 1980).

The city's age-old reputation as a regional transportation center enjoyed parallel boom. In a manner similar to writer James Baldwin's oft-repeated line, "You can't get up South or down South without passing through Atlanta," southerners liked to joke that, whether you're going to heaven or hell, you have to change planes in Atlanta. Expansions made to facilities at the old Atlanta airport—renamed Hartsfield International Airport—were simply not enough to keep up with the surge of new air travelers capitalizing on cut-rate fares resulting from airline deregulation. Hartsfield was now the nation's second busiest airport. Two major carriers, Delta Air Lines and Eastern Air Lines, made Hartsfield a hub for their operations. The airlines collected passengers from cities around the country, flew them to Atlanta, where they would scurry to connecting flights, which then flew them out again.

By 1978, according to the *Wall Street Journal*, Hartsfield was "handling more than twice as many passengers as it was built for." The solution was to build a new airport. That same year, construction on a $750 million airport began. The new Hartsfield Airport would be completed on time and *within budget*, ready to receive passengers in September 1980.

By far, though, Atlanta's most significant infrastructural accomplishment during the 1970s was the opening on July 2, 1979, of 6.7 miles of a proposed $3.3 billion rapid rail transit system. The contract with the Metropolitan Atlanta Rapid Transit Authority (MARTA) called for fifty-three miles of track serving thirty-seven stations. The federal government was committed to picking up 80 percent of the construction costs for the system because the planned system was part of a larger transportation package being carried out in consultation with representatives of the city's black poor, who were expected to have the greatest need for cheap, reliable transportation. This consultation was not undertaken "out of purely altruistic motives," however, wrote Fred Powledge (1973, 33), since the residents of the central city possessed enough political power to "shoot down" any referendum they thought "would treat them unfairly."

The driving force behind Atlanta's rapid rise to prominence was the city's white power structure, its economic center regime. The power structure was made up of an old guard of business and commercial elite whose successor generation in the 1960s and early 1970s remained remarkably intact since first studied by sociologist Floyd Hunter (1953, 1980) in the late 1940s and early 1950s. The power structure that Hunter and others (e.g., Jennings 1964) observed consisted of a narrow old boy network that ruled Atlanta in the manner of a benevolent dictator. Members made unilateral policy decisions on vital matters affecting all aspects of Atlanta's public life. The "machinery of government," Hunter wrote, was "at their bidding." Moreover, "they control large industries in which they reign supreme in matters of decision affecting large numbers of the citizenry. They are persons of dominance, prestige, and influence. They are, in part, the decision-makers for the total community. They are able to enforce their decisions by persuasion, intimidation, coercion, and, if necessary, force" (Powledge 1973, 35).

Up through the end of the 1960s, total power in Atlanta, both political and economic, was concentrated in the hands of this small group of well-educated, well-heeled white men in banking, real estate, stocks, architecture, and retail. The men were not robber barons, though, all things considered. Rather, they were a business elite who arguably "felt a genuine responsibility to their city," as put by Powledge (1973, 35). In perhaps no other major twentieth-century American city could an identical phenomenon of an autonomous, corporate governing power elite be found.[3]

The conduit for exercising this kind of hegemony was the power structure's all-white Atlanta Chamber of Commerce—and also a liberal white press, which, under the likes of *Atlanta Constitution* editor Ralph McGill, always enjoyed a sort of "associate-member status" in the power structure. From its position of uncircumscribed dominance, the Atlanta Chamber of Commerce controlled, managed, and directed just about everything having to do with Atlanta's growth and development.

Chamber of Commerce members were astute, pragmatic, and propitiously farsighted on the troublesome issue of race. As the writer Fred Hobson felic-itously put it, Chamber of Commerce members knew that Atlanta could not afford to keep "lynching its Negroes" (as was openly done in the infamous 1906 Atlanta race riot) and "hope to make money, too." Commerce members stead-fastly held that the city should not get "bogged down" in the storm of deseg-regation, test cases, and protracted legal battles. "After all, business was busi-ness, and business required that Atlanta give up the outward signs of racism" (Hobson 1981, 49; also Baylor, 1996).

When, for instance, a U.S. Supreme Court decision disallowed the city's pro-longed efforts at token integration and required that Atlanta instead desegre-gate its public schools by fall 1961, the city peaceably acceded. Without a fuss, school officials threw open the doors of select all-white public schools to cho-sen young black souls. This unique occurrence in a Deep South town took place after extensive preparations (which included sensitivity sessions between white and black parents) and deliberate public relations management—all planned and carefully executed by an efficient, enlightened chamber of commerce. The city power structure had determined beforehand that Atlanta would not be an-other Little Rock, Arkansas, or Grenada, Mississippi, where in the battle over racial rights burly white men were seen in broad daylight, and in full view of television cameras, using chains, clubs, sticks, and stones to attack little black children trying to enter the state's public schools. Atlanta's operating principle was "desegregation with dignity." The city, in Mayor William Hartsfield's immortal words, was "too busy to hate."

Analysts would indeed attribute Atlanta's phenomenal economic success to the racial pragmatism practiced by white Atlanta city fathers. The conservative economics writer Warren Brookes compared the economic histories of Atlanta and its nearest big-city neighbor and rival, Birmingham, Alabama. In 1940, both Atlanta and Birmingham, though identical in size, were a study in contrasts. Atlanta was a "somewhat somnolent trade center for the rural South" with no industrial economy to speak of. Birmingham, by contrast, was the industrial capital of the Southeast, home of southern steel, and a railroad center "with grand prospects for the future." Thirty years later, the cities' positions were reversed. Atlanta was the economic and social capital of the New South. "Birmingham meanwhile had fallen far behind the rest of the Sunbelt economy, both in jobs and population growth and in family income." This tale of two uneven cities resulted from Atlanta's "willingness to open social, political, and economic opportunity to the city's black residents." While Birmingham was fighting battles over racial rights in the street with bullhorns and bullwhips, "Atlanta was getting ready to become the economic capital of the South" (Brookes 1982, 43–44).

Up through the late 1960s, the Atlanta power structure would have one of their own directly govern the city as mayor or they would anoint an acceptable outsider for the office. In the post–World War I administration of Mayor Asa Candler, patriarch of the Coca-Cola Bottling Company, the power structure had one of their own at the head of city government. The same would be true for Ivan Allen Jr., scion of the Ivan Allen Company, who served as mayor from 1961 through 1969. In William Hartsfield (1937–1961), the power structure was content to exert behind-the-scenes control through a mayor they regarded as "not really one of ours" but an accepted center regime player nonetheless.[4]

Following the Second World War, the power structure controlled and directed city politics by Hartsfield and Allen regularly receiving the black vote—a process that was enhanced in 1946 by the abolition of Georgia's whites-only primary. In their mayoral campaigns, both Hartsfield and Allen, assured of black Democrat votes, would typically articulate progressivist positions on race, thereby favorably pitting themselves against a variety of hostile white working-class forces, who, like archsegregationist Lester Maddox, regularly sought citywide office. Once in office, both Hartsfield and Allen, working closely with and often through a client class of Atlanta's black bourgeoisie, would make symbolic gestures at placating the mass of black voters—who were not benefiting in any meaningful way from their political alliance with the white power structure.[5]

At best, what the black masses got was a government that was perhaps *less* hostile to their interests (than if, say, Lester Maddox were mayor), while the white business class got a free hand in running the city.

But this relationship was to undergo significant, if not exactly fundamental, change as the sixties ended. It all began when the white power structure lost their man in city hall: Ivan Allen announced that he would not seek a third term as mayor. What followed was evolution in the city's political life of what Omi and Winant (1986) termed a "racial state"—a political state of affairs they defined as one of conflict and racial accommodation that "takes shape" around "racially based social movements and the policies and programs of the state."

In the mayoral contest of 1969, with Allen out of the picture, Atlanta's black community rejected, for the first time, the power structure's candidate. The power structure had wanted insurance magnate and alderman Rodney Cook to replace Allen. But the black community rallied around the candidacy of Sam Massell, a wealthy maverick Jewish realtor who had been vice mayor for eight years under Allen. Massell won the election.

"Why the white business elite passed over Massell for the mayoral nomination after supporting him in his successful [vice mayoral] campaigns in 1961 and 1965 is not clear," wrote then Atlanta University political scientist Mack Jones (1978, 99). Massell was certainly a member of the business elite, though not of the established power structure. Jones believed that anti-Semitism might have been a factor. But far more significant to the wider black community than the election of Massell as mayor was the election of Maynard Jackson, a young black lawyer, as vice mayor. Jackson's election served notice that, if Atlanta's black population continued to grow, in the next election—set for fall 1973—Jackson could successfully challenge Massell and become Atlanta's first black mayor.

Demographics were indeed turning out in Jackson's favor. At the start of 1973, Atlanta's black population was 52 percent of the city's total 497,000. Hidden within these figures was a dramatic population shift that had been occurring since the 1969 election. Two of the fastest population growth areas were the city's black near west and south sides. This increasing black concentration meant that in an election, a black challenger appealing to racial solidarity could win the city's top political job. Jackson did challenge the incumbent Sam Massell in 1973. After a bitter race-baiting contest—mostly on Massell's part, according to reliable observers[6]—not only did Jackson handily defeat Massell, but the results of the municipal races changed the racial balance of the eighteen-member city council. For the first time, an equal number of black and white council members were elected, although a white man, Wyche Fowler, was elected council president.

Jackson was reelected by a landslide to a second term in 1977. This time, black lawyer-businessman Marvin Arrington assumed the presidency of the Atlanta City Council. Black political empowerment had come to Atlanta; it had come "to a vibrant rather than a decaying city" (Jones 1978, 99). In fact, emergence of a racial state in Atlanta coincided with achievement of many of the growth plans laid out earlier by the white power elite. When blacks came into political power in Atlanta, the city was thus riding a tide of economic euphoria—a phenomenon not soon repeated in urban politics.

Little wonder that all across the nation, but particularly in the black media, Atlanta was being hailed as one of a small number of cities that actually worked for blacks. Black circulations (e.g., *Ebony*) at the time referred to Atlanta as the "Black Mecca of the South." United Nations ambassador Andrew Young (and later mayor of Atlanta) offered that, in comparative terms, "If they had a chance to get what we have in Atlanta . . . all Africa would buy it." Limiting their comparison to the national scene, writers of a special 1970 *New York Times* piece dubbed Atlanta the "capital of black-is-bountiful" (White 1982, 203). Indeed, in the early and mid-1970s a greater number per capita of sociologist E. Franklin Frazier's (1957) "black bourgeoisie" lived in Atlanta than in any other major American city (Patterson 1974; Thiel 1991).

When a black takeover appeared imminent, why, cynics asked, did Atlanta's white power structure decide to stay *in* the city and not "cut and run" to the outskirts, as the business classes in several other major cities had been doing? Besides, members of the Atlanta power structure disliked the new mayor personally and "really did not need much more than skin color" as a reason to leave (Gulliver 1981).[7]

So why did they stay? One obvious answer is that the means for accumulating wealth (mostly buildings and other real estate) into which the power structure had heavily invested in the boom years of the 1950s and 1960s could not have been easily, or lightly, abandoned.[8] The other not quite so obvious answer is that select power structure members had envisioned even greater economic gains for themselves if they were to stay inside the city and work out realistic, mutual arrangements with agencies of the new racial state.

Be that as it may, the nominal control that blacks came to assume over city government energized black expectations, especially among Atlanta's black poor and working classes. It was primarily their vote, after all, which had put in political power leaders who had been nurtured in the movement politics of the sixties. The city's black poor thus expected a dramatic reversal of the inequitable status quo that had long benefited mostly white interests—a sentiment that many within the white power structure described as scary (Eisinger 1980).[9]

In reality, though, the type of power arrangement into which an educated black elite had entered did not allow for a reordering of existing priorities. Accommodation was the operative principle. The old white Atlanta guard had peacefully acquiesced, with "pragmatic acceptance," to use the political theorist Antonio Gramsci's term (1977), to joint control of the city on the understanding that black officeholders would do the following:

1. Contain the demands of the black poor and working class, or at least keep these demands within the bounds of "normal" protest politics.

2. Show competence in the management of city affairs, particularly in the management of things like crime.

A self-perpetuating white power structure in turn would do the following:

1. Continue to invest in downtown, thereby helping to ensure the viability of an elite class of black political leaders, who among other things needed a reliable tax base from which to implement redistributive policies that would keep them in elected office.

2. Vacate the arena of electoral city politics, leaving it exclusively (or almost exclusively) to up-and-coming blacks.

The transition to black rule, then, did not signal fundamental change in the ordering of economic priorities. If anything, it meant "settling for a more equitable share" of economic goods for a black client class *within existing priorities* (Jones 1978, 116). The priorities over which a black political class was to preside revolved around making Atlanta a safe, attractive place for capital, where a small business elite could continue to accumulate super profits while dominating the producing classes, black and white (see also Reed 1981).

As the power structure became more diversified in social composition and business interests, particularly in the late 1970s and early 1980s, the class grew well beyond the core group observed by Hunter in the late 1940s. But the foundation, which guaranteed wealth accumulating to the top, while filtering down negligible benefits to the producing classes, had already been laid.

More significantly, the onset of black political empowerment did not bring any bold initiative for creating economic opportunities for the black nonproducing classes. Rather, the exercise of black political power was subordinated to three essentially formalistic maneuvers:

1. Insisting that black entrepreneurs, black contractors and subcontractors, and other representatives of a black middle class be "cut in" on whatever deal was going down.

2. Reorganizing and making personnel changes in city government to increase the number of black officeholders, giving agencies the appearance, if not always the substance, of "our people" in control.

3. Using blocking tactics, or exercising "negative power" (Burman 1979), in negotiations with the power structure.

We will summarily examine how each of these maneuvers worked and affected the city's sociopolitical relations.

A much-touted legacy of the 1970s was Mayor Maynard Jackson's insistence on black participation in major capital ventures, explicitly in ventures over which city hall exercised some measure of direct control.

From 1973 to 1979 the percentage of city contract businesses going to minority firms zoomed from 13 percent to 24.5 percent. Minority firms probably got no more than a relatively small percentage of the total amounts involved in formal, sealed-bid contracts—no more than 14 percent, according to some estimates. But they got 35 percent of the funds from "negotiated contracts." In the construction of the new Hartsfield International Airport, for example, Jackson had insisted that it be a joint effort that would involve significant representation of black contractors and subcontractors. As a result, 20–25 percent of all airport-construction contracts ended up going to minority firms. And when the airport opened in 1980, Jackson got 40 percent of the concessions—the shops and duty-free businesses—for minority operators.

In areas where the city had no direct control, the mayor resorted to using the traditional bully pulpit, from which he would pressure major financial power centers—including the city's five largest banks—to increase the number of blacks in managerial positions. "There must be 380 or 390 vice presidents of downtown banks, and not one is black in a city that is 55 to 60 percent black," the mayor declared in his January 1979 state of the city speech. Of course, the mayor was less successful at bringing about affirmative-action hiring in the Atlanta banks than he was at obtaining minority contracts for the new airport. At the end of 1979 the only sign of movement within the banks was an announcement by First National Bank of Atlanta that Atlanta University's black president, Cleveland Dennard, had been named a director of the bank and its holding company. At Fulton National Bank, spokesman James Hixson explained his bank's inability to promote blacks into top management as resulting from the lack of necessary zeal on the part of black employees. "Most of your blacks are in departments such as bookkeeping and clerical work," Hixson said he had observed. "They seem to want to go into that field more" (*WSJ* 1979a.)

Jackson's second maneuver was to reorganize city government, especially the Atlanta Bureau of Police Services (ABPS). Up until the 1940s, mere mention of the Atlanta police would strike fear in the hearts of the city's black residents. For generations of black Atlantans, the police had been "the most racist bunch of lawmen in the entire South," as the black-owned *Weekly Defiance* put it in a special October 1881 issue.

Police commissioners often encouraged their men to "kill every damned nigger" they had a "row" with (Watts 1973). Not only were blacks arrested more often than whites, but young black males were singled out *by the police* to be beaten, abducted, or killed. The 1881 Defiance editorial stated, "We have lived in Atlanta twenty-seven years, and we have heard the lash sounding from the cabins of the slaves, poured on by the masters; but we have never seen a meaner set of low down cut throats, scrapes and murderers than the city of Atlanta has to protect the peace" (Gossett 1965, 453).

In the Atlanta race riot of 1906, Atlanta police officers had actually joined white mobs in attacking blacks. In one instance, black residents of nearby Brownsville had requested police protection. What they got was a contingent of county and city lawmen who charged into homes and immediately began arresting black men found with arms (Williamson 1984, 216–18).

Twenty-five or so years after the Atlanta riot, violent racist forces were still exercising undue power within the ABPS. According to former police chief Herbert Jenkins (1970), an enlightened professional whom William Hartsfield had given the job of cleaning up the force, Atlanta policemen had to join the Ku Klux Klan if they ever hoped to become accepted members of the force. The Klan hierarchy worked behind the scenes with the Atlanta City Council's police committee. And policemen who failed to join the Klan had little authority or influence. Rookie policemen were subjected from their first day on the force to ever-increasing pressure to become Klansmen. They were regularly assessed fifteen dollars for bedsheet "uniforms." And it was accepted tradition that they would all be gathered up one night and carried to Stone Mountain to recite the pledge of allegiance in front of the Klan's flaming cross.

In 1973, the problem with the Atlanta police was not quite on the order of racist magnitude portrayed by Jenkins and others (e.g., Mathias and Anderson 1973; McMillan 1961), although popular belief was that several Atlanta police officers had merely exchanged their Klan sheets for police uniforms. This belief, like the one articulated by the *Defiance* almost a hundred years earlier, was not without foundation. According to news accounts, twenty-three black persons were killed under questionable circumstances by Atlanta police officers between July 1973 and July 1974, and a number of others had been similarly wounded (Jones 1978, 109).

Change in police conduct would come only by rapidly increasing the number of blacks on the force, Jackson's people reasoned. In 1974 blacks numbered only 355, or 23 percent, of the 1,545-person police force (Jones 1978)—an unacceptably low number for a city that was more than 50 percent black. Jackson determined that he would implement a recommendation by the city personnel board that two-thirds of all new police officers be chosen from a black applicant pool until the racial imbalance was eliminated. But he ran into stiff opposition from the police chief, John Inman, white aldermen, and the white Atlanta press.

The conflict came to a head when Jackson moved to put through a reorganization plan calling for a public safety department within which police, fire, and civil defense responsibilities would be housed. The heads of these units would be responsible to a commissioner of public safety. The mayor wanted to put John Inman in a subordinate role to his, Jackson's, handpicked commissioner of public safety. A legal battle and at least one reported physical scuffle, involving threatened use of a gun, ensued between the Jackson and Inman forces. Eventually, after a high court ruling against Inman, the mayor appointed his chief administrative assistant and former Morehouse College classmate, A. Reginald Eaves, as commissioner of public safety. This appointment was roundly opposed by the business and commercial elite and the local media, but it found favor with Jackson's black constituency, especially within the all-black communities that were most directly affected by both crime and police misconduct.

Commenting on Eaves's personal popularity, *Village Voice* writer Stanley Crouch (1981, 19) noted:

Even after it was revealed that Eaves's secretary had a heroin conviction in New York, his popularity in the black community was undiminished, primarily because he announced that he would personally charge with murder any police officer who killed without reasonable cause. Police homicides ceased. Over a two-year period, Eaves got press by going on police raids, rigged to allow him to kick in doors and collar criminals for the cameras, much as J. Edgar Hoover had done in his day.

In "Reggie" Eaves the black community believed that, for the first time, it had the Atlanta police on its side.[10] Facts on reported crime tended to support that belief: during Eaves's tenure, rates of street crime actually decreased.

By the end of Jackson's first term, city government, especially at the ABPS, was indeed showing signs of "our people" running things. In addition, the mayor's personal credibility among the black poor and working class had been solidified by his having done all the right symbolic things. He had marched with striking sanitation workers when he was vice mayor, and shortly after being elected mayor he had moved into a public-housing project for a weekend stay with a welfare family.

But the mayor's deliberate symbolic overtures to the black community and his new blackened look of city government represented little more than a triumph of form over substance, which leads to the third and final formalistic maneuver: the mayor's use of negative power.

Jackson's relative successes at reorganizing city government—or at least the ABPS—failed to carry over in matters affecting the flow of wealth inside the city. On matters touching on "big" economic projects, the mayor could do little to prevent the power structure—or any other significant group of white economic interests, for that matter—from doing whatever they wanted to do.

When, for example, the manufacturers of Arrow Shirts wanted to move their factory out of Atlanta and sell the land to the city's transit authority, MARTA, the mayor "knew it would cost the city 800 jobs and dwindle the tax base further," recalled onetime Jackson aide Eugene Duffy. Jackson called the management of the firm into his office and "let them know that if they tried to leave, he would inform the Transit Authority [and that] they would be denied a demolition permit. Arrow agreed to relocate inside Atlanta," Duffy told Stanley Crouch (1981, 24).

Similar blocking moves would get the new Hartsfield Airport built in the southern, or black, part of Fulton County, near the mayor's "natural" political power base, instead of on the northside, as the power structure had wanted.

Throughout his two terms as mayor, then, Maynard Jackson's political actions consisted mostly of trying to answer simultaneously to the city's downtown business elites and to a heretofore disenfranchised black population. To stay in power he constantly had to give currency to racial themes. Equally important, though, he could not afford in doing so to deliberately antagonize, or *appear to deliberately antagonize,* powerful white economic interests. The mayor needed to keep the power structure and other economic elites happy so they would choose to stay and continue to invest in the city.

2

Two Deaths Against the Backdrop of Racial Troubles

> As mayor, what I wanted to do was to lead us ... into an era where we truly could begin to point at progress.
>
> —Maynard Jackson

> Effectively isolated from the economic center of Atlanta, the youth of Atlanta have no sense of what it means to participate in building the future of society.
>
> —Jill Nelson, Pacific News Service

Inevitably, many of the balancing acts that Maynard Jackson was forced to perform with Atlanta's white power structure were seen by blacks as betrayal. In fact, several of the mayor's actions were viewed as "sell-outs." So throughout much of Jackson's second term, a context of racial strain persisted.

One often cited example of betrayal was Jackson's apparent surrender to white demands that he ask for the resignation of A. Reginald Eaves, his black commissioner of public safety, because of Eaves's alleged improprieties on a police examination.[1] But on the day that a press conference was called, ostensibly to allow Eaves to announce his resignation, a group of black leaders "physically restrained the commissioner from making the announcement and condemned the mayor for capitulating to white interests" (Jones 1978, 114).

Eaves was still given the boot. He would go on, nonetheless, to acquire a significant political following among the city's black poor. That following grew from, among other things, his readiness to say certain "injudicious" things. He would frequently imply before large black audiences that the reason he had been booted out of city office was because of a residual, color-coded "racism" that was endemic to Atlanta's privileged black bourgeoisie. He, an unarguably *black* man,[2] had thus been racially victimized by the light-skinned Jackson crowd. This reflexivity to air in public an uncomfortable truth about race in black Atlanta only added to Eaves's popularity among the city's dark-skinned poor and working class—a popularity that six years later he would parlay into a respectable bid to become the next black mayor of Atlanta.

One year after firing Eaves, Jackson submitted a reorganization plan to the city council. The plan would have eliminated three of the existing departments, established a number of new offices, and transferred several bureaus from one department to another. The mayor insisted that the proposed changes were designed to enhance efficiency. However,

> members of the council and other black leaders noted that two of the departments to be eliminated, administrative services and community and human development, were headed by black commissioners out of favor with the white business and commercial elite . . . [and that] the commissioner of the department of community and human development had been denounced for not acceding to the wishes of the business and commercial elite to spend community development block grant funds primarily on projects in the downtown business districts (Jones 1978, 114).

Despite the mayor's reasonable explanation, black leaders, led by civil rights activist turned Georgia state representative Hosea Williams, organized the Coalition to Save Atlanta. The coalition's publicly stated purpose was to oppose the mayor's reorganization plan. Jackson withdrew his plan when it became clear that he did not have the votes on the city council to approve it.

By far, though, the most striking example of what black and poor Atlantans would see as a breach of trust was the mayor's handling of a strike by the city's mostly black sanitation workers, with whom Jackson had marched when he was vice mayor. The workers' average earnings lay below the poverty threshold, so in March 1977 they initiated a strike action against the city. The workers were demanding pay increases of fifty cents an hour.

The mayor said that, although the workers' request was justified, the city simply did not have the money to meet the demand. After negotiations broke down, the mayor announced that workers who did not return to their jobs would be fired. He was roundly supported by the black civic leadership elite. "Several black organizations and prominent black political personalities held a press conference in the offices of the Atlanta Chamber of Commerce, where Martin Luther King, Sr., whose son had been slain [on April 4, 1968] while supporting black workers in a similar strike, announced that the assembled group supported the mayor and that he should 'fire the hell out of the striking workers'" (Jones 1978, 115)—which the mayor subsequently did.

The episode is worth recalling because it brought to a head underlying class contradictions and tensions in Atlanta's black polity. Black middle-class leaders and representatives of the white power structure stood with a black mayor in opposing a group of black workers.

In the end, the sanitation workers lost because they were unable to marshal sufficient broad-based support for their cause. But the way the mayor chose to deal with the standoff took off part of his shine with folks at the grassroots, folks who shared a condition of deepening black impoverishment—as was evident in nearby Miami, Florida.

The seemingly optimistic picture of racial progress painted by University of Chicago sociologist William Julius Wilson (1978) in his classic, *The Declining Significance of Race,* was not at all reflected in the mood of ghetto America in 1980. In Miami's Liberty City, with its depression-level unemployment, high rates of crime, and "crackling resentment against the police" (to use *Newsweek*'s [1980a] grim depiction), three days of rage claimed sixteen lives, left four hundred people injured, and wreaked millions of dollars in property damage.

The Miami "riot" of May 1980 was quickly suppressed by an occupying army of 3,600 state militiamen and by the promise of federal attention to the grievances that had set it off. In the classic 1960s pattern, Liberty City blew up in a rage at the agencies of ghetto (in)justice, specifically at a group of white policemen who had beaten a black insurance man, Arthur McDuffie, to death and at an all-white jury who freed four of the officers.

But the fires in the Miami night illuminated a store of deeper, more dangerous problems for blacks all across America. The people in the nation's ghettos were, at the beginning of the 1980s, in worse shape economically than in the hottest of the bygone summers of the 1960s. One in eight blacks was unemployed. The "stagflation" of the Jimmy Carter years was quickening and deepening, and "governments at every level were in a penny-pinching mood." A national "insensitivity to the needs of black and poor people" characterized the times, observed National Urban League president Vernon Jordan (*Newsweek* 1980a, 32).

In Atlanta, the other side to a story of impressive economic growth were feelings of neglect and frustration. To widely divergent segments of Atlanta's black community, much of the building boom of the 1960s (the building of the new Atlanta-Fulton County Stadium and Civic Center, for example) symbolized misplaced priorities. In the highly touted "Plan of Improvement" of the 1950s, "municipal ills were 'cured' with the axe, not the scalpel," wrote White and Crimmins (1978, 13). Neighborhoods were obliterated, families uprooted, and small businesses destroyed, creating—in the typical third world manner—huge "cordons of misery" (Schwendinger and Schwendinger 1985).

The goal of Atlanta's "urban renewal" was not so much to renew the historic city as it was to create a new one from scratch. Slum clearance became city clearance. In a study of "system bias" in Atlanta's urban renewal program, author Clarence Stone (1976, 3) pointed out that, when Atlanta's economic growth was at its height (in the mid-1960s), "the city pursued a policy under which one-seventh of its population was displaced by government action. Some neighborhoods were simply demolished to make way for commercial and other forms of nonresidential redevelopment." Stone concluded that neglect, overcrowding, and "unaverted racial tensions" changed the social and economic character of many areas.

Despite Mayor Jackson's attempts at "playing ball" with the white business elite, Atlanta lost 6,681 jobs between 1972 and 1978, and the city was the only major jurisdiction in the contiguous seven-county region to show job losses. At the close of the 1970s, the percentage of the region's workers employed in Atlanta dropped to 43.5 percent, from 55.8 percent (Georgia Department of Labor 1980; *WSJ* 1980). Enough jobs were simply not being provided by the number of new office buildings going up in town. (Noted travel authority and urban critic Arthur Frommer warned an elite Atlanta luncheon audience at the Atlanta Historical Society, "No office building has ever improved the quality of life or generated a long-lasting supply of jobs to a city.")

A larger transformational dynamic in the way that capital was being organized in the city was also at work, however. While the rich Piedmont Club set still controlled a considerable chunk of Atlanta real estate, beginning in the 1980s they no longer dominated the ranks of prime property owners. Sharing the ownership spotlight were large insurance companies, pension fund pools, and foreign capital. More important, while new business ventures were moving into the Atlanta area, they were not moving inside the Atlanta city limits. They set up operations instead in the rapidly expanding faraway suburban fringes. One result of this trend was that downtown Atlanta was losing its metropolitan hegemony and "becoming just another one of the region's urban-village cores," Christopher Leinberger and Charles Lockwood pointed out in a thoughtful analysis of how the expansion of business was "reshaping" America.

Government, professional services, finance, wholesale trade, and the convention business were still in downtown Atlanta. However, as prestigious high-rise buildings were completed at, say, Perimeter Center and Cumberland/ Galleria (on the northern end of Atlanta's circumferential highway [Interstate 285]), downtown Atlanta continued to lose much of its "price-conscious . . . tenants" (Leinberger and Lockwood 1986, 46).

Whatever job growth the Atlanta metropolitan region experienced in the late 1970s through early 1980s occurred primarily in the newer, outlying areas. But these jobs were technically demanding. And they were coming when the city's unskilled black population was rapidly growing. Mayor Jackson's own poverty task force would attribute the city's growing unemployment problem particularly to the loss of low and semiskilled blue-collar jobs to "other locations" and to "mismatch" between skills needed for available jobs and the skills possessed by those in need of the jobs. The task force's report was sweeping and particularly relevant to the larger point being made here relative to the economic disfranchisement of a growing segment of Atlanta's black population in the late 1970s and early 1980s.

> Between 1970 and 1975, the number of firms located in the City of Atlanta decreased by 5%, from 17,000 to 16,900. The total number of persons employed . . . declined 4%, from 338,000 to 324,000. While white-collar jobs were increasing, blue-collar jobs decreased from approximately 146,000 to 131,000. Fourteen percent of its warehousing employment and 21% of its manufacturing employment were lost to the City during this period. . . .
>
> New manufacturing and warehousing operations . . . have been locating in suburban and other areas for greater efficiency of land use, lower operating costs, . . . and better access to what many view as a more productive and less unionized labor force. Development of interstate highways, particularly the circumferential freeway, has reinforced this trend. Furthermore, the City itself is almost fully built out; relatively little vacant land remains in the City for new industrial and/or warehousing development. At least half of the existing warehousing and manufacturing structures in the City, while not structurally substandard, are obsolete. New firms are not attracted to these facilities, and existing firms are leaving because of functional inefficiencies. . . .
>
> Complicating the loss of jobs has been the City's inappropriately skilled workforce. The metropolitan Atlanta economy is one of the most highly skilled in the nation. Approximately 72% of the metro labor force is skilled, while only 12% is semi-skilled and 16% unskilled. Moreover, demand in the economy is increasing for white collar and skilled workers. The City's resident workforce . . . is not highly skilled. Fifty percent of this workforce has blue-collar jobs; more than half of the workers lack high school diplomas. They cannot compete for most of the jobs that are being created in the City and regional economy. (Atlanta City Government 1981, 14–16)

So, following a national trend, many traditional blue-collar jobs in manufacturing were leaving Atlanta's city limits and locating in areas north of the city, beyond the reach of the city's public transportation system[3] and where no affordable housing existed.

In September 1980 unemployment nationally for blacks of all ages reached a record 16.3 percent, compared with an average of 7.5 percent for all adults and

6.5 percent for adult whites (U.S. Department of Labor 1980; U.S. Department of Commerce, June 1980a). For the fifteen-county metropolitan Atlanta area, the 1980 unemployment rate for all groups was 6 percent. But when examined in terms of race, minority unemployment was more than double that of whites. For the white workers, 4.9 percent were unemployed in 1980, whereas blacks and other racial minorities had an average unemployment rate of 10.7 percent.

The problem was greater for black teenagers, especially those trapped in the city's cordons of misery. While 11.6 percent of white youngsters ages sixteen to nineteen were unemployed in the greater Atlanta region in 1980, black teenagers had an unemployment rate of 35.6 percent. For the city of Atlanta proper, in 1980 the unemployment rate was 39.8 percent for black males ages sixteen to nineteen and 27.9 percent for men ages twenty to twenty-four, compared with rates of 9.6 percent and 0.1 percent, respectively, for white males (Georgia Department of Labor 1980). The result was that, by the end of the 1970s, the economic gap between black and white Atlantans had widened considerably. The ever-watchful *Wall Street Journal* (1980) noted that the contrast between the affluence of Atlanta's convention enticements and the surrounding poverty of numerous public housing projects "appears to be worsening."

Sociologist Gary Orfield and *Chicago Tribune* reporter Carole Ashkinaze reinforced the point in a penetrating analysis of economic trends in Atlanta from the early 1970s through the middle 1980s. "The concentration of poor families in the central ghetto increased substantially. Between 1970 and 1982, a period of enormous population increases for metro Atlanta, the percent of central city households that were poor doubled" (Orfield and Ashkinaze 1991, 17).

In 1980 some 30 to 40 percent of Atlanta's population lived below the national poverty level, a percentage second only to that of Newark, New Jersey (U.S. Department of Commerce, 1980a). In 1969, 13,276 Atlantans lived in the fifteen poorest, predominantly black census tracts of the city; in 1979 the number increased by 18.6 percent. Of the 20,005 persons ages twenty-five and over living in fourteen of those poorest tracts in 1979, only 4,879 (24.3 percent) had completed four years of high school, and a mere 33 percent of persons ages sixteen and over were employed full or part time (U.S. Department of Commerce 1980b, 1980c).

Reflecting humanitarian as well as pragmatic concerns for this desperate situation, the editorial board of the *Atlanta Constitution* observed the following in a poignant lead editorial to a special series, "Black and Poor in Atlanta":

> If you measure Atlanta's prosperity in terms of new office towers that are changing the skyline, then Atlanta is the pacesetter in the Southeast.

If you measure Atlanta's progress by the number of bright professionals and skilled and educated workers who are moving into the city, then Atlanta must be rated among the nation's brightest urban centers.

If you measure Atlanta in terms of "the Beautiful People," fine restaurants, big-league sports and first-rate entertainment, then Atlanta is the "in" place to be.

But if you measure Atlanta in terms of being poor and being black, you will find this is a city of despair. (*AC* 1981u)

And commenting specifically on the series, associate editor Bill Shipp wrote that they showed "yet another face of Atlanta, but one so scarred that most of us dare not look too long" (Shipp 1981a).

So, despite formal black political empowerment, in the late 1970s and early 1980s Atlanta had a distinctly "surplus" *black* population. Its members formed that sector of the Atlanta order which, to use the apt phraseology of sociologist Stuart Hall (1978, 375), was "consigned to a position of wagelessness." The group's continuous disadvantaged position relegated them to a permanent sub-proletariat, the most vulnerable strata in society.

It was the children of this displaced, "wageless" class of Atlantans who were constantly being subjected to violent crime. The mysterious Atlanta murders were therefore part of a larger story of whole communities and families in distress. At its existential core, the Atlanta tragedy was a story of the world of sad children being forced to grow up much too fast; children from dreary, neglected homes worth escaping, even at odd hours of the night; children from neighborhoods without parks and recreation; children who had to take a bus for long distances, past countless liquor stores and juke joints, to catch a movie, use a swimming pool, or buy a loaf of bread or carton of milk. The story was about mostly young boys being pushed— and sometimes pulled—into dubious "manhood," their yearning to escape a life of poverty and boredom driving them into streets where they had become "available" (Headley 1981).

Several of the Atlanta youngsters who were murdered were last seen out on city streets miles from home trying to make a dollar. Some were doing so as beseeching helpers or petty entrepreneurs in the walkways and parking lots of the area's great urban malls. Others were engaged in the sort of "own-account" activity not likely to win conventional, middle-class approbation. Yet others were out there holding fast to an unwavering belief in their own "natural" abilities: that they could sing and compose lyrics and that, if given a chance, they could become overnight sensations—another Prince, another Michael Jackson.

Of all the things having the most disastrous impact on Atlanta's black poor and working class in the late 1970s, none was more serious—and indeed more deadly—than ordinary street and domestic crime. In 1979 official crime statistics made Atlanta the nation's murder and crime capital. "There have been 140 murders so far, 69% more than a year earlier," reported the *Wall Street Journal* (1979b), referring to the city's midyear homicide numbers.

Statistics released by the Metropolitan Atlanta Crime Commission also told of an escalating street-crime problem (table 1). The number of all serious or Index crimes committed in the city in 1978 was 18 percent higher than for the previous year (*AJ* 1979a). And the number in 1979 increased by 9 percent over 1978's rate.

As calculated from table 1, Atlanta's homicide rates of 34.1 and 53.3 per 100,000 population in 1978 and 1979, respectively, were the highest for the forty largest U.S. cities, including many with far worse crime images. In terms of overall street or Index Crime rates, Atlanta's was the highest for the nation's seven largest cities (see table 2).

This upward swing in crime greatly concerned the city's white ownership class. The "horrifying" statistics would, in their view, scare away businesspeople, especially white conventioneers. A more jaded fear was being expressed by middle- and upper-income white suburbanites. Media surveys reported them saying they believed that the rapes, robberies, and murders of inner-city Atlanta might soon be spilling over into surrounding white neighborhoods. Such a

Table 1. Number of Reported Index Crimes for Atlanta, 1976–1980

Year	Total Index Crimes	Percent Change	Homicide	Rape	Aggravated Robbery	Assault
1976	49,538	1.3	155	477	3,410	3,518
1977	45,604	-7.9	138	514	3,357	3,598
1978	53,865	18.1	144	592	4,119	3,992
1979	58,724	9.0	231*	656	5,189	4,639
1980	59,765	1.8	200	680	4,735	5,470

Source: Crime in Metropolitan Atlanta, 1976–1980 (Atlanta: Metropolitan Atlanta Crime Commission, July 1981).

*Differs from data supplied by Atlanta Bureau of Police Services, which recorded 263 criminal homicides for 1979.

Table 2. Overall Index Crime Rate per 100,000 Population for Seven
Largest U.S. Cities, 1978 and 1979

City	1970 Pop.	1978 Index Crime Rate	1979 Index Crime Rate	Percent Change
Atlanta	421,103	12,732.1	13,879.4	9.0
Boston	599,582	4,151.0	11,713.3	7.4
Chicago	3,060,801	6,234.1	6,100.6	-2.1
Detroit	1,258,924	8,778.2	8,795.2	0.2
Los Angeles	2,863,412	8,149.2	9,032.4	10.0
New York	7,109,420	8,025.5	8,736.4	0.8
Philadelphia	1,757,368	4,151.0	4,699.4	13.0
Washington	656,000	7,766.8	8,602.1	10.0

Source: Calculated from *FBI Uniform Crime Reports* (Washington, D.C.: Government
Printing Office, 1978–79).

problem, they believed, would be of little concern to a black city administration that was already "insensitive" to the high level of personal crimes being perpetrated against the city's white minority—such as downtown merchants being held up in broad daylight.

Such fears were, of course, groundless. A crime-containment strategy of ghettoization (intended or not) was fully operational in Atlanta. Crime, especially violent crime, was being kept within the confines of the city's depressed areas. Data on race of violent crime victims and on victim-offender relationships for 1979 showed a pattern of poor black Atlantans violently victimizing other poor black Atlantans—"black-on-black crime" the troubling, nationwide phenomenon was being called in the national media, black and white.[4]

The one agency that seemed least able to cope with Atlanta's worsening crime problem was the Atlanta Bureau of Police Services. Many Atlantans were in fact attributing the city's high crime rate to the demoralized state of the ABPS, whose personnel had shrunk by one-fourth between 1975 and 1979. A "summit on crime" in July 1979, involving leaders of the city's political and business communities, focused almost exclusively on the problems within the city's police force. To fight the increasing crime problem, suggestions ranged from "providing bright, white hats for Atlanta's policemen to calling out the military" (*AJ* 1979b). (The military option—and the idea of having outside forces intervene in the city's crime problem—turned out to be not at all far-fetched: the governor called on state troopers to patrol Atlanta streets that same year.)

After the crime "summit," Jackson said he would soon announce a "major plan" to fight crime. "We don't intend to sit back and let things drift. We intend to act," the mayor said. But a six-year fight over the racial makeup of the force had severely slowed promotions and recruitment. In addition, a mass exodus of white officers—which occurred earlier when Eaves took over as public safety commissioner—had drastically reduced the number of active-duty officers. (Many white officers had simply "defected" to the newly established, and mostly white, Fulton County police department.) A lawsuit brought against the city by disgruntled white officers remained unsettled. On more than one occasion, Jackson publicly rebuked the federal district court judge handling the suit for not acting quickly enough. The judge's inaction, the mayor said, had delayed hiring and promotions within the ABPS for several years.

As a consequence of these combined forces, in July 1979 Atlanta had a shrunken and unhappy police force, which the Teamsters Union was busily trying to organize.

Jackson had replaced his friend A. Reginald Eaves with a disciplined professional, Lee P. Brown ("No Rap" Brown, folks on the street would call him), as commissioner of public safety. And for police chief he appointed an equally regarded academic criminologist, George Napper. Both men were black, and both had earned doctorates in criminology. Neither one, however, commanded the respect of the people trapped behind ghetto walls. Folks instead tended to view the city's two top cops as inaccessible, aloof, and totally lacking in those qualities which had endeared them to the down-to-earth, regular guy, "Reggie" Eaves.

Official white Atlanta was not any more supportive of either Brown or Napper. Although both men did offer scholarly analyses of crime, they were frequently derided by white opinion makers. Regular columnists for Atlanta's two dominant newspapers frequently lampooned them as "the big thinkers," "people with advanced degrees" who "didn't know the first thing about street crime" (e.g., Ingle 1981).

Two murders took center stage in Atlanta in 1979. Both "shook" the city's "multibillion-dollar-a-year convention industry to its roots," according to an Atlanta public radio documentary (WABE 1981).

On Thursday night, June 28, 1979, Dr. Marc Tetalman, a white thirty-five-year-old Ohio research physician, was gunned down by two armed robbers near the Civic Center. As reported in the *Atlanta Journal* and the *Atlanta Constitution*, Tetalman had been in town attending a convention on nuclear medicine. He had dined at the Abbey restaurant at the corner of Piedmont Avenue and

Ponce de Leon with his wife and three other persons. The group decided to walk back to the downtown Hilton Hotel, the site of the convention. They were strolling south on Piedmont Avenue when two men approached them. Witnesses said that one of the men pulled a pistol from his waistband and demanded the out-of-towners' wallets. Tetalman refused. The robber then shot Tetalman in the chest before turning the gun on one other person in the party, wounding him in the chest and right arm and hand. Tetalman died an hour later in surgery at Grady Memorial Hospital. His associate responded well to surgery and was reported in good condition shortly after the incident. The gunman was described as a "short black man."

Official reaction to the Tetalman killing was swift and furious. The Atlanta Chamber of Commerce offered a $10,000 reward for information leading to the conviction of the guilty parties. Chamber members and other white elites heaped blame on Jackson for a soaring crime problem, which had now claimed the life of a prominent visitor. The mayor and his public safety commissioner called a press conference the day following the murder, "not only to offer condolences to the Tetalman family, but to attempt to quell the increasing adverse publicity about Atlanta's rising homicide rate" (*AJ&C* 1979).

In a show of support for Jackson, the illustrious Benjamin E. Mays, then president of Morehouse College and a mentor to the mayor (as he had been to Martin Luther King Jr.), wrote a strongly worded letter to the editor of the *Atlanta Journal and Constitution*. The letter was as much a denunciation of the white Atlanta press as it seemed intended to morally strengthen the mayor's hand.

> We are all saddened by the recent unmerciful attack and murder of the distinguished nuclear physician. . . . [But] the implication that the mayor is to blame for this very complex problem of crime is not fair. Your newspapers, above the vast majority of all other institutions in our community, know full well that all urban police departments, especially ours, place very high priority on insuring the safety of out-of-town visitors. . . .
>
> To suggest that Mayor Jackson is feigning a concern for our crime problems . . . is in my estimation a disservice to the mayor, the citizens of Atlanta and our visitors. (Mays 1979)

The Tetalman murder was left unsolved, although Atlanta police believed his killer died in a drug shootout.

Four months later, on October 17, 1979, a white woman on her way to celebrate her twenty-sixth birthday at lunch was shot and killed before a crowd in Margaret Mitchell Square. The gunman then put the pistol to his head and killed himself. Patricia Barry worked as a legal secretary with the prestigious Atlanta law firm Troutman, Saunders, Lockerman and Ardmore. Her assailant was a thirty-two-year-old black man from Pleasantville, New Jersey, who was believed to have had a history of mental illness, yet he was able to purchase the murder weapon from an Atlanta pawnshop (AC 1979).

Official white reaction to Barry's killing was, again, swift. Former Georgia governor Carl Sanders, a senior partner in the law firm for which Barry worked, announced plans to call a news conference the next day to "discuss the city's spiraling crime problem." He demanded "less jawbone and more backbone" in local law enforcement. *Atlanta Constitution* columnist Lewis Grizzard (1979) asked, "Why doesn't somebody get the drunks and punks off the streets of Atlanta? Why doesn't somebody do something until we can go an entire week without a citizen getting blown away?"

In the dramatically publicized Tetalman and Barry murders, white Atlanta had suddenly caught a glimpse of the horror that was an everyday reality inside Atlanta's poor black and forgotten neighborhoods, where life was (and still is) nasty, brutish, and short.

Somewhere between the murders of Marc Tetalman and Patricia Barry, two other killings took place in Atlanta. On a muggy afternoon in July 1979, the bodies of two teenage boys were found 150 feet apart in a wooded section of a mostly black middle-class Atlanta neighborhood. For these victims there were no outraged press conferences, no ferocious columnists demanding that the city "do something," even if it meant bringing out the national guard. Their deaths barely made it onto the back pages of the Metro section of one of Atlanta's two major newspapers.

The reason why the slaying of Edward Hope Smith and Alfred James Evans did not make the big headlines was that they were from among the city's black *and* poor. Their deaths would not stymie the onward march of medical research. No prestigious law firm or former governor would miss them. These two unnoticed and only procedurally recorded murders would nonetheless serve as the starting point for a series of events that, in the months to come, would impact just about every aspect of Atlanta life.

The killing of twenty-seven more black males would trigger a new dimension to the crisis already existing in the Atlanta racial state. At issue was whether elected black political authority would decisively respond to the urgent troubles of a significant segment of the people who had put them in office.

3

Where Have All the Children Gone?

Who has him is not important to me. Just let him come home.
—Camille Bell, in a plea to the unknown abductor(s) of her
nine-year-old son, Yusef

What follows is a narrative of the known facts behind the disappearance of nine black children. Any reconstruction of the Atlanta murders would have to begin with the July 28, 1979, discovery of the bodies of fourteen-year-old Edward Hope Smith and thirteen-year-old Alfred James Evans. Their names would be the first and second, respectively, to appear on the city's special police task force list of murdered and missing Atlanta youngsters (see appendix A).

Although fiercely attacked by some, the special police task force list is still *the* essential guide to what happened in Atlanta.[1] So in retelling and analyzing details, I will be staying within the broad definitional scope of that list. I therefore accept as valid the official claim, belated though it might have been, that sometime in the spring of 1980 Atlanta authorities were presented with a set of peculiar crime facts: a number of black youngsters from particular areas of the city had been slain, and the slayings had features that differed from the city's usual run of murder cases.

I also accept that, between July 1979 and June 1981, no other known killings fitted key pattern elements observed for the officially listed twenty-eight (later twenty-nine) victims. This concession could be viewed as foolhardy, since others, notably ex-Atlanta police Chet Dettlinger and reporter Jeff Prugh (1983), asserted that a number of other killings of young black Atlantans—including several females—did indeed occur in the city during the period in question. But for various extraneous reasons (such as degree of activism on the issue by their mothers), these victims' names were never added to the official list of Atlanta's missing and murdered.

But the contention was specious. Given the extent of Atlanta's persistent violent crime problem, the city must have experienced several unsolved, and even mysterious, slayings in the late 1970s and early 1980s. Not much would be gained from getting into what could be a lengthy side discussion about all the puzzling homicides that took place in the city over a fairly long period. One can take on only so much in one narrative.

On the afternoon of July 28, 1979, an elderly woman rummaging for redeemable aluminum cans in a wooded lot just off Niskey Lake Road, in a mostly middle-class and solidly black southwest Atlanta neighborhood, stumbled onto a frightening sight. She saw the partially clothed body of a black male youngster lying halfway buried beneath some brush. Police found another body 150 feet away. One month later they identified the first body as that of Edward Hope Smith, who had been missing for a week. Eventually, after almost a year of dispute, investigators concluded that the second boy was Alfred James Evans.[2] Both had been murdered.

The two homicides were treated in the normal procedural way: routine examination and photographing of the crime scene, followed by removal of the bodies to the county morgue for autopsies, then wait for a relative to come and claim the bodies. Additional investigation in search of a murderer or murderers would be carried out by the homicide division of the Atlanta Bureau of Police Services.

Atlanta's dominant news media showed little, if any, interest in the two killings. The editors of the city's dominant newspaper organization—the *Atlanta Journal and Constitution*—must have looked at these deaths in the same way as the police. The boys were part of a "delinquent subculture," their deaths having little or no meaning to newspaper readers. Had the two boys not been murdered, few readers would have even known of their existence. But that still did not matter very much, because the killer was probably not someone who could prove a threat to decent people. The Atlanta news media's self-assured judgment resulted in the story of the two Niskey Road deaths being all but ignored by the Atlanta public.

Black Atlanta did not seem any more perplexed or worried over the two deaths than were the white media or the Atlanta police. "Nothing excites us anymore," commented the black-owned and grassroots-based *Atlanta Voice*, in its front-page cover story. This apparent indifference puzzled *Voice* writer Harvey Gates. "There is something strange about the death of those two black boys," yet no one in the black community is "bothered" by them, he wrote. "Who are these boys?"

We don't know Where they come from? We don't know Why were they there? How did they get there? And why were they killed? We do not know the answers to any of these questions. The overriding question is why don't we know any of these answers? The answer to this question is that somebody somewhere is not talking. There is no way under God's creation that somebody hasn't missed these boys. Black people have a lot of children, sometimes they can't even think of their names and ages but they know when one is missing for a day. To say nothing of a whole week. This is not one child, there are two. . . . They maybe from different homes or they maybe from the same home. We don't know but somebody does know and this is what is disturbing. (Gates 1979a, 3)

Ten days later, Gates wrote an even more stinging editorial:

Thus far the Niskey Lake two . . . have not been identified nor claimed nor buried. They are still laying on a cold slab somewhere in the police dominion waiting to be claimed.

They cannot stay out of the grave forever, they died an ignominious death. They maybe buried in an anonymous grave. There will be nothing to put on their marker. If these were white boys the white community would rise up in righteous indignation but they are black. This single fact maybe their greatest sin. Where are our pulpits? Where are our pens? Where are our conscience and community concern?

These boys did not come here from outer space. Some body know who these children are. Somebody saw them riding or walking. Some body know how they were killed. Some body know why they were killed.

Now, if these children were white, the state, the city, the community would show some concern. They would offer rewards. They would keep the issue before the public's eye. (Gates 1979b, 5)

On the evening of July 20, fourteen-year-old Edward Smith walked to the Greenbriar Skating Rink in southwest Atlanta from his home in the Kimberly Court housing project, almost three miles away. Teddy came to the skating rink on Stone Street practically every weekend. He left the rink with a girlfriend at about 12:30 A.M., July 21. They parted at the corner of Campbellton and Fairburn Roads. Edward told his girlfriend he was headed home, up Campbellton Road. Somewhere along the way he vanished.

Rink owner Eddie Eugere would later tell investigators that he remembered Edward wearing a black football jersey with red numbers. (Edward loved football and planned to try out for the school team when he returned to Therell High School as a ninth-grader in the fall.) When Edward's body was found, the jersey was missing, as were his socks and a leather sun visor. An autopsy revealed that he died of a gunshot wound to the upper back from a small caliber pistol, possibly a .22.

Thirteen-year-old Alfred Evans had lived in the East Lake Meadows housing project, on the other side of town (in the southeast quadrant of the city's vast black south side) from where Edward Smith had lived. Alfred played on the school basketball team and boxed at a nearby club, Warren Memorial Boys' Club, at 790 Southeast Berne Street. Alfred also had a passion for professional wrestling; he would often go to see wrestling events at Atlanta's downtown Municipal Auditorium. And he liked karate movies.

It was to see a karate movie that Alfred left home with three dollars in his pocket on Friday, July 25. He told his mother he was headed for the Coronet Theater on Peachtree Street in downtown Atlanta. The next morning, when Alfred still had not come home, Lois Evans phoned the DeKalb County police. She was instructed to notify the Atlanta police. She then tried to call the city's missing persons unit, part of the ABPS. But the short-staffed unit was closed and would not be open again until 9:00 A.M. Monday. An entire weekend would pass before an official missing person report on Alfred Evans was filed.

No one knew for sure what happened to Alfred between his home and the Coronet Theater. Investigators would dismiss as a suspect in his death a young man who knew Alfred and admitted giving him a ride to a bus stop on Glenwood Avenue the day he disappeared. Alfred's mother told the police that her son would have caught one of two MARTA buses that passed along Glenwood Avenue, either of which would have dropped him off in downtown Atlanta.

In the year that Alfred Evans disappeared, drug trafficking raged through the "Meadows," as residents ironically called the barren sprawl that was the East Lake Meadows housing project. The drug scourge did not spare Alfred, who was known to friends as Q. Little Q, they said, had relatives in the trade, and he helped out as a runner. So at first official figuring was that the youth's death resulted from a drug overdose and that his body was dumped by a panicked acquaintance—the man who had given Alfred the ride the day he left his home. But teacher Rosalind Williams told investigators that, although Alfred probably experimented with drugs, he was too bright, too alert, and too athletic to have been the victim of heavy drug usage.

Another drug-connected theory was that both Edward Smith and Alfred Evans had attended a pot party free-for-all. Edward, too, had friends in the trade: friends who might have had reason to kill him. In addition, Edward associated with some older boys who had criminal records, and he had friends on County Line Road, where the supposed pot party took place. But the theory began to crack when an anonymous caller failed to show up for a scheduled meeting with an Atlanta detective. The caller claimed she had been at a party where one boy was shot and another strangled. Investigators could find no one else who knew anything about such a party.

Medical examiners concluded that Alfred Evans had died of "probable asphyxia," resulting from "probable strangulation." For two and a half years, his and Edward Smith's murder would remain officially unsolved.

Edward Smith and Alfred Evans came from two of Atlanta's most disadvantaged communities. They also grew up in less than "intact" families. They probably did hang out with the "wrong" crowd. And despite their tender ages, they were uniquely experienced in the ways of the street. None of this was true for fourteen-year-old Milton Harvey. In the tree-draped corner of northwest Atlanta that enclosed the Nash Road community, Milton Harvey was "about as far removed from slum violence as two hardworking parents of modest means could get him" (*AJ&C* 1981).

Milton was not quite eight years old when his mother and stepfather, Patricia and Roy Ellis, moved out of the Leila Valley housing project—in depressed southeast Atlanta—in 1973. The couple worked long and hard to maintain a nice little house on Nash Road; they had even managed to build a swimming pool in the backyard.

Milton liked to shoot pool and play basketball at a nearby park. The odd jobs he picked up were the type any typical youngster would have: he mowed his neighbors' lawns, helped a local landlord paint old houses, and babysat his older sister's children.

Milton Harvey vanished on the morning of September 4, 1979, six weeks after the discovery of the first two bodies. It was a quirk of pride that kept Milton from attending the first day of school. The night before, his mother had bought him a pair of sneakers he didn't like. So he asked to stay home until she could get him the "right" kind the next evening. She relented but asked Milton to use part of his day off from school to go pay her MasterCard bill.

Roy Ellis recalled that his stepson took the $100 check from his mother to pay the credit card bill. He borrowed a yellow ten-speed bicycle from a friend, then headed in the direction of the Citizens and Southern Bank, about three miles away on Old Gordon Road, just off heavily traveled Fulton Industrial Boulevard. Bank records indicated Milton made it to the bank and paid the bill. What happened before and after that is shrouded in mystery.

A week after Milton disappeared, a neighbor found the borrowed bicycle beside a pine tree just off Sandy Creek Road, a dirt road running off Fulton Industrial Boulevard between the bank and Milton's home. An employee of a drilling company across from Sandy Creek Road remembered seeing two boys just north of the road around lunchtime the day Milton disappeared. The boys were pushing a bicycle south along Fulton Industrial Boulevard.

On November 16, a man picking up aluminum cans to sell came upon Milton's skeletal remains just off Redwine Road in East Point, an adjoining city south of Atlanta and near the airport. This was more than a dozen miles from Milton's home.

For a time, East Point authorities doubted that Milton had been murdered, since they found no visible marks on his bones to indicate foul play. But later, when Atlanta authorities were brought into the case, they suspected asphyxia as a probable cause; they also believed that the boy's killer might have been a house painter, since specks of paint were found on the white T-shirt and blue cutoff shorts Milton was wearing when his remains were found. Investigators discarded that theory when they learned that Milton had stopped off briefly to help a friend paint an old house. Curiously, evidence technicians never found Milton's knee-length socks with stripes at the top or his old blue sneakers.

In the end, primarily because of the badly decomposed condition of Milton Harvey's body, medical authorities were unable to conclusively determine the cause of his death.

Eula Birdsong could vividly recall her last encounter with nine-year-old Yusef Bell. He had an "air about him," the elderly neighbor remembered. Sometime in the late afternoon of Sunday, October 21, 1979, she had asked the proud "little man" to go buy her a box of Bruton snuff. An adult asking a neighborhood youngster to run an errand was not at all unusual in communities like Yusef's. Running an errand was one of several ways that children could earn pocket change.

The bright-eyed boy Ms. Birdsong had summoned to her porch pronounced after her the *t* in Bruton with precision. He was slightly offended when she asked him if he thought he had enough money. Yusef held out two quarters, more than enough to cover the cost of the snuff.

Yusef, his two sisters, and one brother lived with their mother, Camille Bell, in the McDaniel-Glenn housing project, a stretch of dilapidated buildings situated in the shambles of the Mechanicsville neighborhood, just below Interstate 20 and west of the Atlanta-Fulton County Stadium.

Yusef was one of twenty-five students at Dunbar Elementary enrolled in a gifted students program. At the Warren Memorial Boys' Club (frequented by slaying victim Alfred Evans), Yusef would astonish audiences with his rendition of Martin Luther King Jr.'s "I Have a Dream" speech. Yusef was a quick-witted child who seemed destined to climb from his depressed surroundings on brain power alone. Folks in the neighborhood treated the fifth-grader like a walking electronic calculator and encyclopedia wrapped in one.

Yusef never returned. After purchasing the snuff at Reese Grocery on Mc-Daniel Street, he vanished. A store employee recalled seeing him leave the store at 4:45 P.M. A neighbor reported seeing him getting into a blue car on Fulton Street with someone she believed was his mother's estranged husband. But after interviewing Camille Bell's husband and a lady friend of his, the police gave little credence to the alleged sighting.

When word got out of Yusef's disappearance, the entire Mechanicsville community shared his mother's terrifying ordeal. In newspaper bulletins, set against a passport-size photograph of the smartly dressed, studious-looking, handsome young man, Camille Bell urged the abductor, or abductors, of her son "not to be afraid" to let him come home. "The police may be interested in finding out who took him, but from my point of view, I just want my son back," Ms. Bell pleaded into TV cameras. "Even if it's tomorrow, even if it's next week, dress him up differently and put him out by a phone booth."

Camille Bell clung to the belief that her son was not dead or hurt. "I do feel that he is out there somewhere and unhappy. I just want him back home" (AV 1979).

On November 8, eighteen days after Yusef was last seen alive, a janitor looking for a place to urinate discovered the boy's body; it had been hidden in the crawl space at an abandoned school not far from the Bell home. Yusef was clad only in the cutoff shorts he had on the day he disappeared. He had been strangled, according to medical examiners. On his throat were bruises and fingernail punctures consistent with strangulation by hand.

Investigators surmised that he was killed somewhere else and then carried into the building. They also noted that the floors to the abandoned building were dirty but the bottom of Yusef's feet were clean. His body, they believed, was probably washed or bathed after death. At the seat of his cutoffs, though, was a small piece of masking tape. And sticking to the tape were some textile fibers; one was a green carpet fiber.

The recovered fibers would prove auspicious to investigators looking into Yusef Bell's death. Fifty years earlier, the French forensic scientist Edmond Locard (1930) had published his findings on the transference of fibrous particles. Locard concluded that fabric and other textile fibers were important trace material because they transferred, or "exchanged," easily between objects. Thus, whenever two clothed people touched, for instance, they would exchange minute fibers onto each other's clothing.

Similarly, if someone had been in contact with, say, a carpet, blanket, towel, or rug, that person's body would likely have minute textile fibers clinging to it. Forensic scientists had discovered that in virtually every instance of physical contact in which textile material of one form or another was present, exchange, or transference, of traceable fibrous material likely occurred.

Investigators would eventually reason that, if Locard's exchange principle was correct, the fibers found on slain Yusef Bell's cutoffs should point to the physical environment in which he had likely been killed.

News of Yusef Bell's slaying stunned black Atlanta. Particularly incensed were folks in his neighborhood. The Greater Mount Calvary Baptist Church at 388 Southwest Glenn Street overflowed with family, friends, and believers—including local pols and celebrities. They all came to memorialize and to bury Yusef. The Reverend Timothy McDonald, an associate pastor of Ebenezer Baptist Church and an expert on problems of inner-city Atlanta youth, sermonized: "Yusef's death bespeaks the violent nature of our society. . . . Taking the life of a child is inexcusable. [Yusef's] potential to liberate his people was blighted out." A telegram sent to the Bell family from Mayor Maynard Jackson and the Atlanta City Council extended "sincerest condolences" and assured Camille Bell that the Atlanta Department of Public Safety would do "everything within its power to expeditiously resolve this tragedy" (AV 1979).

Following the funeral, Camille Bell pressed for a broad investigation of the four unsolved child murders. She and community leader Grace Davis, head of Atlanta Women Against Crime, a new inner-city advocacy organization, warned the police and others in the local political authority structure that the strange murders were not isolated. The police should treat the murders of Edward Smith, Alfred Evans, Milton Harvey, and now Yusef Bell as special cases.

But the two women, both articulate onetime foot soldiers in the civil rights movement, were unable to budge the Atlanta authorities. They complained that Mayor Jackson and the Atlanta police were not concerned about the killings. Jackson cared "more about convention dollars than he did about black children's lives," charged Camille Bell. And it didn't help much that the mayor's cool, dispassionate commissioner of public safety, Lee Brown, saw "nothing out of the ordinary" in the child murders.

Not everyone within the Atlanta Bureau of Police Services shared Brown's view. After Milton Harvey disappeared, the officer in charge of missing persons asked that more investigators be assigned to the three cases. She was ordered to "hold off" because the ABPS was short-staffed.

Camille Bell, Grace Davis, and other community women continued to voice their dissatisfaction, picking up the support and encouragement of others within reawakened statewide grassroots protest movements. Mayor Jackson learned of the bubbling unrest over the slayings in much the same way that news reporters and the public later did: from the rumor mill in the streets. "There is talk," the mayor complained to Lee Brown in a March 1980 memo. The memo instructed Brown to look into the matter (*AJ&C* 1981).

But at this time the ABPS was being taken to task for continued increases in crime in the downtown business district and for the "bad press" the city was receiving. Disheartened representatives of the power structure were mounting increasing pressure on city officials to "do something" about the "soaring crime problem," because "scare stories" about crime were "crippling" downtown in a "sort of self-fulfilling prophecy" (*AJ&C* 1980a).

Brown and Central Atlanta Progress (a pro-downtown business advocacy organization) executive director Dan Sweat concluded that what Atlanta police most needed was a public-relations consultant. In early March the city hired an expert with a national public relations and advertising firm. "We're not trying to do a slick PR job," Brown told reporters. He and the business establishment only wanted "improved communications between the police and the public" (*AJ&C* 1980a).

No puzzling deaths of Atlanta children occurred between November 1979 (when Yusef Bell's body was discovered) and March 1, 1980. The police, in the meantime, said they had not been able to establish any "common denominator, similarities, patterns, or trend" in the four slayings. Neighborhood folks thought differently. Their darkest fears that more disappearances and killings would follow were soon realized. On March 10, another body was discovered— the fifth within seven months.

Venus Taylor moved from Chicago to Atlanta in early 1980, bringing along her playful twelve-year-old daughter, Angel Lenair. Ms. Taylor supported herself and her daughter as a cocktail waitress at the Mahogany Club on Campbellton Road in southwest Atlanta. But this single source of income dried up when the club lost its liquor license.

On Tuesday, March 4, Angel completed her English homework and left her apartment to visit a girlfriend. Angel never made it to the friend's house.

Angel had "steady habits," her mother later would tell investigators. The sixth-grader always did her homework when she came home in the afternoon before going out to play. And Ms. Taylor knew something was terribly wrong when Angel did not return from visiting her friend to see *Sanford and Son,* a television show she never missed.

Six days after Angel Lenair disappeared, her body was found in a forested vacant lot along Campbellton Road. She was still wearing the clothes she left home in: blue jeans, a blue shirt and blue vest, green socks, black shoes, and white panties with a tiny blue pattern. A second pair of white panties, which Angel's mother said was unlike any Angel owned, was stuffed in the dead girl's mouth. Investigators believed that an electrical cord, which bound Angel's hands, was pulled around her neck until she died. They also thought that she might have been sexually molested, but later they determined she was not.

The death of Angel Lenair was initially considered as one of the ten or so murders of children that Atlanta police investigated each year. Early investigations led to a male suspect—an acquaintance of Angel's mother whom investigators believed was involved in drugs. This led to official speculation that Angel's murder was somehow connected to her mother's involvement with drug traffickers. The police eventually cleared all "likely suspects" but were left not knowing who had killed Angel.

Jefferey Lamar Mathis was a conscientious, dependable child. He was the youngest of four boys and two girls born to Willie Mae Mathis. Jefferey's story dramatically illustrates the mysteriousness of the Atlanta tragedy and allows perhaps the most intimate, painful glimpse of the horror experienced by victims' families. The story, as related by writer Steve Oney (1981), deserves extended retelling.

Early in the evening of March 11, Ms. Mathis asked her older son Frederick, a shy, quiet fourteen-year-old, to run up to Gordon Street in the West End neighborhood where the family lived to buy her a roll of toilet paper and a money order. As the boy burst out the front door, his mother called after him from her bedroom, "Get me a pack of cigarettes, too."

When Frederick returned home and handed his mother her money order, she found that he had forgotten to pick up the cigarettes. She asked him to go back and get them. Frederick said he could not because he had to leave for church choir practice; the church bus was waiting in front of the house.

"Who's back there in the den?" Ms. Mathis remembered asking Frederick.

"Jefferey and Wanda," Frederick answered.

"Jefferey," Ms. Mathis called out. "Come here and go get Mama a pack of cigarettes."

Jefferey, a wry eleven-year-old with a high forehead and a winning smile, got up from where he was parked with his sister in front of the television set, waiting to watch *Three's a Crowd*. It was nearly seven o'clock when his mother handed him a dollar and sent him on his way.

In Oney's reconstruction, Jefferey probably began walking north on East Ontario Avenue, the street right outside his front door. The Mathis home was about one hundred yards south of the intersection of East Ontario and Gordon Street. Jefferey would have passed a half-dozen houses and a vacant lot before reaching the intersection. Before him, on the north side of Gordon, he would have seen a row of single-story brick buildings housing a barber shop, a beauty salon, and a hardware store. When Jefferey reached the curb, he would have had to make a left past a row of stores, and then cut across the street to reach his likely destination, the Star Service Station, a yellow concrete-block building. Star offered the lowest-priced cigarettes in the vicinity.

At about 7:30 P.M. Ms. Mathis began to wonder what was taking Jefferey so long. But by 8:30, an hour and a half after Jefferey had left, she was starting to worry. "Jefferey wouldn't have stayed away willingly that long with his mama's dollar," she thought out loud. She sent Frederick (who had by this time returned from his choir practice) and two older sons, Stanley and Reginald, out into the neighborhood to look for their brother.

Willie Mae Mathis directed their efforts from her porch. As the night wore on, a beat policeman drove by. Ms. Mathis told him that Jefferey was missing. The officer told her he would keep an eye out for the boy, but if he hadn't come home by morning, she should call Atlanta police's missing persons unit.

Early the next day, Ms. Mathis made the call. Even though an officer did come out to her house, she got the impression that a missing child was not a high priority with the Atlanta police. Missing persons investigations were a "joke," especially for missing kids, a detective familiar with the Mathis case told Steve Oney. The police felt that most kids reported missing were simply runaways who would "turn up sooner or later" (Oney 1981, 19).

But Jefferey was not the sort of boy who intentionally stayed away from home. Like many other boys his age, he worked the typical round of odd jobs, like carrying grocery bags for shoppers at Kroger's on Cascade Road, nearly a mile from his home. And while he was tough and aggressive (on the day he disappeared and on the day before that he had fought with a classmate over a girl, winning both matches), he was known as a dependable, cautious child.

In the days following Jefferey's disappearance, members of the Mathis family continued to look for him in the neighborhood. For a while, they thought that W. A. Williams, a barber whose shop on Gordon Street was one of Jefferey's hangouts, was the last person to see him. Williams recalled that Jefferey had twice rapped on his window the evening of March 11, a signal that told him the boy was headed to the store and wanted to know if the barber needed anything. Williams remembered shaking his head no, and Jefferey walked on by.

As spring turned to summer, life around the Mathis house subsided into a kind of numb normalcy. Jefferey's brothers and sisters continued to go to school and church, and Willie Mae Mathis kept busy doing housework and paying the bills. "Yet her world seemed out of focus, and despair hung heavy in the atmosphere." She kept Jefferey's clothes neatly folded away in his drawer. Every time the phone rang, she hoped he was calling.

By June 1980, after three months of waiting, Ms. Mathis, still believing that Jefferey was alive, "lapsed into depression." Everything seemed wrong, tragic, senseless. She would sit on her sofa listening to gospel music, lighting cigarettes, puffing on them, stabbing them out, then lighting others. Born the daughter of an Atlanta truck driver, Ms. Mathis had worked as a maid at Peachtree Center. She also had held a job with a microfilm company, winding recording tape onto cassettes. When the company declared bankruptcy, Willie Mae Mathis found herself on the unemployment line. Such disruptions were disturbing but not out of the ordinary for her and most of the women she knew. What was happening to her now, though, seemed inexplicably bad.

In May 1980, two months after Jefferey's disappearance, Willie Mae's cousin came from Alabama and had moved into the house on East Ontario Avenue to keep Willie Mae company. The cousin brought her son, Garrick, along. Four weeks later, on a warm Saturday in June, Garrick went swimming at the Mozley Park pool. He got into difficulty swimming, and before a lifeguard could pull him from the water, the boy drowned. Willie Mae, "who had always believed strongly in Christ, began to feel as if she were coming undone," wrote Oney (1981, 20).

Months following Jefferey's disappearance a girl reported seeing him getting into a blue car with two men. One of the men, she said, was black; the other could have been white, or he could have been a light-skinned black. Whatever might have happened to Jefferey Mathis, no one really knew. Almost a year would pass before anyone would at least have a clue.

Fourteen-year-old Eric Middlebrooks was given up by his mother when he was four months old. He would not see her again until he was five years old. He never knew his father. Eric was reared by his mother's family and friends. In the spring of 1980, Eric had just moved into an apartment at 345 Howell Street in southeast Atlanta, behind the Moreland Avenue exit off Interstate 20, to live with a male guardian.

Shortly after 10:00 P.M. Sunday, May 18, Eric answered the telephone at his home. The call was apparently his. He then hurriedly left the apartment complex on his bicycle, carrying a hammer and several hand tools. He left as though someone on the phone had summoned him.

Around 7:30 the next morning, Eric's murdered body was found next to his bicycle behind the "Hope-U-Like-It" bar at 247 Southeast Flat Shoals Avenue, a few blocks north of his home on the opposite side of the Interstate. His pockets were turned inside out, but he probably had no more than a dollar or two when he died. Caught in a rip in his tennis shoes was a clump of red fibers, which, along with the shoes, a crime-scene technician collected and sealed in an evidence bag.

Eric's chest and upper arms showed two slight stab wounds. The Fulton County medical examiner's office ruled, however, that Eric Middlebrooks died of "brain injury due to a blunt instrument."

Eric Middlebrooks seemed to have died the way dozens of black teenagers across the country died: he was beaten to death in a murder that seemed motivated by revenge or robbery. But Eric's case persisted as unsolved, despite the fact that his body was found within twelve hours after he was last seen alive and no more than eight hours after he had been killed. Also, the medical examiner looking into Eric's death was able to determine a specific cause of death and general type of weapon used. Someone had bashed in his head with a blunt, flat instrument. Moreover, investigators had discovered a possible motive. A few weeks before his murder, Eric had testified against three juveniles in a robbery case.

But none of these circumstances would prove helpful to Atlanta homicide officers. Because there were only minor blood stains found around Eric's body, the police concluded that he was not killed behind the bar at the spot where his body was discovered. No murder weapon was found, and the place of the killing remained a puzzle. So, too, did the telephone call Eric took just before dashing out of his home at what would seem—for a fourteen-year-old, anyway—a late hour.

The police questioned the juveniles against whom Eric had testified, but released them when their alibis checked out. Eric's most recent guardian, Robert Miller, with whom he had stayed the longest, also at first suspected that Eric might have been killed by someone involved in the robbery or someone else who knew him. But Miller had no specific evidence to support his hunch. In fact, he didn't even have a good idea who Eric's friends were. He only knew that Eric would sometimes go swimming at the neighborhood boys' club by borrowing a friend's membership card. Miller notified Eric's mother of his death, but she did not attend the boy's funeral.

Twelve-year-old Christopher Phillipe Richardson lived with his mother and grandparents in a comfortable one-story house off Memorial Drive in Decatur,

Georgia, just east of the Atlanta city limits in DeKalb County. Relatives and school officials spoke of Christopher as a "quiet, stay-at-home" child. Christopher's teachers described him as an average student who didn't make trouble. They had nevertheless decided that Christopher should repeat the sixth grade because his reading skills were at the fourth-grade level.

At about 1:30 P.M. on June 9, 1980, Christopher left his home to walk one and one-half miles to the DeKalb County Midway Recreation Center for a swim. Just before leaving, he argued with his mother, Sirlena Cobb, about whether he could wear his new shirt to the pool. She said no, and she prevailed. Ms. Cobb then gave Christopher the fifty cents he would need to get into the center's pool. Christopher left his home wearing walking shorts, not swim trunks, since he didn't own any. Then he simply vanished. Christopher was last seen outside the Krystal Hamburgers fast-food restaurant on Memorial Drive, near Belvedere Mall. He was walking toward the recreation center.

Early on Sunday, June 22, 1980, one day before Latonya Wilson's seventh birthday, her parents called the Atlanta police to report her missing. The girl was the victim of an early morning kidnapping from her home at 2261 Northwest Verbena Street. At least that's what her parents believed.

According to the police report, when her mother, Ella Wilson, went to Latonya's bedroom at 6:30 A.M., to check on her and her eight-year-old sister, Latonya was not there. In her brother's room next door, a recently replaced pane of glass was missing from one window, and the window next to it was open. The apartment's back door was open, and the missing pane of glass was found in an open Dumpster about twenty feet away. But investigators reasoned that, if a kidnapper had removed the pane of glass, opened the other window and crawled in, then gone into Latonya's room, snatched her, and escaped through the back door, he would have had to crawl over one of Latonya's sleeping brothers, walk past her parents' bedroom, and take her without awakening her sister or anyone else in the house. The scenario seemed unlikely.

But a neighbor, Gladys Durden, told the investigators that she saw two men near the Wilson apartment at about 4 A.M. the day Latonya disappeared. She later saw one of the men "carry" Latonya out of the apartment under his arm, she said.

On the day Latonya Wilson was reported missing, her mother and father led groups of neighbors on searches of their Dixie Hills neighborhood. They didn't find any clues. Neither did the Atlanta police.

The disappearance of Latonya Wilson would mark the emergence of a potent dynamic inside the communities that were mysteriously losing their children. Nine black and mostly poor children had disappeared since July of the previous year. Six bodies had been found. To a number of residents, a pattern of randomly snatching, then murdering, black children was now well established. The horrific incidents were related in some way. And they were being carried out by a force, or forces, from outside the neighborhoods in which the youngsters lived.

Victims' families took the Atlanta police's seeming ineffectiveness at solving the cases and their indifference as signs that they would have to bring concerted pressure to bear on the Atlanta authorities. Mobilization through collective, or at least joint, citizen action would be necessary. Three of the mothers of slain or missing children and an itinerant Baptist minister, the Reverend Earl Carroll, whose motive the mothers never completely understood or trusted, came together one evening in June 1980 at Paschal's Restaurant, near the Atlanta University Center. The mothers were Camille Bell, mother of slain Yusef Bell; Venus Taylor, mother of slain Angel Lenair; and Willie Mae Mathis, mother of missing Jefferey Mathis.

The choice of Paschal's as a place for mothers from Atlanta's black inner city to meet and plan strategy against the Atlanta authorities was filled with historical irony: Paschal's Restaurant was one of the key venues where, in the heyday of the civil rights battles, Martin Luther King Jr. and his lieutenants often would plan, from the "safety" of Atlanta, details of their next nonviolent direct action against the citadels of southern white supremacy. Maynard Jackson's supporters had met at Paschal's to fine-tune a political blueprint for Jackson's bid to become the first black mayor of Atlanta. And when the new mayor's grip on the reins of city power seemed most unsure, his people would regroup at Paschal's over coffee and toast and devise ways to deal with reactionary elements within the city's white power guard.

Now, in June 1980, three ordinary Atlanta women came to meet at a place woven into the memory of the struggle for racial justice in America. Like the movement people of times past, they also came to plan collective action. This time, however, the action would be directed not against some southern segregationist order but against a black city administration and black political class. The action was deemed necessary because aspirations for, and achievement of, black political empowerment seemed not to have translated into demonstrable understanding of, and less so concern for, the troubles and fears of the black poor.

The three Atlanta mothers came to Paschal's to lay plans for the founding of an organization that would dedicate itself to the unheralded cause of the children of the disinherited. They later would call their organization the Committee to Stop Children's Murders, STOP for short. No one in the media took note of the meeting, save for a lone reporter with the *Atlanta Voice*. The paper's editors viewed the meeting and the mothers' objectives positively and urged all parents and concerned citizens to support them (*AV* 1980b).

The apparent kidnapping of Latonya Wilson would broaden, somewhat, the scope of official investigation into the three other disappearances. Local law enforcement authorities asked the FBI to look into the case of the missing girl. The agency's involvement would be purely procedural—and only so because kidnapping was suspected. On June 26, the FBI's Atlanta office sent a routine teletype message to FBI headquarters in Washington, D.C. It read:

> Victim abducted from her residence . . . early morning hours, June 22, 1980. Entry to residence allegedly gained from removing pane of glass from window permitting unknown subject entry to bedroom where victim's two brothers sleeping. Unknown subject then walked past parents' bedroom to victim's bedroom where victim and two sisters sleeping.
>
> Neighborhood investigation determined witness who was awake and claims that she observed unknown subject enter victim's residence three times through window where pane was missing and on fourth occasion depart residence with victim.
>
> No ransom demands made to date and parents of victim not affluent and live in low rent housing area. Interviews of parents negative regarding motive of suspects. [OBLITERATIONS][3]
>
> Victim described as black female, date of birth June 23, 1973, three to four feet tall, 55 to 65 pounds, black hair, brown eyes, slightly protruding teeth.
>
> No information to date of federal violation, however, Atlanta following closely . . . in event same develops. (FBI n.d.)

The message was routinely processed and the case, seen at the time as just another of the myriad of "probable kidnapping" cases that local law enforcement jurisdictions around the nation regularly asked the FBI to look into, entered into the bureau's vast files. The case of the missing Wilson girl, however, would be the first in an immense nineteen-volume investigative log that the FBI would compile and label "ATKID," for Atlanta's missing and murdered youngsters, who, as the terminology suggested, were presumed to have been kidnapped somewhere along the terrifying route to their untimely deaths.

4

A Summer of Death

He was a ghetto child, sure enough, but I took care of my baby. He may not have had fine clothes, but he had clothes.

> —Atlanta mother Vera Carter, mother of nine-year-old Anthony Carter

Led by Camille Bell, whose son was found dead in November 1979, the mothers' organization founded at Paschal's Restaurant immediately sought to pressure not only the Atlanta city government but also an unlikely sector of Atlanta society. Claiming they were getting nowhere with city officials, the Reverend Earl Carroll, Camille Bell, and other mothers took their case to corporate Atlanta; they met with representatives of the white power elite. But these were not the "good old days" of unbridled power structure dominance, when any power structure member could simply call up city hall to have his wish instantly granted. With the rise of the new racial state, the power structure had quietly determined—especially in light of the imbroglio over the Eaves and sanitation workers' firings—that it was in their best interests to stay as far away as possible from matters of internal racial grievance.

The mothers nonetheless went to see Dan Sweat, head of Central Atlanta Progress, a highly regarded business organization. After promising them that he would see what he could do for them with the mayor and the public safety commissioner, Sweat directed the mothers to Joel Goldberg, chairman of the Atlanta Business Coalition. Goldberg recalled to reporters that the mothers were asking for financial support. He told the mothers that he couldn't help with money, but he would discuss their plight with black members of the MARTA board, on which Goldberg served.

By early summer 1980, however, Mayor Maynard Jackson's own concern was growing. The rumors had not ceased. Nine black Atlanta children had mysteriously disappeared; six of them had turned up dead. The mayor sent another memo to his public safety commissioner, instructing him to look deeper into the matter.

On June 24, less than two weeks after the Committee to Stop Children's Murders (STOP) was founded, the seventh body was discovered. Ten-year-old Aaron Wyche's body was found one day after the boy was last seen at Tanner's Grocery Store on McDonough Boulevard in southeast Atlanta.

His body was found face-down beneath a highway overpass on a railroad track near Constitution Road and Moreland Avenue in DeKalb County. For the next several months, his death would be treated by investigating authorities as an accident, not as a homicide. Aaron might have simply fallen to his death from the overpass while walking like a tightrope walker or running along its edge, DeKalb County police investigators believed. But the overpass was shielded on both sides by two-foot concrete abutments topped by twin guardrails, which all but eliminated the likelihood of someone accidentally falling from it.

Furthermore, pointed out DeKalb County's truculent public safety director, Dick Hand, the boy's body bore no signs that anyone had tried to "strangle or smother him." Hand and Dr. Joseph Burton, DeKalb County's medical examiner, concluded that Aaron had been alive as he fell onto the railbed. They attributed his death to "positional asphyxiation" from injuries to the rear of his neck. Trees leaves in the dead boy's hand bolstered the theory that Aaron was alive on the way down and died when neck injuries prevented him from lifting his head to breathe. The nagging question remained, however: Did Aaron Wyche fall off the overpass, or was he pushed or thrown off?

The youngster could have slipped off, had he been sitting on the guardrails. Traces of tar found on the rails (the road having recently been tarred) indicated that someone may have been climbing on the rail. But Aaron's mother and grandmother held that the boy's death was no accident. The boy was afraid of heights, so he would not have been climbing on the guardrails. His death was as mysterious, they insisted, as that of the six other cases of black child killings known thus far. The authorities would eventually agree. Dick Hand would reassess his initial conclusion. Aaron "may have been attempting to get away from a captor, ran away, climbed the bridge and fell," Hand would finally conclude (*AJ&C* 1981).

Barely two weeks after Aaron Wyche's death, another black child was discovered murdered.

Friends described nine-year-old Anthony Carter as a shy boy who masked his reticence with playground bravado. Like most of the youngsters he knew,

Anthony ran errands for older people in his near southwest Atlanta neighborhood, and he picked up odd jobs around nearby West End Mall.

Neighbors in the redbrick apartments along West End Avenue did recall, though, that Anthony often spent evenings roaming the neighborhood. "Lots of time he would stay until 10, 11 P.M. watching television with my children," remembered neighbor Eula Collins. "I'd always send him home then. Sometimes he'd ask for something to eat, and if I had it, I'd feed him" (*AJ&C* 1981).

On a warm summer night, sometime around 1 A.M. on Sunday, July 6, the end of the Fourth of July holiday weekend, Anthony Carter disappeared while playing hide-and-seek with a cousin.

His body was found the following day. It had been dumped behind a neighborhood warehouse a little more than a mile from Anthony's home. Medical examiners determined that Anthony had been stabbed at least four times with a two-inch pocket knife.

Vera Carter would tell reporters that, months after her son's death, FBI agents considered her a prime suspect in the murder of her only child.

Until the end of June 1980 the number of child murders was not unusually high. Atlanta police records showed that ten children were murdered in 1975, nine in 1976, seven in 1977, and ten in 1978.

So the eight unsolved murders between July 1979 and July 1980 didn't appear to police authorities to be exceptional. No need, therefore, to treat them differently. But Camille Bell, Grace Davis, and other mothers pressed for a single, coordinated investigation into the now eight unsolved child murders. There was something frighteningly different about the murders, the women kept saying.

They were not off base. Had Atlanta police taken a closer look at their own data on child murders over the most recent five-year period, they would have indeed seen something unusual. From 1975 through 1978, only two Atlanta children had been murdered by strangulation. But in just one year, from July 1979 through July 1980, two deaths had already been attributed to strangulation. In most of the city's child-murder cases, the victims died of shootings, stabbing, or beatings—usually at the hands of a relative or someone known to the child.

Although not exactly aware of these bits of criminological details, folks within the city's cordons of misery had grown impatient with the way Atlanta authorities were dealing with the murders. They accused police of treating poor black people with contempt.

Encouraged by former public safety commissioner Reginald Eaves (later elected Fulton County commissioner), who kept encouraging the community at loss to "organize,"[1] aggrieved mothers embarked on a multitiered, community-grounded oppositionist project. With help from volunteers, the mothers set up shop at a local mall and established a twenty-four-hour telephone hotline. They drew up safety rules for children, which they communicated to parents in a variety of better-parenting instructional settings.

More controversially, the mothers recruited some former Atlanta cops and a private security specialist. The ex-officers—all white males—had been announcing publicly that the child murders were not murder as usual.[2]

The men began their independent investigation by announcing that they were private detectives hired by STOP cofounder Willie Mae Mathis to find her missing son, Jefferey. These investigations didn't turn up anything particularly helpful, although the detectives' apparent overriding objective was probably accomplished—providing additional ammunition that critics could use to heap ridicule on the work that Atlanta police had thus far done on the cases.[3]

As the level of organized activities in the affected neighborhoods intensified, and as word got out of the "shoddy" work that Atlanta police were doing, pressure was on Mayor Jackson to do something substantial.

On July 17, eight days after STOP had held a well-received press conference, Commissioner Lee Brown announced that he was forming a special police task force to investigate the string of child murders and disappearances (see appendix B).

The task force would comprise one ABPS sergeant, who would serve as supervisor, and four investigators. They were given a list of ten Atlanta children who either had been murdered or were missing. Their specific assignment was to investigate the deaths of Edward Smith, Alfred Evans, Milton Harvey, Yusef Bell, Angel Lenair, Eric Middlebrooks, and Anthony Carter. (Aaron Wyche's name would be added to the list later.) In addition, they would look into the disappearance of Jeffery Mathis, Christopher Richardson, and Latonya Wilson.

In announcing the formation of the task force, Brown made no concession to the mothers' contention that black youngsters were being snatched at random. The task force, Brown said, was simply a specially appointed entity with responsibility for looking into a set of unsolved murders. As if to reinforce the point, Governor George Busbee offered a $1,000 reward, per case, for information leading to separate indictments. Like Atlanta's police brass, Busbee did not believe there was a single controlling pattern to the mysterious cases.

The community at risk favored the creation of a task force—even though, as Willie Mae Mathis commented, "It took another death [of Anthony Carter] to get them to do what they should have done four kids ago." Something would have been done sooner if the children had been white or from families of the middle-class blacks who ran Atlanta, folks in the neighborhoods were saying. "It takes a little bit more to get people [in Atlanta city government] concerned about a child out of the ghetto," said Camille Bell at one neighborhood meeting.

Two weeks following the announcement of the task force, another child disappeared.

Ten-year-old Earl Lee Terrell was not at all a "street kid." But neither was he quiet or shy, nor someone who always stayed close to his home at 1930 Browns Mill Road in southwest Atlanta. Earl was in the third grade at Lakewood Elementary School, which meant he was as much as two years behind the grade most students were in at his age.

Earl had been at the South Bend Park swimming pool, across the road from Lakewood Fairgrounds, on Wednesday, July 30. He and another boy started wrestling on the pool deck. They were stopped by lifeguard Olivia Hickson. When she caught the pair wrestling again, she threw them out. One of Earl's sisters told him to wait for her on a bench outside the pool. Earl sat cooling his heels, then took off on his own. One woman said she saw Earl after 3:30 P.M. that same day standing on the corner near Jonesboro Road crying. Another woman said she saw him buying some Freeze Pops in a grocery store about a block away from his house. The freelance detectives working with STOP learned that after Earl left the pool area, he stopped at a nearby house to look for a boy, but the boy was not there.

When Earl didn't come home, his relatives scoured their neighborhood looking for him. They were about to call the police when his aunt, Vickie Terrell, who lived next door to Earl and his mother, received a baffling phone call. On the line was "a man who sounded like a middle-aged white man with a Southern drawl." Earl's aunt listened to the caller, whom she quoted as saying, according to Dettlinger and Prugh (1983, 78), "I've got Earl."

A few minutes later, the phone rang again. The same voice said, "I've got Earl. He's in Alabama. It will cost you two hundred dollars to get him back on Friday." Ms. Terrell and Earl's mother, Beverly Belt, took this to mean the man would call back on Friday. At 2:00 A.M. Thursday, twelve hours after Earl had disappeared, Ms. Belt reported her son missing. She told Atlanta police of the ransom demand. The police placed a wiretap on Vickie Terrell's phone, anticipating the Friday call-back. But the call never came.

The disappearance of Earl Terrell marked the second missing Atlanta child case showing evidence of possible kidnapping. The other was that of seven-year-old Latonya Wilson, whom a neighbor claimed she had seen being carried away by a man in the early morning hours of Sunday, June 22. Both cases demonstrated the typical kidnapping earmarks that would normally serve to bring the FBI into a seemingly local crime case—Earl Terrell's more so than Latonya Wilson's. In Earl's case, Atlanta law enforcement had reason to believe, based on the mysterious telephone call, that he had been forcibly abducted and transported *across state lines.*

Acting on a direct request from local authorities and information provided by the newly formed special Atlanta police task force, on July 31 the FBI's Atlanta office sent a teletype message to Washington regarding Earl Terrell's disappearance. The message was simultaneously transmitted to the FBI's Mobile and Birmingham, Alabama, field offices.

By this time, though, other reasons became apparent for publicly bringing in the FBI. With black residents clamoring for more concerted investigative effort, Mayor Jackson's people felt that bringing in the FBI would serve a compelling public interest. For this reason, it would have to be done in a decidedly dramatic way. Not much public or civic (and certainly little political) good would be served if the FBI were to come into the Atlanta cases in a quiet, purely procedural way. So city officials kept up a loud, steady drumbeat about how much the FBI was needed.

On August 14, for instance, Deputy Police Chief Morris Redding held a well-publicized conference at the ABPS's Decatur Street headquarters. Although he was prepared to discuss child murder cases similar to Atlanta's, Redding told reporters that he had specifically asked the FBI special agent-in-charge for Atlanta, John Glover, a black man, to come to the conference "to assist." Assisting in an essentially consultative way (mostly providing scientific analysis of crime-scene data) was about all the FBI seemed willing to do in the Atlanta cases. The mayor's people were fast learning that getting the FBI more integrally involved would require sustained pressure on the bureau and on the U.S. Department of Justice.

As the months wore on, no reliable word was heard, and no good evidence was found, concerning the whereabouts of Earl Terrell. His name was added to the task force list. Earl was now the fourth youngster listed as missing; seven others were listed as slain. Earl Terrell would not be the last, however.

Twelve-year-old Clifford Emanuel Jones was a "smiley, round-faced kid." He had lived in nearby Chattanooga, Tennessee, until his mother moved to Cleveland just a few months earlier. They were visiting his maternal grandmother in Atlanta when he disappeared.

Clifford had been in Atlanta long enough to be warned about the danger. It was a warning his mother repeated the afternoon of August 20, when Clifford left his grandmother's house—at 1153 Lookout Avenue in near northwest Atlanta—with his cousin to scavenge for aluminum cans to sell.

"Mama," Clifford had yelled over his shoulder. "We'll find some cans and make some money so you can wash the clothes."

Clifford got separated from his cousins in his search along Hollywood Road. He was last seen at the intersection of St. James Drive and Lookout Avenue around 8:00 P.M., apparently headed back to his grandmother's house.

Clifford's body was found early the next morning beside a Dumpster at Hollywood Plaza Shopping Center in an area his relatives had searched the previous night. He had been strangled with what medical examiners speculated was a ropelike object, possibly a piece of cloth, which was used to jerk him up and then strangle him. He may have been strangled, the examiners believed, by the very shirt he was wearing. Clifford suffered bruises to his lips and a cut inside the corner of his mouth.

Besides the red-and-blue striped shirt he was wearing at the time he disappeared, Clifford's body also was clad in red-and-blue jogging shorts and white tennis shoes that were not his. The shorts and underwear he had on when he left his grandmother's home were missing. On the unfamiliar pieces of clothing on the dead boy's body state crime lab technicians found some synthetic carpet fibers.

Clifford Jones was the second victim, after Angel Lenair, to have died of ligature strangulation, that is, being choked to death by some narrow, telltale object.

The month in which Clifford Jones's body was discovered, August 1980, saw the official launching of the Committee to Stop Children's Murders. STOP organizers formally presented their program and objectives at another of their news conferences. They also used the occasion to sum up what they knew so far about the murders and disappearances. They were sure, first of all, that the cases were related. The victims were approximately the same age, size, and build; they all lived in poor black Atlanta neighborhoods; and, except for Clifford Jones, their bodies were found south of Interstate 20. More than likely they had been killed outside their respective neighborhoods.

Organizers said they wanted the American people to see the issue of Atlanta's missing and murdered children within a larger social and political context. They stressed the bigger problem of children at risk—risk of neglect, drug abuse, parental and family abuse, homelessness, prostitution, illness, disappearance, and untimely death.[4]

STOP's broad array of concerns and objectives were best articulated by Camille Bell in one of the group's brochures and later published as an op-ed piece in the *Washington Post*. Camille Bell wrote:

> Our tragedy in Atlanta has focused the nation's attention on the unsolved murders of 26 young black people. Yet the nationwide coverage, the progress (or lack thereof) of the investigation and the statements of many individuals connected with the case have more often than not clouded over the real issue in Atlanta.
>
> The tragedy in Atlanta is only the most prominent example of a sickness that plagues the entire nation. More than 4,000 children are murdered annually in the United States, with many of these crimes going unreported. . . . These are children of different races and economic levels brought together by the cruel bond of murder, sexual assault, and neglect. . . .
>
> We, the mothers of Atlanta's slain children, share a bond with the parents of missing and murdered children everywhere in this country. We know that our children were not hoodlums or hustlers, but were ordinary children engaged in ordinary children's pursuits. Many were gifted children, destined to lead their brothers and sisters when we are gone. . . .
>
> Although we in Atlanta want an end to the killings in our city, these very killings have opened our eyes to the plague in this country—and it is not limited to Atlanta. . . . We must all unify if we are to protect our children; we must all stand up, so that America's future leaders have the opportunity to grow up and serve. (STOP n.d.[a]: 1–2)

STOP had already organized "block groups" in several of Atlanta's inner-city neighborhoods. Their main task was to watch out for neighborhood children. But, organizers contended, if the murderer or murderers were to be brought to justice, then grassroots political organizing had to go hand-in-hand with block watches and other neighborhood safety-first initiatives. Only by integrating neighborhood crime-prevention strategies into a larger political project could communities at risk hope for action from the downtown political directorate.

To force the authorities to take them (or at least the potential political power they represented) seriously, in late August STOP set up what their leaders termed "political awareness teams." The teams' central task was to "educate voters to the necessity of voting for those people who have demonstrated a special concern for children." A larger political plan called for organizing communities into "manageable cluster groups," each having a leader who would bring together a variety of other related interest groups—"from parents and clergymen to store keepers, beauticians, and barbers" (STOP n.d.[b]).

A major kickoff rally for this rising political counterforce was held a month before STOP's formal launching. The venue was historic Wheat Street Baptist Church. Encouraged by a receptive audience, Camille Bell and a succession of mothers railed from the church's ornate pulpit against an insensitive city administration, which they said had waited much too long to do anything about the killings and disappearances of black Atlanta children. This preaching occurred after the church's revered Reverend William Holmes Borders had firmly and heartily chastised the "establishment."

After Clifford Jones's name was added to the special Atlanta police task force list, in late August, Commissioner Brown told reporters that Atlanta police would not "leave any stone unturned in pursuing the investigation." He promised, "We're going to work on these cases twenty-four hours a day, seven days a week. The department's commitment to these cases is unparalleled" (*AC* 1980a).

The mayor simultaneously expanded the special police task force; it now had four supervisors (up from one) and thirteen investigators (up from four). Atlanta authorities, furthermore, began talking publicly about the "obvious pattern killings." They now seemed to have figured that the murders were committed by the same person or persons—something STOP had been saying all along.

Jackson received stepped-up, direct assistance from the governor. In addition to lending four Georgia Bureau of Investigation (GBI) agents to assist the special Atlanta police task force, Busbee instructed the GBI to help by making available to the Atlanta authorities state computers and the Georgia crime laboratory. Busbee also asked the GBI to assess any funds they might have on hand to see if they could be channeled into the Atlanta investigation. He then announced a flat $10,000 reward for information in *any* of the listed thirteen cases, reflecting his own changed opinion of the cases: the governor now seemed convinced that the cases were indeed related.

Summer dragged on into fall, and less than a month after the slaying of Clifford Jones, another child disappeared.

Fannie Mae Smith was on the telephone when an operator broke in with the message: "I have an emergency call from Darron Glass." Then the line went dead. That was the last time, a few hours after he disappeared, that the eleven-year-old foster child apparently tried to contact the woman he called Grandmama and whom the county government paid three dollars and ninety-five cents per day to rear. More than seventeen years have passed since anyone last saw Darron Glass. He disappeared, without a trace, on the evening he walked away from a church bus bringing him home from an outing to an Atlanta Braves baseball game.

According to police records, Darron was last sighted around 5:30 P.M. on Sunday, September 14, 1980, as he left the bus at the corner of Glenwood and Second Avenues in southeast Atlanta, within a block of the intersection where Alfred Evans apparently vanished fourteen months earlier. (Alfred had planned to catch a MARTA bus at that location to go see a movie on Peachtree Street in downtown Atlanta; he was found dead on July 28, 1979.)

But Darron, at four-feet nine-inches tall and weighing seventy-five pounds, had a history of running away. Although both his parents had died, and he had been in several foster homes, he had a half-dozen relatives in metropolitan Atlanta to whom he would go whenever the mood struck him. A sister lived near him on East Lake Drive, and an uncle, with whom Darron lived for a while and called his "Daddy-Uncle," lived not far away off Flat Shoals Road. But none of the relatives reported seeing him after the Sunday he disappeared. Nor were investigators ever able to confirm supposed sightings afterward or a telephone call that one of Darron's foster brothers claimed to have received from him as late as November 1980.

Darron apparently knew at least two other children on the list of murdered and missing children. He was not known, however, to have hung out with any of them. Darron was a "troubled kid," according to Smith, the foster mother with whom he stayed longest. Darron's parents had died in violent altercations. But the youngster was in many ways a "typical ten-year-old boy who liked to eat, drink Kool-Aid, and make noise," said Smith, who soon began requesting payment for interviews on the subject of her missing foster son.

Just before his disappearance, Darron was attending a special program for students with behavior problems at Kirkwood Elementary School. His rather difficult life had made him street-tough. "He was well-rehearsed in the streets," Smith told reporters. She described him as a "charmer" who could talk himself out of almost any tight spot. Investigators looking into his disappearance were not so confident.

Whatever happened to Darron Glass has remained one of the truly unsolved mysteries of the Atlanta tragedy, a tragedy that continued to deepen on into the fall of 1980.

5

The Pain of Finding Nothing at All

We realized that finding a body would be as painful as finding nothing at all.
—Linda Field, search team member

In the weeks following the disappearance of Darron Glass, terrified black Atlantans came together as perhaps never before. Church and civic groups organized programs on safety measures for the protection of neighborhood children. The media and other agencies geared toward the public instructed parents to monitor their children's activities at all times, to tell them never to ride with anyone without parental permission, and to know how to reach their children's friends in an emergency. Official law enforcement in the meantime had produced virtually nothing, so a local organization decided to launch a series of weekly searches for the five youngsters missing since March 11, 1980.

The unfolding tragedy now had Mayor Maynard Jackson's full attention. He still had to reckon, however, with other pressing city issues, including continued white fear of crime and its consequences for the economic life of the city. Case in point was a Tennessee company's decision, in early September 1980, to cancel plans to build a $7 million factory outlet shopping mall south of the Atlanta-Fulton County stadium. The company's representatives said the area's reputation for crime had scared off potential investors. At least two families of murdered children lived in the hard-pressed area where the factory would have been built.

In October the leadership of the Southern Christian Leadership Conference (SCLC) joined forces with other concerned community groups in a combined Sunday prayer pilgrimage, march, and rally to "save our children." Ministers led more than eight hundred participants in a litany affirming their commitment to building "a world in which our children can live to become good, honest, and useful men and women" (AV 1980c).[1]

The high point in the rally came when SCLC president Joseph Lowery delivered a brief but fiery oration. Lowery issued a challenge to the Atlanta authorities. "Atlanta must not boast of having the biggest airport in the world," he said. "[It] must strive to be the community with the biggest heart." Looking out into the gathering and seeing only a sprinkling of whites, he chastised white America for being more concerned with the irrelevance of "Who shot J.R.?"—the despised character in the long-running TV series *Dallas*—than with who was "killing our children and the dream of brotherhood and justice."

Lowery also challenged the black community to be more responsible and forthcoming. "There must be somebody," he said, "somebody in Atlanta who has some bit of information" relating to the murders. "There must be someone who has observed something suspicious, either relating to the crimes, or to individuals who might be suspect. People are afraid, too often, to contact the police voluntarily" (Gulliver 1980).

None of the city's elected officials, black or white, showed up to hear the group's complaints.

The special Atlanta police task force charged with looking into the string of mysterious child slayings and disappearances had in the meantime reached an investigative dead end. Tips relating to the cases had slowed.

Perhaps because of this, task force investigators increasingly became more willing to utilize both conventional and unconventional approaches to solving the crimes. They had reviewed the cases of sexual offenders brought to the attention of the police within the past year and had looked closely at all "perverts" who had recently gotten out of prison. Professional behavioral scientists also had analyzed, for the authorities, a number of earlier crimes resembling the Atlanta cases. But the behavioral scientists were unable to offer a "psychological profile" of just who was murdering Atlanta's children, because no clear evidence had emerged to indicate only one person was responsible.

This lack of any noteworthy breakthrough led Atlanta authorities to get in touch with a nationally known psychic, Dorothy Allison, from Nutley, New Jersey. She had been working free of charge helping police solve homicide and missing persons cases since 1967. Within four days in 1978 she had led police in a New Jersey town to the bodies of two missing teenagers. She had also helped with New York's "Son of Sam" murder cases and with a series of strangulations in nearby Columbus, Georgia.

By her own account, Allison had helped solve fourteen homicides, uncovered thirty-eight bodies, and worked with police in connection with more than one hundred cases between 1970 and 1980. Her contact with these "atrocious cases," she told reporters, left her with utter contempt for murderers and child molesters. That contempt, she said, was the reason she had been volunteering her extraordinary service to cities requesting it.

Allison said that when she first learned of the Atlanta youth murders in early September, the "image of something clear, like a glass," came into her mind. A few days later, Darron Glass was reported missing. She knew nothing about his disappearance until well after her "vision," Ms. Allison said (*AC* 1980b). She wanted to come to Atlanta to "get" the killer. "I don't care where he's at. I've helped the police capture fourteen killers, and I'm going to get fifteen" (*AC* 1980e). The Atlanta law enforcement community decided to bring her to Atlanta.

The city's white elites supported the decision, even though they had some "minor" reservations. "We are a little skeptical about using psychics to catch criminals," editorialized the *Atlanta Constitution*. "Ordinarily, that has the ring of something you find in a B movie plot on late-night television. But we applaud the Atlanta police for considering the use of a well-known and apparently successful psychic in trying to track down the Atlanta child killer—or killers. This is no ordinary case and no stone should be left unturned" (*AC* 1980c).

In early September the independently operating detectives—who ostensibly were working on the missing Jefferey Mathis case—were beginning to develop a theory. Mike Edwards brought the theory to life by driving writer Steve Oney on a route consisting of secondary roads.

First, Edwards drove Oney along Gordon Street, then Fulton Street, then Memorial Drive. To travel from the spot on Gordon Street where Jefferey Mathis disappeared to the intersection of Memorial Drive and Interstate 285 in DeKalb County, fifteen miles away, Edwards had only to make one left and one right turn. As Edwards drove along, it seemed to Oney that "his course flowed as easily as a river."

> Passing a Dempsey Dumpster behind a warehouse, he [Edwards] pointed out where Anthony Carter's body was found. Hard by Atlanta Stadium, he showed where Yusef Bell had disappeared and then drove by an abandoned schoolhouse where the boy's tiny corpse was discovered. On Memorial [Drive], he pulled to a halt by a glass-littered lot behind a tiny bar; it was there that Eric Middlebrooks's body was found only a few months after Jefferey Mathis disappeared. And as he proceeded down Memorial, he pointed out spot after spot where one of the missing and murdered children had either lived or disappeared. (Oney 1981, 26)

The notion of a geographic pattern to the killings was one that the Atlanta authorities weren't quite ready to put much stock in—at least not at the end of summer and into early fall 1980.[2] Before they saw anything to "this map thing," and before Dorothy Allison came to town, another black Atlanta child was reported missing.

Ten-year-old Charles Stephens was like any other child of the projects. On almost any afternoon he could be seen shooting basketball near his apartment on Pryor Circle in southwest Atlanta. Charles sometimes helped neighbors empty garbage cans for a small tip. At other times he would withdraw to his living room, where he liked to draw and tinker with plastic models. But other details of Charles's life revealed that he was no stranger to trouble. A neighbor had reported to police, sometime in early 1980, that Charles had killed her watchdog and then stolen her television (Dettlinger and Prugh 1983, 135).

Charles was last seen alive on October 9, 1980. He had been sketching and watching television at home after missing the school bus. His body was found the next morning lying on a grassy hill off Norman Berry Drive, near the entrance to the Longview Trailer Park in East Point, a suburb on Atlanta's southwest boundary. The body was placed where it could be easily found.

When he disappeared, Charles was wearing a T-shirt, dark pants, and his sister's shoes. Missing from his dead body were the shirt and one shoe. He had been smothered by something like a blanket or a strong hand placed over his face. Rub marks found on his nose and mouth reinforced this conclusion. On his body, medical experts and police investigators found some carpetlike fibers.

Within a few days of Charles Stephens's murder, another incident occurred that made it more difficult for black Atlantans to, as *Time* (1980) put it, "fight off" the suspicion that the murders might be "part of a ghastly racial vendetta."

On Monday, October 13, an explosion went off at the Gate City Day-Care Center in the Bowen Homes housing project in near northwest Atlanta. Experts said it had the force of fifty pounds of dynamite and was as powerful as a huge fragmentation grenade. Adjacent buildings shook and windows shattered in the aftershock. A metal door from the center was blown completely over the top of the housing complex, landing five hundred feet away; a car parked in a nearby lot was flipped over. The day-care center itself was blown inside out. When the wreckage was cleared, four children and one adult—all black—had been killed.

The next night a frightened, angry group gathered at the Greater Fairhill

Baptist Church on Hightower Road to demand answers from the mayor. Jackson tried to speak, but the group jeered and booed when he explained that the explosion was an accident.

"Listen," Jackson pleaded to the gathering, which was about to transform itself into a mob. "Just hear me for a minute. I know the frustrations here. I feel the same frustration. Just a minute. Just a minute. That's the God's truth" (ABC *Nightline*, October 20, 1980).

Political writer Frederick Allen, who covered the meeting for the *Atlanta Constitution*, wrote: "The people of Bowen Homes were convinced that a bomb had been planted, that some racist individual or group had murdered their children, and they were not to be quieted by reassurances from any of their familiar leaders" (Allen 1981a).

The mayor gave up trying to speak. So did the other mainline black leaders assembled for the occasion: former Atlanta city councilman Arthur Langford Jr., Greater Fairhill pastor J. E. Jones, and SCLC president Joseph Lowery. Only the plain-speaking, impolitic state representative Hosea Williams, Martin Luther King Jr.'s field general, could successfully reach the angry horde. After taking control of the pulpit, Williams ordered the television camera crews and the newspaper photographers to leave. Then, rather than try to reason with the crowd, Williams spoke directly to their fears. He preached about the racism that was loose in the land. Finally, he led the shouting throng on a march to city hall. "Five miles and a couple of hours later, standing in the deserted streets of downtown Atlanta, the crowd had exhausted its emotions. The moment of violence that threatened Atlanta had vaporized in the chilly night air," wrote Allen (1981a).

Hosea Williams's move, though openly combative, still angered more militant activists, who thought his actions belittled the people's cause and thwarted their moral right to a "revolution."

The official report on the day-care center explosion stated that the building's boiler blew up. The explosion resulted from "poor work" by the Atlanta Housing Authority, whose work crew had lighted the building's boiler less than a half hour before it exploded. But questions persisted and doubts lingered. Black folks wanted to know why, for instance, it took the Atlanta police a full half hour to arrive at the scene of the explosion.

The police, curiously, said they responded as late as they did because they were tied up answering all the bomb-threat calls they were receiving right after the explosion at the day-care center. Twelve certifiable threats were made that day to the city's predominantly black public schools. Added to this, an international meeting of neofascists had convened in Atlanta a few days before the explosion. The meeting had been called by known rapists who had been implicated in the killing of four black girls in the 1964 Birmingham, Alabama, church bombing.

In late fall the prevailing belief within Atlanta's poor black neighborhoods was that the tragedy of their missing and murdered children was connected in some way to the day-care center explosion. The source of both tragedies, folks were saying, was a pervasive current of violent racism.

Mayor Jackson and other black city officials tried to find ways to neutralize such talk. The mayor's approach was to publicly yield to the truth of hate groups being vile and despicable. At a heated news conference the day after the explosion, Jackson specifically denounced activities being waged by Georgia Klan adherents, whom he called "renegades." The mayor pointed out that if blacks also were to train with submachine guns and at paramilitary bases (as the Klan was reportedly doing in the hills of north Georgia), "they'd be under the jail." He added, "Black folks running around with machine guns saying they're going to kill white folks—and cops, too? Are you kidding me? Mister, that never would have been tolerated" (*AC* 1980j).

Jackson's black nationalist bluster was clearly intended to restore a measure of credibility with his rapidly fracturing "natural" black grassroots constituency. His remarks were a partial concession to the expressions of ordinary black Atlantans. But he was especially careful not to even appear to agree with notions of the Klan, or any other white hate group, being behind either the killings and disappearances or the day-care center explosion.

As it turned out, though, the mayor *did* secretly fear that recent "growth of the Klan might spark racial violence in Atlanta" (*AJ* 1980). So right after the day-care center explosion he privately asked Governor George Busbee to step up an ongoing GBI probe into Klan activities in and around Atlanta. In a letter, Jackson urged Busbee to "immediately investigate [the] Ku Klux Klan in Georgia and take whatever steps are necessary to insure the safety of all Afro-Americans, Jews and others in this state who are threatened by the vicious hatred and outlaw tactics of the Ku Klux Klan" (*AC* 1980j).

Atlanta's white elites had an entirely different view. A coalition of Atlanta businesses announced in mid-October that it was undertaking a campaign aimed at providing Atlanta's 70,000 downtown workers (who were mostly black) with "safety tips for protecting children." The Atlanta Business Coalition included the Atlanta Business League, Atlanta Chamber of Commerce, Atlanta Convention and Visitors' Bureau, and Georgia Hospitality and Travel Association.

What was happening to the black children of Atlanta, coalition representatives said, need not be tied to race or place. They were "senseless crimes" that could affect any group. "This is not a problem confined to the city limits," said chairman Joel Goldberg. "Crimes against our children are taking place throughout the metropolitan area. This is not a problem that concerns only black residents. It concerns all residents. Children are our greatest asset, and all of us must do our part to help police solve these senseless crimes" (*AC* 1980d). The explosion was "unfortunate," Goldberg said. His group soon had the day-care center rebuilt—free of charge to the city.

While investigations continued into the explosion and the most recent murder, a novel approach to finding the still-missing five youngsters came on the scene.

The United Youth Adult Conference of Atlanta (UYAC), headed by the Reverend Arthur Langford Jr.,[3] organized volunteer Saturday searches—that is, groups of people joining forces and going out, squadronlike, to fan bushes, search vacant lots, and interview residents. Organizers hoped that they also would gather vital information that could help identify suspects.

Founded in the spring of 1972 as an advocacy agency for crime prevention, better working conditions, and community improvement, the UYAC's first project was working with a group of black striking employees of Holy Family Hospital (later named Southwest Community Hospital) in Atlanta. Strikers had called on Langford, a seasoned activist, to "investigate their complaints of unfair working conditions." Langford and a committee thought the strikers' demands were just, so they organized a picketing campaign against the hospital. While demonstrating on the hospital grounds, Langford was shot. "During his recovery," according to a UYAC booklet, "leaders of the United Youth Adult Conference rallied to form community support from the city and the nation. The day after the shooting, more than 2,000 concerned citizens held a massive demonstration on the hospital grounds. . . . The demonstration proved to be successful and the dispute between the strikers and the hospital was settled" (UYAC, n.d.).

In an interview Langford told me that his group had organized the Saturday searches because folks in the community, including students from the Atlanta University Center, had asked, "What can we do?" Communal frustration was all the more palpable, Langford said, in view of the Atlanta police "just dragging its feet on these cases."

The searches began Saturday, October 18. Search teams fanned out into the neighborhoods from West Hunter Street Baptist Church at 1040 Southwest Gordon Avenue.[4] Wearing orange vests and arm bands, they searched abandoned buildings, hollow tree trunks, and stream beds for shreds of clothing, fresh digging, stacked rocks, or any other clues.

A biracial group of several hundred volunteers stumbled onto skeletal remains in the Dixie Hills neighborhood of near northwest Atlanta. The broken bones were quickly carted away for forensic analysis by task force investigators. Dental records revealed that the remains belonged to Latonya Wilson, the seven-year-old girl reported missing for the past four months—since June 1980. On the morning of her disappearance, Latonya's parents had told police they believed their daughter had been abducted.

The bones were discovered in a fenced-in, wooded area near the intersection of Verbena Street and Sewanee Avenue—within eyesight of the Hillcrest apartment complex in which Latonya lived. Dr. Saleh Zaki, associate medical examiner for Fulton County, said the cause of Latonya's death could not be immediately determined, but he suspected foul play. No "soft tissue" was left because the youngster had been dead for several months. Zaki told reporters that, because the body was thoroughly decomposed, it would be difficult to determine whether Latonya had been sexually assaulted (*AC* 1980f). Latonya Wilson became the eleventh murder victim on the list of Atlanta's missing and murdered children.

Finding dead bodies was not exactly the kind of outcome that organizers of the Saturday searches had anticipated. They hoped to find live children who were simply too dazed, lost, or bewildered to find their way back home. But finding a body was a measure of success, however macabre, because finding nothing at all would have been almost as painful. This was agonizingly brought home to search team members when they confronted the mother of missing Jefferey Mathis after that first Saturday search.

"I'm Willie Mae Mathis," the sad woman said in between sobs as she walked up to a search team, which included *Atlanta Constitution* journalist Linda Field. "I heard you found a child."

"Yes, ma'am, we did," Field replied.

"It was a girl," said another team member.

"Twin tears streamed from her eyes, her body shaking with emotion," recalled Field.

"I thought you found my child," said Mathis.

"Hold on, sister," another team member encouraged. "God is with you, and so are we" (AC 1980g).

Encouraged by their qualified success on their first day—and the widespread praise for their efforts—Langford and his followers vowed to conduct more searches in coming weeks. To avoid tipping off the killer(s), search organizers said they would not disclose the location for their next search.

On the following weekend, three thousand searchers showed up—including Mayor Jackson and other local pols. This time the searchers scoured the East Lake Meadows community, in which two of the still-missing children, Christopher Richardson and Darron Glass, had lived. Both boys were last seen alive on Memorial Drive, which ran through southeast Atlanta and the East Lake Meadows community. Alfred Evans, one of the eleven dead youths and second on the task force list, also came from the East Lake Meadows community.

The mayor called the response to the UYAC appeal for volunteers for the second search effort "most heartwarming." Not one to miss an opportunity to "show off" the social remarkableness of Atlanta, nor downplay his own growth on the issue of the murders and disappearances, the mayor continued: "There are two stories to be told here. One is about the tragic attack on our children, but the parallel story is about the greatness of the people of Atlanta" (AJ&C 1980b).

The white Atlanta establishment, particularly its liberal white-owned media, agreed. In an editorial, aired on October 28, the management of WGST News Radio 92 applauded the search parties.

> The 3,000 people who turned out on Saturday to search the East Lake area for the missing four black children are a tribute to the responsiveness of the Atlanta community in times of stress. The gathering was reminiscent of the sixties—even some of the same faces and some new faces of young people who would have been in the movement of the sixties. The spirit that first made Atlanta great fifteen to twenty years ago . . . was again evident on Saturday. . . . Many prominent Atlantans came—not looking for publicity. Just to help. That the search this week was fruitless is not important—it is the effort and concern that matter. Mayor Jackson may have said it best when he indicated we are proud of our buildings, our transit system, our heritage, and our landmarks, but when the chips are down it is the people of Atlanta who make this the city that it is. (WGST 1980b)

The second Saturday search yielded a stolen bank safety deposit box, a gun, and some animal remains—but no dead bodies or live children. Langford called, nonetheless, for more volunteers for the following weekend.

The Saturday searches gave well-meaning whites an opportunity to engage in a goal-oriented activity *in behalf of black people.* "All over the city," reported the *Atlanta Constitution,* "whites noticeably absent from earlier marches and rallies [i.e., those organized in the wake of the slayings and disappearances] are making an about-face. They now are planning to join search parties." Commented businessman Dan Sweat on the Saturday searches: "I think we had seen a growing apart of blacks and whites. If any such thing is possible, maybe something positive has come out of the tragedies if it has brought the community together again" (*AC* 1980h).

The community at risk didn't see things quite that way. They could hardly be expected to be impressed with what they viewed as "goody-goody" embraces. They weren't exactly moved, either, by Jackson's symbolic participation in *one* Saturday search. Folks held that the mayor's presence was purely political, an act intended only to get black folks to "cool down."

Police assist Helen Pue, mother of murder victim Terry Pue (*Atlanta Journal-Constitution* /George A. Clark)

Save Our Children March on Auburn Avenue in 1980. Camille Bell and her daughter Tonia are at left, next to Evelyn Lowery. Rev. Joseph Lowery is third from right, and Rev. Earl Carroll is at extreme right. (*Atlanta Journal-Constitution* /W. A. Bridges Jr.)

Police Chief George Napper and Commissioner Lee Brown hold a press conference in front of the Fulton County Jail (*Atlanta Journal-Constitution* /W. A. Bridges Jr.)

Mayor Maynard Jackson displays part of the $150,000 reward offered for information on the missing and murdered children (*Atlanta Journal-Constitution* /George Clark)

JOIN US!
The Committee to Stop Children's Murders

525
STOP
COMMITTEE TO STOP CHILDREN'S MURDERS

Sᴀᴠᴇ Tʜᴇᴍ Oʀ Pᴇʀɪsʜ!

859½ Martin Luther King Drive

· **Atlanta, Georgia 30314** ·

Pamphlet distributed by citizens' group responding to Atlanta child slayings and disappearances

Wayne Williams talks to the press (*Atlanta Journal-Constitution/* Kenneth Walker)

Cobb County police and Atlanta Task Force officers recover Nathaniel Cater's body from the Chattahoochee River (*Atlanta Journal-Constitution*/Jerome McClendon)

Williams leaves the Fulton County Courthouse after entering a plea of not guilty (*Atlanta Journal-Constitution*/Jerome McClendon)

CAN YOU ??

SING OR PLAY

AN
INSTRUMENT

★

If YOU Are Between "11-21" (male or female)
And Would Like To Become A
Professional Entertainer,

"YOU" Can Apply For POSITIONS With
Professional Recording Acts
No Experience is Necessary, Training Is Provided

All Interviews Private & FREE !!

★

FOR MORE INFORMATION CALL
3 PM - 7 PM
404 / 794-8980

Flyer distributed by Wayne Williams in Atlanta public housing project
(from the FBI's case file)

Homer Williams, father of Wayne Williams, wards off photographers (*Atlanta Journal-Constitution*/W. A. Bridges Jr.)

Judge Clarence Cooper and Fulton County district attorney Lewis Slaton (*Atlanta Journal-Constitution*/W. A. Bridges Jr.)

Mary Welcome, Williams's attorney, holds a press conference (*Atlanta Journal-Constitution*/George A. Clark)

Defense attorney Mary Welcome signs an autograph for Earl Williams, a Connecticut lawyer (*Atlanta Journal-Constitution*/Nancy Mangiafico)

6

Select Outsiders Only

Atlanta's Black leaders . . . were made to look bad, and the overall impression
of the program to those outside this city must have been that Atlanta is a
criminal city living in constant fear.

—Editorial, WGST News Radio 92

Intent on alleviating the mounting tension, Mayor Maynard Jackson tried
every conceivable thing. In addition to having his public safety commissioner
assign increasing numbers of the city's police officers to the special investigative task force, the mayor insisted on, and eventually got, more than usual FBI
involvement in the Atlanta cases. He brought into the city five supersleuths who
had recently cracked some of the nation's most notorious murder cases. In the
meantime, state authorities tried to learn more about militant activities of the
Ku Klux Klan in hopes of "heading off" racial violence in Atlanta. In late October 1980, the ABC TV programs *20/20* and *Nightline* sent production teams
to cover what was happening in Atlanta.

From the moment word began to spread around the nation of the puzzling
murders and disappearances of black children in Atlanta, the reflexive reaction
was: In one way or another, race was the motivation behind the terrible incidents. The national news media made much of this angle, emphasizing the paradox of Atlanta as a southern city with a history of racial enlightenment—and
where many of the nation's successful blacks lived—with "something like this"
happening there.

Nightline opened its October 20 story on the Atlanta murders by connecting
them to the seemingly racially motivated killing of six black men in Buffalo,
New York, earlier that year. The killer had ripped their hearts out of their bodies. "Understandably," host Ted Koppel said in his opening note, "in the black
communities of both cities, the fact that all the victims have been black raises

a lot of fearful questions." To reinforce the point, Koppel related SCLC president Joseph Lowery's contention that the murders of blacks in Atlanta and Buffalo were "part of a general national pattern of assaults on blacks." Lowery had also stated, Koppel reminded viewers, that all these killings were "the result of an increase in right-wing extremism throughout the country."

In the program's lead-in, correspondent Al Dale focused on the tension in Atlanta's terrorized black and poor neighborhoods. The horror and deception of Atlanta as a "city too busy to hate" was now shown on national TV. The picture was one of residents voicing anger that it had taken *this long* for Atlanta police to connect the cases of the murdered and missing children or for them to have made any effort beyond normal police work to solve them. "There is something wrong with the heart of Atlanta," one man said. "There is something wrong with the spirit of Atlanta."

Dale pointed out that Atlanta's poor black children and their parents were afraid. "Along with that fear, there is an undercurrent here of suspicion that the deaths may be part of a broader campaign against black people. Mayor Jackson cautioned against such conclusions last week after an explosion at a day-care center took the lives of four more black children and a black teacher."

Strangely, when Public Safety Commissioner Lee Brown was interviewed on the program, he indicated that he was still not convinced that the unsolved cases were connected. "Being that we have not solved the cases, we're unable to determine the motive," he said. "We know that there [are] certain characteristics that are similar. . . . So because we do not even know the motive . . . we have no way of saying what they're related to." Koppel interrupted and asked if "after fifteen months" Atlanta police had nothing other than "ten dead children and four missing?"

Brown replied: "Well, we're operating under the premise that they [the murders] could be related, that one or more could be related, all could be related, and none could be related. . . . We do not know at this point."

Brown seemed to have been backing away from an earlier position he and other investigating authorities had taken right after the death of Clifford Jones. The commissioner had said then that the Atlanta authorities were taking a unitary approach to the killings and disappearances. His apparent flip-flop two months later on national TV could only have been interpreted as an attempt to neutralize an insistent nationwide tendency to see racial conspiracy in the Atlanta cases.

The news magazine program *20/20* aired its first story on the Atlanta child murders on October 23. The largest segment of the hourlong broadcast was devoted to the unfolding events in Atlanta. Host Hugh Downs described Atlanta as "a city of fear," its black community "aroused." Correspondent Bob Sirkin pointed out that one of the "ironies" of the tragedy is that Atlanta was a city run by a black administration. "The mayor here is black. The police chief is black. The commissioner of public safety is black. And tonight those men are bearing the brunt of the black community's anger and frustration over these child murders. Blacks accusing blacks of doing too little too late to stop the murders."

A cross section of Atlanta's black community, from Reverend Lowery to mother Camille Bell, expressed fear, anger, and frustration. "The children who [are] being killed," Camille Bell said, "are primarily poor, primarily black, and no one gets terribly concerned." When asked how she could fail to trust a black police chief and commissioner, Bell's trenchant reply was that the race of these officials was of "little consequence" in alleviating the facts of black dispossession.

As if all this weren't bad enough for Atlanta's long-treasured good image, the program went on to tell of a local TV station's investigative report on the Ku Klux Klan. A voice-over to footage showing stepped-up Klan activity in the Atlanta area, and of Klansmen saying they were "preparing for guerrilla war," said developments like these had raised the "paranoia level" of Atlanta's blacks, who were "already frightened and angry because of the child murders."

Atlanta's white establishment was livid. The next day, civic and business leaders demanded a meeting with ABC representatives to express their dissatisfaction with what they considered "unfair reporting." The management of WGST News Radio delivered an irate denunciation:

> *20/20* was something like 20/200 in eyeglass terms. But without the benefit of lens correction. . . . Atlanta's Black leaders were made to look bad, and the overall impression of the program to those outside this city must have been that Atlanta is a criminal city living in constant fear. . . . The use of footage on the Ku Klux Klan was immaterial to the story [of the child murders], and [was] a case of managed news clearly designated to create a false impression. (WGST 1980a)

In a way, this kind of vituperative reaction to "meddlesome outsiders," especially the northern liberal media, was not entirely new. In the height of the civil rights era, few things irked the southern segregationist order more than the northern media "coming down here and telling us how to treat our Negroes." Although issues of race had always been politically and ideologically different in Atlanta, the general sentiment against outsiders still firmly held. The last thing the Atlanta establishment wanted was to have ABC—or any other northern medium, for that matter—projecting *their* interpretation of what was happening with black Atlanta children.

Only those outsiders who, like psychic Dorothy Allison, would not try to recharacterize the tragedy or wrest control of its definition from the Atlanta establishment would go unchallenged. Allison arrived in Atlanta on October 21 to much fanfare. "I guarantee there will be no more murders while I'm here," she told reporters at a packed press conference. She envisioned the Atlanta killer being of the same race as all the slain children: black. "I'm very hopeful," Police Chief George Napper said, "that Mrs. Allison's presence will bring to a quick conclusion the nightmare facing this city" (*AC* 1980i).

City officials spared no expense at making Allison's whirlwind five-day stay comfortable. Her book, *A Psychic's Story*, went into its third printing while she was in Atlanta. Still, she was unable to lead investigators to any missing children, to any dead bodies, or to the person or persons responsible for the murders and disappearances. The city's excessive kindness and too much publicity, she said, was preventing her divining powers from getting into full gear. She departed Atlanta leaving only "tips" for the city's special police task force to investigate, Deputy Chief Morris Redding told reporters. Atlanta police were not giving up on psychics, however. They were "continuing to talk with a number of other persons who claimed unusual powers," Mayor Jackson admitted to reporters.

Interestingly, despite WGST's ranting over *20/20*'s playing up of the Ku Klux Klan element, Atlanta officials could not deny their concerns over the Klan and other hate groups' possible involvement in a number of violent racial incidents in the Atlanta area.

City officials had hurriedly scheduled a late October conference, which included officials with the U.S. Department of Justice (DOJ), to "assess local racial attitudes" and to "head off a possible confrontation between blacks and whites." Ozell Sutton, regional director of the DOJ's Community Relations Service, said a series of slayings in several cities and the slayings and disappearances in Atlanta were part of a national concern that blacks were being victimized. Asked to send representatives to the conference (which was closed to the public and the media) were the NAACP, the SCLC, the B'nai B'rith Anti-Defamation League, and several other civil rights and civil liberties organizations.

Tensions further prompted state authorities to successfully resist the DOJ's decision to move to Atlanta the trial of a white former Miami policeman charged with violating the civil rights of black insurance agent Arthur McDuffie, whom police officers had allegedly beaten to death (*AC* 1980j).

At a press conference, Georgia governor George Busbee announced a GBI investigation into "militant activities of the Ku Klux Klan in Georgia." His aim, he said, was to "head off racial violence." GBI director Phil Peters noted, "We have every reason to believe there is an increase, certainly in the visibility of the Ku Klux Klan" (*AC* 1980j).

While the governor had been holding his press conference, leaders of a group of black veterans vowed to arm themselves against the Ku Klux Klan or anyone else who threatened black people. "If it takes our blood to run in the streets, let it be," said James W. Tibbs, national adjutant of the group U.S. Veterans, which included former members of the Black Panther Party. Tibbs said that as many as eight hundred black veterans could be called to arms in Atlanta if blacks were put in a position of having to defend themselves. Armed veterans would "watchdog" the streets of Atlanta (*AJ* 1980b).

The idea of possible "race war" in Atlanta because of the string of unsolved murders and disappearances was not taken lightly by state and city authorities. But no records were available to indicate exactly how long the Georgia state-led investigation into Klan, and Klan-inspired, activities continued after its October launching and just what was learned from that investigation. The Atlanta mayor increased his special police task force to thirty-five full-time investigators. That did not prevent another black Atlanta child from disappearing, however.

Nine-year-old Aaron Jackson Jr. stayed away often from the little green cinder-block house on Norwood Road in southeast Atlanta where he lived with his father and two older sisters. Neighbors wondered why Junior was forever wandering about. They would often see him scampering through the Atlanta woods, sometimes for days at a time, "like an inner-city Tom Sawyer." "I'd see him in the park at 11:00 P.M. with no shoes, just walking around," Geneva Sims, manager of a neighborhood supermarket, told *Washington Post* staff writer Art Harris. Aaron "would go wherever someone would give him a meal" (*WP* 1981b).

Aaron was wandering in the early morning hours of Saturday, November 1, 1980, when he disappeared. He was last seen alive at the Moreland Plaza Shopping Center, near the intersection of Custer and Moreland Avenues in southeast Atlanta. His body was found the next day not far from his home; it was lying just off Forest Park Road on the bank of the South River beside a bridge. Investigators concluded he had been smothered to death. Aaron was wearing a silk shirt, blue jeans, shoes, and socks when he disappeared. All but his socks remained on his murdered body.

Around the time of the discovery of Aaron Jackson's body, task force investigators were deliberately searching for similarities and whatever common elements seemed to link the killings and disappearances. Aaron's murder allowed for comparisons with at least two earlier murders: Charles Stephens and Clifford Jones. Both Stephens and Aaron Jackson turned up dead the day after they disappeared. Both died of asphyxial suffocation—that is, they had been smothered, possibly by a blanket or strong hand placed over their faces. Both bodies were placed so they could be easily found, and both bodies were missing clothing.

Although Clifford Jones was strangled rather than smothered, investigators decided that the bruises on his lips indicated that he had been attacked in a manner similar to Jackson and Stephens. Also, investigators found some carpetlike fibers on Jackson's clothes—as they had found on Jones and Stephens.

In reaching for some kind of explanation for the death of her child, all Benny Jackson could say was, "He was a free-spirited child, but he was a loner. That's what bothers me. Aaron didn't talk to grown-ups. Whoever killed him had to catch him off guard" (*WP* 1981b).

Up through the end of October, the FBI had assumed a minimalist role in the Atlanta investigations. Technical assistance from the bureau was first sought in the apparent June 1980 kidnapping of seven-year-old Latonya Wilson. The agency's help was solicited again a month later, when ten-year-old Earl Terrell disappeared.

Documents obtained from the Department of Justice under the Freedom of Information Act indicated that, between March and October 1980, Atlanta officials kept the FBI Atlanta office fully informed of developments. The FBI would in turn advise the Atlanta authorities on forensic leads, as its lab experts in Washington saw them.

But Atlanta officials desired much more than token help from the FBI. From the moment he sensed racial trouble, Mayor Jackson publicly indicated that he wanted, and indeed expected, definitive FBI involvement. Throughout the summer the mayor tried to get the agency to formally "sign on" to all aspects of the Atlanta investigations. But bureau officials steadfastly resisted.

Jackson's persistent beseeching of the FBI was in itself curious. A history of disinterest in enforcing federal laws intended to protect blacks from violent racist attacks—especially during the era of the civil rights campaigns—and known campaigns of dirty tricks that the agency had waged against civil rights leaders, notably Martin Luther King Jr., had made the FBI probably the most despised federal agency among American blacks.[1]

Besides, by late fall, rumors were wild in the nation's inner-city streets that the FBI was involved in the Atlanta murders. The FBI, word had it, was collaborating with the CIA in obtaining the bodies of the dead children for the national Centers for Disease Control, located in Atlanta, or they were covering up for racist whites—namely, Klan members who were committing the murders. Why, then, would Atlanta's black political authority want "heavy" FBI involvement in the investigations? Two politically racialized reasons were evident.

The first was that, while blacks were saying they suspected the FBI of not exactly having clean hands in the Atlanta slayings, they also were saying that if the victims had been white, the federal government would have shown greater concern. (That contention would be expressed eloquently by Washington mayor Marion Barry.) Had white Atlanta children been murdered, Atlanta's black elected authority would have called in the FBI. Why shouldn't poor black Atlantans get the same high-order protection that the city's white community would have unblinkingly demanded—and received?

The imperative tugged at the Jackson forces. No tried and true elected black official could ask less from the federal government for "his" people than he would have for white folks—even if the federal agency to which he had to turn was the hated FBI.

The second reason for wanting in the FBI was that the Atlanta mayor's demanding—or sounding as though he were demanding—federal involvement in a local matter was a well-established way to show political clout and to consequently enhance the bona fides of an elected local official. Jackson understood perfectly well that political power had a lot to do with being able to mobilize the resources of the federal government to act in behalf of local interests. He knew that the measure of his success as mayor and eminent black leader would lie not only in his having demonstrated common cause with people in distress but in having enough clout to secure help from a powerful federal agency.

Jackson's own moral and political agendas were not enough, however, to bring in heavy FBI involvement. Under federal statutes, a legal basis had to be established under which the FBI could be authorized to enter the investigation. But this was, as far as the Jackson people were concerned, trifling legalism about which the bureau was being excessively difficult.

Presidential appointees in Washington understood the larger political picture in Atlanta; midlevel professionals and other bureaucratic managers within the FBI and DOJ apparently did not, or they refused to cooperate. This much can be deduced from the following undated FBI memorandum:

> On 11/3/80 George Napper, COP, Atlanta, Georgia, contacted the SAC of the Atlanta Division, John D. Glover, to request additional investigative assistance. SAC Glover advised the COP the facts to date have not determined a Federal

violation; therefore, no additional FBI assistance could be forthcoming at this time.

SAC notes that political pressure has prompted local leaders to react to this tragic situation in an emotional manner. As a result, they are creating the impression that the FBI is being less than cooperative in this matter.

The U.S. Attorney, Northern District of Georgia, is attempting to schedule a meeting . . . to once again explain the position of the FBI and the DOJ in this matter. [2]

Another memorandum stated: "SAC, Atlanta, has repeatedly informed Mayor Jackson, Commissioner Brown, and Chief Napper that the FBI lacks jurisdiction in this matter and, therefore, is unable to provide the kind of investigative assistance [they wish]."

Jackson did not take these dismissals quietly. Shortly after the November 3 meeting between FBI officials and his chief of police, the mayor sent telegrams to Georgia congressional leaders and to the White House. He also telephoned presidential aide Jack Watson, an Atlanta native. Watson passed the mayor's comments on to U.S. Attorney General Benjamin Civilietti.

At a news conference, Jackson fired off angry criticisms of FBI Director William Webster. Although the bureau refused to claim jurisdiction in Atlanta, the mayor said, it had intervened in the cases involving attacks on blacks in Buffalo. "We want them to send us every living agent that they can to Atlanta. Lindbergh was one child and we're talking about fifteen here," the mayor said, referring to the 1932 kidnapping of the infant son of aviation hero Charles Lindbergh, whose case benefited from mammoth FBI involvement.

The outburst was vintage Jackson. The presentation was of a black elected official standing up for *his* people to the larger political powers that were to deliver on promises of fairness and justice.

The gambit paid off—somewhat. On November 6, the day following the mayor's heated press conference, Civilietti authorized a *preliminary* investigation by the FBI to determine if the four missing youngsters—Jefferey Mathis, Christopher Richardson, Earl Terrell, and Darron Glass—were being held in violation of the U.S. Code (Title 18) on kidnapping. If kidnapping, particularly across state lines, was suspected, then the FBI's jurisdiction in the Atlanta cases could be legally established.

Of no minor significance in Jackson's being able to bring into effect this course of action was his access to outgoing President Jimmy Carter, a former Georgia governor who had many black friends in Atlanta politics. The mayor wanted yet greater participation from the FBI, though. As if to underscore his point, during the time it had taken him to wrench the FBI's stepped-up but still rather limited involvement in the Atlanta cases, another black Atlanta youngster vanished.

Sixteen-year-old Patrick Rogers liked karate and music more than he liked school. Patrick and a friend wrote several not-yet-ready-for-Motown songs in their Thomasville Heights housing project.

According to one story, "Pat Man," as he was known to friends, was last seen shortly before 7:00 A.M. on November 10, 1980. He was walking his seven-year-old brother to a bus stop on Henry Thomas Drive in the Thomasville Heights area of southeast Atlanta. But Mary Harper, whose nineteen-year-old son, Joe, collaborated in writing songs with Patrick, said Patrick came by her apartment around 7:30 A.M. asking for her son. A guy wanted to record their songs, Patrick told Ms. Harper. Joe was absent when Patrick came calling. Patrick hurried off, but not before instructing Ms. Harper, "Tell Joe if he come, I be back" (*AJ&C* 1981).

Patrick never made it back to the Harpers. On December 7, Patrick's clothed body—his brown pants pinned together at the waist—was pulled from the Cobb County side of the Chattahoochee River, near the Paces Ferry Road bridge. Medical examiner Joseph Burton found evidence of some type of injury behind the youngster's left ear. Patrick's death, he said, was due to a skull fracture. The youth's body was so decomposed, Burton said, that he could conclude nothing else. But, Burton cautioned, there was no way to determine whether Patrick "sustained this injury through a fall, or whether somebody zapped him in the head and shoved him in the river" (*AJ&C* 1981).

A burglary warrant had been issued against Patrick two days after he disappeared, and some investigators believed that he could have been killed in a dispute with his criminal associates. An Atlanta detective said "Pat Man" ran with a tough crowd. "They had an attitude that they could go where they wanted, and do what they wanted, because they were so many, and mean enough, that nobody would mess with them," the unnamed detective told a reporter (*AJ&C* 1981).

At first, Atlanta authorities thought that, in addition to Patrick's criminal connections, his age might rule out murder at the hands of a child killer. So for more than two months they resisted community pressure to include him on the special police task force list.

Investigators looking into Patrick's disappearance learned that a young black Atlanta man claiming to be a musical talent scout had been in the Thomasville

Heights neighborhood one week before Patrick's disappearance. The man had been distributing fliers for a talent show he was organizing. The fliers announced auditions for aspiring musicians and listed a telephone number to call. The number belonged to a residence in the Dixie Hills area of the city, that of Faye and Homer Williams, both retired Atlanta school teachers.

While the circumstances of Patrick's death could not be linked conclusively to any of the special police task force victims, a number of curious coincidences had brought the boys together in life. According to Patrick's mother, he knew victim Aaron Wyche rather well because Aaron lived in an adjacent apartment building. When Aaron's body was found beneath an overpass in June 1980, Patrick told his mother the killings were "getting closer to home." Patrick also knew Aaron Jackson, who often visited friends in Thomasville Heights.

Like Aaron, Patrick carried grocery packages to customers' cars at the Moreland Plaza Shopping Center. Two other Atlanta boys who would later turn up dead were also known to the wily "Pat Man" Rogers. Despite these seeming connections, however, investigators were unable to establish a well-defined chain of circumstances that could have brought the youths together in death.

Two weeks before Patrick Rogers's body was found, FBI officials had agreed that forcible abduction—if not necessarily across state lines—had occurred in the Atlanta incidents. The bureau would henceforth involve itself more substantively in the investigations. But it would not be part of the Atlanta mayor's special police task force.

The FBI's stepped-up (though still quite tepid) involvement signaled a new stage of federal interest. But more FBI agents in Atlanta would hardly meet the city's massive and costly needs. Atlanta would need lots more help from Washington.

The year ended with Jackson appealing for more donations to a special reward fund he had established. Atlanta police, meanwhile, were tailing the Reverend Earl Carroll, a cofounder of the mothers' group STOP. Carroll cried "political harassment." The authorities were following him around, he said, as reprisal for his having brought the Atlanta cases to the public long before Atlanta police were willing to acknowledge that a problem existed. As it turned out, Carroll was suspected of purloining funds. City authorities were wondering about all that money going to victims' mothers and whether Carroll might be profiting from the grief. Carroll was arrested months later and charged with improper solicitation and writing bad checks.

In the larger sphere of things, many black Americans worried that the right-wing tide in the 1980 elections—bringing to power Ronald Reagan—would wash away even more of the social and political gains they had made. "It seems that a conservative element in this country is looking at the election as a mandate for retrenchment," fretted Representative William Gray III of Pennsylvania, a member of the Congressional Black Caucus. Gray worried that coalitions of "ultraconservatives" were at work "turning back the clock" on racial tolerance (*Newsweek* 1980b). His concerns seemed saliently borne out that November. Shortly after the presidential election, six Ku Klux Klansmen and Nazis accused of killing five black and white demonstrators at a Greensboro, North Carolina, rally the previous year were acquitted of all charges brought against them.

7

"We've Got to End This"

He had a wonderful little ten years here. I know he's gone to a better place.
—Willie Mae Mathis

In January 1981, with news of the Atlanta murders rapidly spreading across the land, solidarity groups were being formed everywhere. And it seemed that suddenly everybody became more concerned about the problem of missing children, black and white.

Practically everyone in Atlanta had been touched by the ongoing tragedy. You could hardly hold a conversation with anyone in the city "who hasn't a theory on the crime or a concern about its lack of resolution," reported PBS's Charlayne Hunter-Gault, in her lead-in to *The MacNeil/Lehrer Report* (January 8, 1981) in its first of many full-length news stories about what was happening in Atlanta. All around town folks were moaning, "We've got to end this."

Child experts were saying that the impact of the tragedy had permeated almost every aspect of the lives of the "unmurdered" and "unmissing." Atlanta's children were so gripped by fears that play activities for some had ceased. Emotional problems were on the rise, social and emotional development were being adversely affected, and some children were "having difficulty trusting other people," according to Atlanta child psychologist Nancy Emmons (1980). From evaluations of a sample of Atlanta school district's 74,400 pupils, conducted during the late weeks of 1980, Emmons found increased references to violence and hostility toward children, disorganization of thought processes, distrust (especially of white examiners), low self-esteem, confused self-image, intimidation, fear, and lack of self-confidence. Ironically, Emmons argued, "these students are also the ones most discriminated against on the standardized tests." The poor, the minorities, and the children were once again the "scapegoats" of Atlanta society, she contended.

But the killings and the disappearances did not end. Three days into 1981, another black Atlanta child disappeared. The Saturday searches continued; the latest one turned up an abandoned house filled with children's shoes, clothing, and a macabre display of drawings and two Bibles nailed to the wall. The Bibles were opened to passages referring to children and violent death.

Restively taking all this in was Atlanta's white establishment. Power structure members were growing ever more concerned about what all these developments would mean for civilized Atlanta, a city which not so long ago they completely owned. White opinion makers in the corporate media were not at all impressed with a heavy-handed curfew that Mayor Maynard Jackson and the Atlanta City Council had instituted. The editorial board of the *Atlanta Constitution* counseled: "It is ludicrous to ask city officials to take all the responsibility of keeping thousands of children off the streets. Once this story is over, maybe parents will reflect on traditional values of the family" (*AC* 1981a).

Lubie Geter was the fifth child born to Annie Geter, a worker with a local dry cleaner, and Lubie Geter Sr., a Veterans Administration hospital chef. Teachers at Murphy High School described the tenth-grader as affable and a good student. Lubie earned spending money by working at a car wash and carrying bags for shopping center customers.

Mrs. Geter last saw her fourteen-year-old Saturday, January 3, 1981. He had spent some of his Christmas money buying car deodorizers wholesale to resell for profit. He was anxious to hawk his wares to shoppers at a mall about five miles from his home, at 129 Dahlgreen Street in southeast Atlanta. After breakfast his older brother, Frank, drove him and a friend to the mall. Lubie was wearing a maroon-burgundy ski jacket, green knit pullover shirt, faded jeans, and his favorite penny loafers.

"Come back before dark," Annie Geter had instructed her son, whom she often warned to be wary of strangers, especially "with all those child murders going on" (*WP* 1981a).

"Don't worry, Mom. They've got to catch me first," Lubie had shot back.

But Lubie did not come home by dark. He had told his brother he did not want to take the bus home when he was finished with his sales. So he would call when he was ready, which would be about 5:30 P.M. Lubie never called. The last time anyone saw him was that afternoon. He was standing outside the Big Star food store at the Stewart-Lakewood Shopping Center on Georgia Route 166, selling his Zep Gel deodorizers.

Annie Geter at first figured that her son had gone to a movie with his profits. But the hours passed, and she began to pace the floor. She stayed up all night
waiting.

In the morning she called Atlanta police. She was referred to the ABPS's missing persons and youth squad unit, where Detective Carole O'Neil did an initial
investigation. O'Neil did not, however, inform the mayor's special investigative
task force of the case. (Informing the task force of any and all reports of missing
black children had by this time become standard procedure.) Deputy Chief Morris Redding, who headed the task force while fulfilling other responsibilities with
the regular force, said he heard of the missing Lubie Geter late the following
Tuesday morning. The case was not formally turned over to the task force until
three full days after Lubie had been reported missing.

Atlanta police brass reacted to the ensuing public furor over this critical delay
by demoting O'Neil and other officers. Commissioner Lee Brown did try to explain, though, that his missing persons unit always took twenty-four hours to
determine whether a child was actually missing or merely a runaway.

On the night of January 8, five days after Lubie's disappearance, the sheriff's
office in Rockdale County (about twenty miles east of downtown Atlanta) received a telephone call. A man (no further description was provided) called to
tell officers to look for a black boy's body on Sigman Road in that county. Up
to that point, the county had not figured in any of the child slayings or disappearances. Believing that the call might be in connection with Geter, early the
next morning close to one hundred county and state police officers combed a
portion of Sigman Road. They did not find a body.

Friday, January 9, a more massive search was coordinated by the FBI for
Lubie Geter, whose disappearance had given the bureau its "first opportunity
to enter a case of a child disappearance simultaneous with local law enforcement" (FBI, n.d.). Up until then, the FBI had entered investigations after the
fact, that is, after Atlanta police had done their initial investigations. Now FBI
agents could be in on the search from the start.

Two hundred and fifty local officers and twenty-six FBI agents combed a
four-square-mile area on both sides of Interstate 75-85 north of Lakewood Free-
way, in the vicinity of the ailing Stewart-Lakewood Shopping Center. The search
party came up with "negative results," according to FBI records. Things did not
look good for Lubie Geter. At least two other listed children, Angel Lenair and
Edward Smith, were last seen alive in the same general vicinity. And the bodies of Lenair and Milton Harvey were discovered not far from where Lubie had
reportedly disappeared.

The task force listed Geter as the eighteenth black Atlanta child to disappear in as many months.[1] Thirteen of the children had turned up murdered. No clear motive could be established for the murder of the youngsters other than—maybe—their race. Investigators wondered, then dismissed, sexual motivation. Consulting experts cautioned, though, that absence of a visible sexual motive should not rule out a sexually motivated killer, since some psychopaths may be sexually motivated, even though they may not appear so; they may experience sexual fulfillment in a violent act.

The massive January 9 search for Lubie Geter did not shed any new light on what might have happened to him. But the effort was not entirely a waste. On that cold Friday afternoon, an East Point police officer suggested that a few men break off from the main search party and comb the woods off Redwine Road near Interstate 285 (the officer remembered the area as a dumping ground for stolen cars). No sooner had the officers begun their search when a man ran up to them saying his hunting dog had come home with "a very bad odor" and "sticky stuff on him, like he'd been nosing into something" (*NYT* 1981a, 1981b).

Lying uncovered on the ground about seventy-five feet from Redwine Road were two sets of skeletal remains. Before long, the entire Atlanta news media, it seemed, converged on the scene. Mayor Jackson also came by late afternoon. Commissioner Brown subsequently announced that the remains "appeared to be that of children." The remains were too badly decomposed, however, for either set to have belonged to Lubie Geter. So the immediate speculation—in both law enforcement and the media— was that they must have belonged to two of the other missing youngsters: Jefferey Mathis, missing since March 1980; Christopher Richardson, missing since June 1980; Earl Terrell, missing since July 1980; or Darron Glass, missing since September 1980.

Some four days would pass before Dr. Robert Stivers, chief Fulton County medical examiner, was able to announce that one of the skeletons was definitely that of Christopher Richardson. The other he tentatively identified (and would confirm five months later) as that of Earl Terrell. The reason Stivers gave for the delay in identifying the remains was that Atlanta investigators not only had failed to properly secure the crime scene but had bagged and labeled the remains without *his* permission.

Key parts of the skeletons were missing, Stivers claimed. His experts had to go back to the crime scene to recover them. On one such trip, they found eleven teeth on the ground. The recovered teeth, he said, were what he had used to identify both youths. Stivers said he was contemplating seeking criminal charges against the negligent Atlanta officers.

Until their remains were found together, no real evidence had emerged to suggest that Richardson and Terrell were connected, except that they were both slightly built and had disappeared during the summer of 1980. They apparently did not know each other. They lived six and one-half miles apart—Christopher in suburban Decatur and Earl in southwest Atlanta. Earl disappeared fifty-one days after Christopher. And stories told by school officials, friends, and parents indicated that the two boys had different personalities and habits.

Yet, because their bodies were found so close together, police investigators speculated that the same person killed Earl and Christopher, then dumped their bodies off Redwine Road. But they had no idea how the bodies had arrived here. They only knew where and when the two boys were last seen alive—Christopher on Memorial Drive walking toward DeKalb County's Midway Recreation Center for a swim, and Earl after he had bought some Freeze Pops in a grocery store about a block from his house on Browns Mill Road, after swimming at the South Bend Park pool.

Because their bodies were so badly decomposed, the medical examiners could not determine cause of death. Several similarities did surface, however, even though investigators couldn't be sure which, if any, would be the key that would unlock the mystery of their deaths. The most notable similarities were the following:

- Investigators found similar fibers on the bodies. This meant that the boys' deaths could be linked to other cases on the special police task force list.

- Both were behind in school, although not enough to be placed in remedial classes.

- Both came from family circumstances that experts described as "unsettled." (Both had moved with their mothers into houses run by relatives.)

- Both frequented the nearest public swimming pools and were on their way to or from the pools when they disappeared.

- Both were last seen alive near a shopping area.

- Both could have been in agitated, if not rebellious, states of mind when they were last seen—Christopher because of the fight with his mother over which shirt he could wear to the pool, and Earl because he had been thrown out of the South Bend Park pool.

- When found, both bodies were missing some of the clothing the youngsters were wearing when last seen alive.

Before investigators could fully sort out the implications of these facts, another missing black Atlanta youth would be added to their list.

Fifteen-year-old Terry Lorenzo Pue was one of eleven siblings. His family had moved from Coweta County, Georgia, to College Park (about ten or twelve miles south of Atlanta). Then they moved into a housing project at Hollywood Court in near northwest Atlanta.

Dressed in beige slacks and a windbreaker with the name "Kim" printed on the back, Terry left his home on the chilly afternoon of Wednesday, January 21. He told his mother he was going to play basketball in East Point. That evening, he stopped at his sister Pamela's apartment in East Lake Meadows in southeast Atlanta. His sister was not home. Terry hung around the Meadows to see a girlfriend and spent the night at a fast-food restaurant outside the Interstate 285 perimeter on Memorial Drive. He spent much of the following day hanging around a shopping center on Memorial Drive trading empty soda bottles for money. Then he vanished.

Friday morning, January 23, a passerby came upon his corpse. It was lying just a few feet off Sigman Road in predominantly white Rockdale County, at the precise spot where a male caller two weeks earlier had told the authorities they would find the body of a black male child.

Pue seemed asleep, one eyewitness said. His body was fully dressed and placed on its side. Investigators found abrasions on his elbow and bruises on his head, indicating a struggle. The state's crime lab director, Dr. Larry Howard, said a "rope or some rough material with a woven pattern" was used to kill Terry; he was apparently garroted. Lab experts processed Pue's fingerprints, and they recovered some dog hairs and some violet and green fibers, which they determined were identical to other fibers found on the bodies of at least four other list victims.

But investigators were unable to trace Pue's associations. He had told a waitress at the fast-food restaurant on Memorial Drive the night before he disappeared that his parents were living their lives and he was living his.

Terry's mother told task force investigators that her son suffered a fractured skull when he was two years old. The injury left him with a learning disability. He had been in juvenile court eight times for truancy and shoplifting and had landed in the Challenge School, a state-run facility for youthful offenders at the West Hunter Street Baptist Church. The school's director told investigators that Terry had been introduced to still-missing Lubie Geter, who had visited the school.

Whom Terry hung out with on the streets remained a mystery. Since he was on the move for money that Thursday night in the far end of DeKalb County, investigators figured that, as he worked his way back to Atlanta, he had met someone intent on doing him harm. Terry's mother thought otherwise. She believed her son's killer had been in contact with him sometime that Thursday and that Terry was therefore on the run. His apparent wandering of the Atlanta metropolitan area was a desperate effort to escape death.

The discovery of Terry Pue's body in faraway Rockdale County meant that another metropolitan Atlanta jurisdiction now figured in the investigation. By law, whenever a murdered body was found in a particular jurisdiction, that jurisdiction had primary responsibility for accounting for the facts surrounding the victim's death. So far, bodies had been discovered inside the Atlanta city limits (i.e., portions of the city in either Fulton or DeKalb County), in East Point, Cobb County, and now Rockdale County.

Curiously, none of the bodies had thus far been found in next-door unincorporated (into the city of Atlanta, that is) DeKalb County, a mostly white, middle-class suburb northeast of Atlanta. One of the murdered boys, Christopher Richardson, did have a DeKalb County address (in the city of Decatur), but his body was found inside the Atlanta city limits, near its southwest border with unincorporated Fulton County. And Aaron Wyche's body also was found in DeKalb County, but his death, up until early February 1981, was not attributed to murder but to an "accidental fall."

DeKalb County authorities, then, had no direct legal obligation to investigate any of the murders—at least not up to this point. For this reason, task force investigators did not feel obliged to share vital information surrounding the child murders with DeKalb police. The county's director of public safety, Dick Hand, thought differently. At a news conference on February 4, Hand blasted the special Atlanta police task force for not passing on information to him. He declared that his agency would have done a better job than the Atlanta police at solving the cases. His men, Hand said, would already have brought in the killer or killers. "We would be the one to catch him—or her, for that matter, or them," he bragged of his practically all-white male police force (*NYT* 1981d). Hand would not have long to wait before his boast was challenged.

On February 5, a man looking for rabbit traps in a wooded area in southwest Fulton County came upon a puppy belonging to a neighbor. The puppy had "something" in its mouth. The man followed the dog's path and saw a corpse lying on its back with its arms out. The body rested along the wooded side of

Vandiver Road, two miles from Niskey Lake Road, where the bodies of Edward Smith and Alfred Evans were found, and four miles from Redwine Road, where the bodies of Milton Harvey, Christopher Richardson, and Earl Terrell had been dumped.

Six hours later, Annie Geter made the trip she had been dreading. She went to the county morgue and identified the remains found along Vandiver Road as belonging to her missing son.

Like eight previous victims, Lubie had been strangled. Dr. Robert Stivers, the Fulton County medical examiner, said his killer squeezed his life away with a powerful choke hold, "forcing his larynx up and back and breaking his neck bones" (*WP* 1981d). The killer left no marks on the victim's neck. "It look[ed] like someone coming up from behind and catching the child in the crook of the elbow," Stivers believed. What puzzled the medical examiner most, though, was the apparent lack of a struggle. Lubie's body was found clad only in jockey shorts. The faded blue jeans, green pullover shirt, and maroon-burgundy ski jacket that he had been wearing when he disappeared were missing.

Investigators discovered various crime-scene items that could place Lubie Geter's death squarely in line with other list victims, including some green carpet fibers.

With Atlanta's mayoral and city council elections set for fall 1981, the political tempo was beginning to heat up. Not removed from political discourse was the issue of what, exactly, was happening in the investigations. Although Mayor Jackson was not up for reelection (he was barred by city charter from seeking a third successive term), on the political chopping block nonetheless was the issue of how elected Atlanta authority had so far responded to the string of killings and disappearances.

Mayoral candidate A. Reginald Eaves fired the first salvo. Eaves had been a political thorn in Jackson's side ever since Jackson removed him from the post of public safety commissioner in 1975. For months Eaves had been criticizing Atlanta police for their handling of the cases, and he made it clear when he announced for mayor in early January that public safety would be a leading issue in his campaign. In a wide-ranging series of public appearances and interviews following his announcement, he directly took on the Atlanta police for mishandling the cases. He further warned that the unsolved crimes threatened to divide the city along racial lines. That would certainly be the case, Eaves said, if white children were to be murdered in the same way as were "these black children." "It would not surprise me if [a killer] turns around and kills a couple of white children and makes [whites] think it's retaliation by the black community. When I become mayor of this city, the problem [of the missing and murdered children] will cease in this city" (AC 1981b).

Remarks like these had resonance in Atlanta's poor black community. But, as expected, they caused much unease in middle-class black Atlanta, where some thought Eaves was pandering to the black masses and in so doing was promoting racial divisiveness. One unnamed black Atlanta official retorted that, although blacks were frightened and angry about the children's cases, no responsible black leader would think of getting up on a platform and saying, "There's a beast on the loose and this is the beginning of a race war" (AC 1981b).

Disapproval over Eaves's comments from the city's white ruling class had a more disguised pretext. Several white business leaders saw the emerging rift as an opening for a white candidate to enter—and win—the mayoral contest, then "take back" the city. They decided, therefore, to stay out of the dispute over Eaves's remarks and allow the city's black politicos to "duke it out" among themselves. White Democratic state representative Sidney Marcus, at the time an unannounced candidate, responded faintly to Eaves's remarks: "To speculate about why whoever is doing it [i.e., the killings], I don't know that it serves any useful purpose" (AC 1981b).

In a sharply worded and lengthy editorial, the editors of the Atlanta Voice tried to put Eaves's remarks in context. Eaves was really calling for "public accountability" in elected officials. The mayor had a moral obligation to account to the people from below, since it was their children who were being murdered. "Many times we are called upon to support candidates for Public Offices. We are inundated during election time by candidates' promises of superb and excellent performance. . . . It is now time to pose the most important question of our time in this city: Who determines Public Accountability?" (AV 1981).

In the opinion of the Voice's editorial board, folks at the grassroots had no idea what, exactly, was happening with "these investigations." They knew "little about the city's criminal justice system and what it was doing in the interest of public safety." And they knew "a great deal less" about the special investigative Atlanta police task force—which, board members felt, was too "academic, scientific, and polite." The Voice asked, "Where is the veteran cop who knows those communities and the people in them, their habits, their awareness, their knowledge, and how to pump information with style, comfort, and effect?" (AV 1981).

The matter of how best to investigate the child slayings and disappearances—scientific versus "on the ground"—was only one of several issues that highlighted the contrasting positions of people in and close to the community at risk with that of official Atlanta. But what pointedly continued to separate the community at risk from black elite leadership was the former's insistence on a racially motivated connection to the murders and disappearances.

One prevalent belief in several black neighborhoods was, for instance, that white racist elements *inside* the Atlanta police bureau were responsible. Reinforcement for that kind of thinking came from word that crime experts from outside Atlanta believed that the killer was someone who could command respect and gain the confidence of unsuspecting youths—such as an Atlanta police officer. Seeming "screwups" in investigative work conducted by the city's special task force were, therefore, manifestations of Atlanta police trying to conceal evidence that could implicate them in the string of murders and disappearances.

A case in point was Atlanta police's apparent blunder in securing the crime scene when the bodies of Christopher Richardson and Earl Terrell were discovered and officers lost valuable evidence. Moreover, a forensic dentist called in to examine the two boys' remains had complained that the task force did not give him pictures of all the missing children until several days after he began the process of reconstructing the skull and mouth areas. This had "seriously delayed" him in identifying the youngsters. How could anyone explain things like these except as deliberate ploys on the part of Atlanta police to hide something?

One final "strange" item folks kept pointing to was Reverend Arthur Langford's having to denounce Atlanta police brass for pushing his Saturday searches off into areas that had already been searched by the police. Authorities admitted that the charge was true, but noted that the searches were being "managed" so as to protect any evidence that might be in an area from being "destroyed" by "untrained" civilians. Folks in the street regarded this as ridiculous, since trained police searches had probably already destroyed valuable evidence.

Patrick Baltazar looked older than his years. And he acted worldly, perhaps because his life was never easy. Patrick was one of fourteen children born to Grace and Russell Baltazar. He was closer to his father, whom he had tagged behind along the streets of Glenmora, Louisiana, when the elder Baltazar held down jobs there mowing white people's lawns. When the Baltazars separated in 1977 and Russell Baltazar moved to Atlanta, he promised to return for Patrick. Russell made good on his pledge in late summer 1979. The following July, the two were joined in their one-bedroom Vine City apartment by Patrick's twenty-year-old brother, Donald.

In his spare time, Patrick liked to hang around the Omni, a short walk from his apartment on Foundry Street. He often played electronic games in the Omni's Galaxy Three arcade; he also sold confections there. For more income he picked up jobs selling newspapers and cleaning at Fisherman's Cove restaurant (in the more affluent and faraway section of DeKalb County), where his father worked as a dishwasher.

Patrick Baltazar was a brash kid who was never afraid to approach an adult for a favor or a job. And he worked hard at the jobs he took. His forged work permit, showing he was sixteen years old, got him another job washing dishes at Papa's Country Buffet on Buford Highway a few hours a week. No one suspected Patrick was only twelve years old.

About 5:30 P.M. on Friday, February 6, Patrick stopped by Fisherman's Cove to get some money from his father to attend a Golden Gloves boxing match at the Civic Center. No one knew whether he ever made it to the match. The police recorded the visit to his father as the last time Patrick Baltazar was seen—although subsequent reports placed him at the Omni until midnight that Friday playing games at Galaxy Three. For several days after Patrick failed to come home, Russell Baltazar, acting on tipoffs, drove all over Atlanta looking for his son; he had a gun on the seat behind him.

When word of the missing child got out, Atlanta police launched a massive search, hoping to find some trace of him before turning his case over to the task force. Investigators speculated that he probably wandered back into DeKalb County after he had already been there to see his father. Someone there could have picked him up. No one knew for sure. Local media had a field day reporting the story. All Atlanta was on edge.

The search for Patrick Baltazar ended one week later, about 2:00 P.M. on Friday, February 13, when his fully clothed body was found *in DeKalb County*. The county's public safety director's bluff of just over a week earlier—that his men would have done better than the Atlanta police at solving the murders—seemed to have been called.

Patrick's body was found by a maintenance man for Corporate Square, a business-office complex located between Buford Highway and Interstate 85. The body was stuck in an overgrown area behind the complex, down an embankment from a parking lot. Investigators figured that a killer drove up to the edge of the parking lot and rolled the body down the grassy embankment. "I'm sure [the killer] meant for it to go all the way to the bottom, but it didn't. It got caught on a bunch of sticks," reported a chastened Dick Hand (*AJ&C* 1981).

DeKalb County medical examiner Joseph Burton speculated that Patrick Baltazar was killed shortly after he vanished. He was strangled, "probably with a cord or a sash," and his body was dumped down the embankment, Burton believed. The body had a few scrapes and bruises that were "consistent with a minor struggle." Georgia crime lab experts recovered dog hairs and green carpet fibers, which they determined were similar to items found on the bodies of other listed victims. Their counterparts in the FBI's crime lab in Washington agreed.

On that afternoon when Patrick Baltazar was found, FBI agents with trained dogs were conducting another of their routine searches for missing—and presumed abducted—Atlanta youngsters. In a briar-covered patch of woodlands off Suber and Cascade Roads in unincorporated southwest Fulton County, they stumbled onto a disturbingly familiar site: the remains of what appeared to be a boy.

Fulton County police detective George Coleman was at the site. All that was left, he told writer Steve Oney (1981), "was a skull and a few bones." No clothing was found near the remains. "We spent hours crawling around on our hands and knees trying to find some clothes or evidence, but we couldn't find a thing," said Coleman (although FBI records indicated agents found pages of a "sexually explicit magazine" near the remains). Some of the nearby ground was gathered into a container for crime lab analysis. The bones were scrutinized over the weekend by county medical examiners. Detailed examination of the teeth confirmed the boy's identity.

The following Sunday morning, Police Chief George Napper stood in Willie Mae Mathis's living room and told her that the remains belonged to her son, Jefferey, who had been missing for almost a year, since March 11, 1980. The authorities had nothing on which to assign a cause of death, Napper told her, but they were "working on it."

Willie Mae Mathis went downtown and claimed the skull and bones of her child. She had the undertakers dress them up and then lay them out neatly in a simple, little coffin. She could now grieve with anguished certainty the passing of her precious, dependable Jefferey.

Jefferey Mathis's funeral was held at West Hills Presbyterian Church, a pleasant red brick sanctuary just a few blocks from where he disappeared. The occasion was a trying experience for his mother. "Every sob, every shudder, every tear, was subject to the scrutiny of men behind television cameras," wrote Oney. "Flashbulbs popped. Reporters scribbled in note pads. Mayor Jackson arrived with his retinue. 'I wanted to keep my composure because there was so much attention,'" Ms. Mathis said. Pictures of her sobbing—and of her remaining children in a moment of wrenching sorrow—were beamed over and over on national television broadcasts and reprinted in mass circulations around the world.

A couple of weeks after the funeral, Ms. Mathis could muster a small measure of solace in her child's demise. "I at least feel better knowing that somebody isn't keeping him somewhere and treating him wrong," she told Oney (1981).

Five days after Jefferey's bones were discovered, another black Atlanta youngster disappeared.

Curtis Walker was a quiet thirteen-year-old. Shy and wary, Curtis seldom strayed from his near northwest Bankhead Highway neighborhood. One of seven children, Curtis was slow in school. He was interested in art, at which he did reasonably well in Andrea Patterson's seventh grade class at A. D. Williams School in the Bowen Homes housing project. Ms. Patterson described Curtis as someone she just could not imagine venturing out into the community to seek work, even to get extra money.

But Curtis did try, even if halfheartedly, to find odd jobs. After school he would sometimes follow his more brazen eight-year-old brother down Bankhead Highway looking for jobs at the shops and supermarkets along the way. Curtis would never really ask for work. "He'd just open the door and stand there and stare at you, until you realized what he wanted," recalled Archie Byron Jr. (*AJ&C* 1981), owner of Byron's Gun Shop.

Thursday, February 19, was the first day that week that Curtis had been to school; he had been out with an upset stomach. He got well enough that afternoon to go out looking for work—the first time anyone could remember that he had done so by himself, a seemingly minor occurrence but one that greatly surprised family members. He had slipped out of the family apartment and appeared at Byron's Gun Shop at around 4:00 P.M. Hearing there was no work, Curtis wandered off to the east, toward a small shopping center. He was not seen again.

Curtis's mother, several relatives, and the gun shop owner combed the neighborhood but found nothing. The next day, tracking dogs picked up his scent and followed it a block to the rear of the Center Hill School, where the trail evaporated. The dog handler guessed that at that point Curtis probably got into a car.

Curtis Walker was the fourth child to disappear since January 1981. Youngsters had now disappeared an average of one every two weeks. Three of the four had turned up dead.

Inefficiencies and disputes abounded within the mayor's special police task force around the time that Lubie Geter's body was discovered. The task force had by then evolved into a full-time multijurisdictional investigative unit, consisting of law enforcement personnel from each neighboring Atlanta jurisdiction in which a murdered body (or bodies) had been found. The operating principle was that the agencies represented on the task force would share resources and leads. More important, the task force would function as the single investigative unit looking into the string of deaths and disappearances; that is, exclusive of the FBI, which, though still functioning independently, had begun in the early weeks of 1981 to take on an increasingly more active—and indeed more prominent—role in the ongoing investigations.

But the team concept was not working out very well. Crime experts whose first loyalty was to their respective hiring agency seemed to be working at cross purposes. And police in one jurisdiction continued to investigate cases independently, causing them to stumble over each other. Atlanta police working on a particular case would, for example, interview persons already interviewed by DeKalb County police working on the same case.

The FBI's go-it-alone strategy only added to the disharmony. Local officials became righteously indignant when, for instance, they learned that FBI agents not only had discovered some clothing belonging to victim Lubie Geter without sharing the information with them but had sent the clothing off to bureau headquarters in Washington for *their* crime lab analysis. Then county and city investigators on the special police task force became angry at Georgia state officials for not communicating "vital information" to them.

Mayor Jackson and Governor George Busbee decided it was time to reorganize the task force's command structure. The mayor freed Deputy Chief Redding, a white twenty-year veteran, of other administrative duties to head the task force. And the governor named GBI inspector J. R. "Robbie" Hamrick, a fifteen-year veteran of the virtually all-white-male state police club, as the task force's "investigative coordinator." Significantly, the FBI essentially was left to continue doing its own thing.

The local press establishment heartily endorsed the Redding and Hamrick appointments. "For the first time, the trackers of the child-slayers are being directed by experienced lawmen," wrote the *Atlanta Constitution*'s Bill Shipp (1981b). "And we hope they will be allowed to conduct their hunt without interference from politicians."

8

Multiple Suspects

We could conceivably have sixteen separate, unrelated cases.
—Commissioner Lee Brown

The mild southern winter months of 1981 would see an Atlanta city government hedged in on all sides by the continuing disappearances and deaths of several black Atlanta youngsters. Routine city administrative activities went unnoticed, and the Jackson administration was giving little attention to anything other than the tragedy. It had become to the mayor what the American hostages in Iran had only recently been to former president Jimmy Carter: the number one concern, threat, and frustration.

In his February state of the city address, the mayor made his feelings plain. He abandoned an earlier draft that concentrated on his past goals and accomplishments. Instead, he dashed through his eight years in office in four double-spaced pages and dwelt, for eleven pages, on the murders. One journalist assessed the speech as "not a proclamation but a plea—a prayer that parents be attentive, citizens be vigilant, critics be reasonable (if not silent), and racial tensions be eased" (Rodrigue 1981). The mayor feared, aides were saying, that the killings might become the one thing for which his administration would be remembered.

Curiously, although investigating authorities had for months conceded that the Atlanta murders were following some type of pattern, they weren't quite ready to accept the idea that a single murderer was somewhere "out there." Commissioner Lee Brown emphatically stated in January on *The Mac-Neil/Lehrer Report*, "We can say—based on the evidence—we do not have one person in our city that's stalking our streets abducting our children. Again, as we look at each case individually . . . , as we carry sixteen cases in the task force, we could conceivably have sixteen separate, unrelated cases."

In effect, the commissioner was saying that several persons could be responsible for committing several unrelated murders. At the end of February, investigators were in fact "working" on several suspects.

For the first two murders on the special task force's list, their investigations were "centering" on a Niskey Lake Road address in southwest Atlanta—a house that was almost directly across the street from where the bodies of Alfred Evans and Edward Smith were found. Investigators believed that the house—a regular drug hangout—could have been where the youths were murdered. Smith had frequented the Niskey Lake Road address.

In the case of Milton Harvey, who was last seen in September 1979 riding his bicycle in an industrial area in southwest Atlanta, task force investigators had no "working suspects."

For Yusef Bell, they were questioning at least three black males about his death; one was scheduled to undergo a "hypnotic interview."

For Angel Lenair, whose body was discovered in a vacant lot near her home, investigators were working on two suspects. One was an acquaintance of her mother who was arrested in the neighborhood following Angel's death for grabbing another child. At the time of his arrest, the man was wearing a belt "fashioned from electrical cord" similar to that used to bind Angel's hands.

For Jefferey Mathis, whose remains were discovered some eleven months after he disappeared, investigations were proving "negative." However, in the weeks ahead FBI agents would polygraph the boy's distraught mother, Willie Mae Mathis, who, according to FBI records, "passed" the test.

In the case of Eric Middlebrooks, investigations were still focusing on the possibility that a gang member, or members, may have killed him out of revenge for reporting a robbery.

For Latonya Wilson, abducted from her bedroom, investigations focused on two black males who were reportedly seen lurking in the vicinity of the girl's home on the morning she disappeared.

For Christopher Richardson, whose remains were not discovered for one year, investigators had no working suspects.

In the death of Anthony Carter, the only victim who was stabbed, investigators focused on family members, with FBI agents insisting that his mother might have slain her only child.

For Earl Terrell, who disappeared after leaving a swimming pool and whose remains were found next to Christopher Richardson's, investigators had no working suspects.

Investigators had a "strong suspect" in the death of Clifford Jones, the youth from Cleveland who disappeared while picking up discarded aluminum cans and whose body was found near a trash container. The suspect was the manager of a Laundromat in the shopping plaza where Clifford's body was found. Three youthful eyewitnesses had come forth to identify him. The eyewitnesses said they saw the manager go into the rear room of his Laundromat with a black boy. One of them said he saw the manager "strangle and beat" the boy, then carry his body out to the trash container, where he placed it sometime between 12:00 and 12:30 A.M. on August 21, 1980.

Two polygraph tests were administered to the Laundromat manager. He "failed" both, according to FBI records—even though he admitted that he knew Clifford and that Clifford was in his Laundromat on the evening of August 20, 1980. Medical experts had determined that the time of Clifford's death was between four and six hours before the discovery of his body, which would have placed the Laundromat manager with the boy around the time he was killed. The authorities had not charged the man with anything, however, because they determined that the youth who said he actually saw Clifford Jones being murdered was "retarded."

For still missing Darron Glass and slain Charles Stephens, investigators had no working suspects.

They had a suspect for the murder of Aaron Jackson, last seen on November 1, 1980, whose body was found the next day lying on the stream bank of the South River.

Up until the middle of February, Aaron Wyche's name was not on the task force list, because investigators still thought his death was an accident.

Investigators had no suspects in the deaths of Patrick Rogers, Lubie Geter, Terry Pue, and Patrick Baltazar. They also had no suspects in the latest case of a missing child, thirteen-year-old Curtis Walker.

Up through February 1981, in sum, investigative authorities were of the opinion that no single "mad-dog" killer was on the loose in Atlanta. "The evidence points to more than one killer. There could be as many killers as cases," said Commissioner Brown (*WP* 1981b).

White opinion makers thought inner-city blacks should take comfort in this bit of information. "There is a psychological difference . . . in knowing that possibly the youngsters who've become victims were not the target of some crazed individual who at certain intervals for reasons unknown roams the streets looking for prey," read an *Atlanta Constitution* editorial (*AC* 1980k).

But the outward embrace of the many killers from inside the neighborhood theory sharply contradicted actions being actively pursued at the time by two of the more relevant law enforcement agencies. Among other things, Atlanta police set up roadblocks near at-risk neighborhoods; they were especially interested in stopping and searching cars driven by nonresident white males. The police in neighboring DeKalb County stopped light-skinned black men—whom eyewitnesses could have mistaken for white males—driving cars with boys.

One stop-and-search operation netted a young black man whom Atlanta police said was attempting to kidnap a five-year-old black girl. The man had picked up the child and was carrying her off in his arms when he saw an Atlanta police officer and panicked. Special police task force investigators questioned the man but ruled him out as a suspect in the string of murders. Atlanta police also placed a lookout in late February for a white man driving a sedan with detachable flashing lights. The man had reportedly been bothering children in the Grant Park area. Nothing further materialized that could have connected him to the string of child killings and disappearances, however.

Investigators on the mayor's special task force questioned another man who was handed over to them after Atlanta police had stopped him for impersonating a police officer. The police had spotted the man in a blue car equipped with flashing light and siren. They pursued him, but he eluded them. Atlanta officers spotted him again and gave chase. This time they apprehended him. When the officers found in his possession what they said was "about an ounce of marijuana," along with a police badge and some lollipops, they called in task force investigators.

While the man was being interrogated, a task force officer described him to reporters as a "good suspect . . . the type of person we are looking for" (*WP* 1981c). The man was subsequently held on drug possession and traffic charges, but without any further allegations of him being connected to the slayings. The man who was actually held in connection with the Atlanta cases sometime in early 1981 was not identified in the official records. But these and similar actions suggested authorities were in fact searching for a killer from outside the neighborhoods from which the Atlanta youngsters were being snatched.

As the crimes continued, people everywhere, it seemed, wanted to do something for the children of Atlanta. Offers of help came from such disparate quarters as the NAACP and, mystifyingly, the Ku Klux Klan.

Meantime, three members of STOP had emerged as effective spokespersons for the bereaved families: Camille Bell, mother of Yusef Bell; Willie Mae Mathis, mother of Jefferey Mathis; and Venus Taylor, mother of Angel Lenair. They were being invited to give speeches, head prayer vigils, and appear on national television and radio talk shows.

In late February, top executives from three national recording companies started a fund to help pay for the police investigation. They raised $23,000 in just two days. Entertainers Sammy Davis Jr. and Frank Sinatra offered to come to town and do a benefit concert. So, too, did singers Stevie Wonder and Gladys Knight. Heavyweight boxing hero Muhammad Ali's manager, Herbert Muhammad, said he would start a fund in the Chicago area with a $25,000 contribution of his own. Ali himself came grandly into Atlanta and pledged $400,000 on top of the mayor's $150,000 reward fund.

Churches from across the nation, many in low-income, black urban neighborhoods, filled collection plates and sent the monies to Atlanta. The funds went mostly to the SCLC's Atlanta headquarters; some went directly to STOP. Actually, STOP had initiated most of the collection drives, the proceeds of which organizers had said would be used to assist grieving families in need. SCLC had merely stepped in to help centralize and give a measure of mainstream blessing to the effort.

On any given week in early 1981, STOP would send out more than five hundred replies to people who had offered support of one kind or another, according to secretary Venus Taylor. The group had heard from concerned individuals in every state except Hawaii.

The seemingly extraordinary amount of money going directly to the mothers did not sit well with several of the city's black politicians. On March 25, state senator Julian Bond and others within the local black political leadership elite stood on the steps of city hall and asked a national television and newspaper audience not to send any more money directly to the Atlanta families (*AC* 1981f; *WP* 1981k).[1]

Activist and Georgia state representative (from an Atlanta district) Tyrone Brooks charged that the tragedy had led to "widespread hustling, massive exploitation, and outright fraud." He questioned whether any money should go to the mothers, especially those whose children were already buried. "Once we bury the children [and] take care of the funeral expenses," he insisted, "I don't think we need to pay the families. We have children dying of leukemia in this city . . . but nobody's rushing to say here's some money to tide you over" (*AC* 1981e).

The white Atlanta establishment loved it. "Brooks Makes Sense," headlined an *Atlanta Constitution* lead editorial.

As the months went by, the popularly regarded Brooks became inexplicably more strident toward the more vocal mothers within STOP. He accused them of trying to make the wider black Atlanta community feel "we owe them something" because they've had a tragedy. Eventually, because of Brooks's insistent demands for greater accountability in the handling of donations to the mothers, city officials urged anyone wishing to make a donation to the cause of Atlanta's children to send it to Economic Opportunity Atlanta, a community-development agency. But Brooks's and other perhaps well intentioned but harsh charges of irregularity would lead in the weeks ahead to sustained state harassment of STOP.

Throughout the winter, as Americans watched Atlantans in distress on television, European press reports played up the killings as part of America's brutality and racism. The most scathing came from the Soviet Union's *Tass*. One of its editorials charged, "The killing of black children in Atlanta shows that the real terror of racist violence is rampant in America. . . . There is every indication that the senseless and cruel killing of children in Atlanta is of little concern to the authorities of the state (of Georgia) and to Washington." Instead of catching the killers, the editorial contended, federal officials "are preoccupied with fanning another anti-Soviet campaign by maliciously imputing to the Soviet Union an involvement in international terrorism" (Associated Press 1981).

Satirist and *Atlanta Constitution* columnist Louis Grizzard offered a quintessential cranky commentary on ABC's *Nightline* (February 25, 1981) on these and other surrealist developments: "So ABC *Nightline* is doing a piece on the murdered Atlanta black children. . . . Everybody else is here too. . . . Another body is found; another mother cries in anguish; and the headlines scream, and the television lights go."

Black Atlantans—including those residing outside the community at risk—were by late February genuinely enraged at what was happening with "these kids." Many instinctively believed that some crazy killer was on the loose in Atlanta and that *he* was *white*, as one incident revealed in downtown Atlanta in early March 1981. A black woman saw, or thought she saw, a black child in the rear of a car being driven by three white people. She hurriedly stepped into an auto parts store and pressed the store's owner, a black man, to "do something." The owner grabbed his revolver and began chasing the car, firing off several shots. When it was all over, the police finding nothing unusual about the car or its occupants, the store owner said maybe he had "overreacted."

White Atlantans living in nearby suburbs and on the city's far north side were, on the other hand, thinking, even hoping, that the Atlanta killer was black, according to a story in the *Atlanta Constitution* (1981f).

These underlying tensions prompted SCLC's Joseph Lowery to warn in early March that violence could erupt in Atlanta unless the killer was found. He and others in the local civil rights leadership hierarchy believed more public demonstrations were necessary to ease tensions and bring people together. Preferably, the demonstrations should be under the guidance and generalship of "experienced leaders."

One such demonstration was a rally on Sunday, March 15, in which 1,600 people marched from the state capitol through downtown Atlanta. The march concluded in a field at Morehouse College. Participating and making zealous speeches were several mainline clerics, civil rights leaders—including Coretta Scott King, widow of Martin Luther King Jr.—and black show business personalities. A throng of black Atlanta children participated. One of them would shortly turn up missing.

9

The Politics of Federal Aid

I think it's just disgusting that this country would have to have entertainers go to Atlanta to raise funds for a police investigation when this country sends millions of dollars to El Salvador and overseas [and] elsewhere.

—Female passenger on bus from Washington, D.C., to Atlanta to participate in solidarity march against Atlanta murders

Apart from the unsolved murders and abductions, Mayor Maynard Jackson's most bedeviling problem was finding the money to pay for the continuing investigations. By mid-February 1981 the probe had consumed over $500,000 of the city's unallocated funds.

The governor said he would help. But the paltry sum of $208,475 he was asking of the General Assembly would hardly be sufficient. Costs for extra personnel were running at an unbudgeted $200,000 a month to the city. The Atlanta Bureau of Police Services had ordered thousands of dollars worth of sophisticated surveillance equipment for the investigation. ABPS was spending thousands more per month for computer services and planned to spend considerably more for things like photocopying and helicopter flights. The city also was paying out huge amounts in rental costs for vehicles used on stakeouts. Added to this was the need for funds to deal with an array of mental-health problems associated with the ongoing tragedy; most affected were the city's poor black children.

The mayor would increase the pressure on Washington; he needed direct financial help. Only a massive federal assistance plan could "save" the city. In pitching his appeal to federal authorities, the mayor did in fact equate the situation in Atlanta to a "natural disaster"—the kind of calamity the national government was best equipped to handle. But equally important in keeping pressure on Washington was that Jackson did not want his administration to suffer public ridicule for not seeming to ever come up with anything on the murders.

In beseeching Washington, one essential item political folks in Atlanta apparently had not sufficiently thought through was this: Would an incoming right-wing Republican administration, which came into power on the wave of a white voter backlash (candidate Ronald Reagan having promised to shrink the social functions of government), come to the aid of a black Democratic mayor of a majority-black city with a problem of missing and murdered black children?

Before his February 1981 state of the city address, Jackson had telegraphed the new president. Jackson asked Reagan for a meeting to discuss the crisis in Atlanta. Reagan delegated his vice president, George Bush, to communicate with Jackson. In answering reporters' questions at a White House news conference shortly after receiving Jackson's telegram, Reagan seemed not to have grasped the fundamental issue of money, which was what the mayor was requesting.

The president went off on a tangent: "Now you recognize, of course, that possibly civil rights [meaning something, anything, having to do with race] would be the only basis upon which we could have any jurisdiction down there in this." The FBI could not get involved, Reagan insisted, since "there's been no evidence of crossing state lines or anything. And yet we want to be helpful because that is a most tragic case" (*NYT* 1981c).

No one, it seemed, had as yet told Reagan that the FBI was already deeply involved with the Atlanta cases, that back in the fall of 1980 his predecessor, Jimmy Carter, had indeed suspected a racial angle to the killings and disappearances. And that the legal ground for Carter sending several agents into Atlanta was that evidence surrounding the disappearance of one child, Earl Terrell, suggested he may have been forcibly taken across state lines.

Weeks passed, and all the Reagan folks seemed prepared to offer Atlanta was $264,000 worth of "services and expertise." Ironically, the services and expertise that Washington was willing to provide would come from an agency the Reagan administration was bent on eliminating: the Justice Department's Law Enforcement Administration Assistance (LEAA) program, created by the Johnson administration as a mechanism for parceling out federal anticrime funds to local jurisdictions.

Black Americans, meanwhile, overwhelmingly believed that police and national leaders were not doing enough about the Atlanta killings and disappearances. This was shown in a national survey of 1,284 blacks conducted by Data Black Public Opinion Polls (DBPOP) in the spring of 1981. Seventy-three percent of those polled said law enforcement authorities were not giving enough attention to the slayings; 58 percent felt black leaders were not doing enough; and 69 percent said there was little attention from national leaders in general, regardless of color. Across the nation, at mass rallies and community forums, black folks lambasted the federal government. The sentiment expressed from rostrums and on protest signs was that, had the Atlanta victims been white, elected federal authority (namely, the president and Congress) would have been moving much more earnestly at mobilizing federal resources to assist; 73 percent of the people polled by DBPOP held that view.

A fitting illustration of this widespread racialized anger was Marion Barry's outburst in early March 1981. Barry was in fired-up form at a memorial service for the Atlanta victims at Shiloh Baptist Church in Washington. "A certain mood exists in the country, encouraged by the leadership," he roared, "that it is all right to do anything to black people. Now I maintain that if those were twenty-one white people [murdered in Atlanta], we would have no problem [getting federal assistance]" (*WP* 1981e).

At a press conference a few days later, Barry repeated the charge in response to a reporter's question, playing up even more haughtily his racial thesis. If the Atlanta victims "had been Jewish," he said, "the federal government would have moved faster" to send money to help solve the crimes. "If they had been anything except black they would have moved faster" (*WP* 1981e). The *Washington Post* denounced the mayor for engaging in "opportunistic race-baiting." In strong language, board members blasted him in a lead editorial for "not trying to make it any easier to find a solution in Atlanta without further panic and anxiety and possibly racial conflict there."

> [Barry] is not trying to assist the hard-pressed and hard-working investigators. . . . He is not trying to bring the facts of the case to the attention of people whose understandable fears have been aggravated by a misunderstanding or lack of knowledge of those easily ascertainable facts. Mayor Barry is not trying to contribute in any way . . . to the overwhelming public good that so many others want and are working so desperately hard to bring about: an end to the killings, a resolution of the crimes . . . and a restoration . . . of interracial amity. (*WP* 1981f)[1]

But less flamboyant pressure on the Reagan administration had come earlier from a surprising and unlikely source. In late February 1981 Strom Thurmond, the powerful Republican senator from South Carolina—and archvillain of the civil rights era—had fired off a letter to Attorney General William French

Smith. The Atlanta cases, Thurmond had written, were "social disaster for all America. . . . I believe federal financial assistance should be offered" (AC 1981c).

Thurmond told reporters that one of his staff members learned on a trip to Atlanta that the financial and emotional costs had surpassed the city's ability to pay. "Money should not be a factor," the senator said, because "our children are our future."

Atlanta's white liberal establishment was dumbfounded. The thought of Maynard Jackson and Strom Thurmond being allies in an effort to "save" black people was just incomprehensible. "There are strange quirks of history," read an *Atlanta Constitution* editorial. "Senator Strom Thurmond, who was one of the strongest fighters in the 1950s and 1960s against civil rights legislation, is emerging perhaps as the strongest national supporter of federal aid to help finance the search for the killer or killers of Atlanta's children" (AC 1981d).

Before Reagan officials could get around to responding to Thurmond's letter, however, a black teenager disappeared.

One of seven children, fifteen-year-old Joseph "Jo-Jo" Bell stayed with his grandmother at 395 Southwest Lawton Street while his mother was in prison for killing his father. But Jo-Jo Bell's life was pretty much lived out on the streets of the city's south side. It was primarily because of youngsters like Jo-Jo that Mayor Jackson and the city council had enacted, in late 1980 and early 1981, a series of increasingly stiffer curfews. The measures—the latest one requiring everyone sixteen and younger to be off the streets between 7:00 P.M. and 6:00 A.M.—were intended to reduce the "risk factor" of likely victims.

Residents of the communities at risk were not at all sure of the usefulness of such draconian measures as the way to protect their children, however. Atlanta's poor black children were "vulnerable any hour of the day," as Grace Davis of Atlanta Women Against Crime put it. All but two of the murdered children had apparently been snatched in daylight hours. Besides, curfews meant elimination of needed recreational evening programs—which often kept youngsters out of trouble.

Out on the city's mean streets, Jo-Jo Bell tried to "act growner than what he was," one of his friends recalled. Jo-Jo spent much of his out-of-school time seeking odd jobs; the rest of it he would spend picking up basketball games.

In January 1981, Jo-Jo had started going to the John Harland Boys' Club on People's Street, next to the Harris Homes project. He would show up at the club in the late afternoon to shoot basketball with his sister. But his most frequent activity was hanging around Cap'n Peg's Seafood, a neighborhood fried fish joint on Georgia Avenue. Jo-Jo's routine was to telephone the restaurant's owner, Richard Harp, early in the day from his school and ask if there was any work. Sometimes he would just come to the restaurant and hang out. So late into the night would Jo-Jo hang out at Cap'n Peg's that Harp often would drive him home.

Jo-Jo stopped at Cap'n Peg's on Monday afternoon, March 2. When he learned there was nothing for him to do, he left, saying he was going up the street to "shoot some ball." Jo-Jo Bell was never seen again. The following day, someone called Cap'n Peg's and said he was Jo-Jo. "I'm almost dead," the person said, and hung up.

On March 6, a DeKalb County fireman crossing the Waldrop Road bridge over the muddy South River in DeKalb County spotted a dead body snagged on a log. The body was subsequently identified as Curtis Walker, who had vanished after seeking work at a neighborhood gun shop two weeks earlier.

Curtis had been asphyxiated, experts believed, then stripped to his underwear and dumped in the river. He was probably killed right after he disappeared, the experts believed. The spot where Curtis's body was found was less than a mile from the Reverend Earl Paulk's church. Two weeks earlier, Paulk, a white DeKalb County minister, had appealed on radio and television to the killer or killers to get in touch with him.

Curtis's body showed "signs of struggle," DeKalb County medical examiner Joseph Burton told reporters. "He did show minimal signs of asphyxia. They were minimal, but they were there." These minimal signs bothered Burton, causing him to wonder if "something else [was] going on other than just asphyxia with these kids" (*AJ&C* 1981). Burton speculated that "the killer" (his words) was using a martial-arts type of maneuver to "dispatch his victims." In several of the other murder cases, Burton said he had found injuries to the upper part of the spine, which would support his martial-arts theory.

Despite Curtis's body being tossed into the water, investigators still managed to recover microscopic fibrous material from his body and clothing.

This matter of fibrous material being found on victims' bodies had become common knowledge, going back to extensive media coverage of the disappearance of Patrick Baltazar and subsequent discovery of his murdered body. At that time, investigating authorities had let on, perhaps unwittingly, that they had been recovering some carpet fibers from victims' bodies. The news media picked up on this bit of accidental detail and publicized it. Finding Curtis

Walker's body in a waterway led investigators to speculate that the killer was now deliberately trying to "wash away" incriminating evidence.

Within hours of the discovery of Curtis's body, the federal government responded to Atlanta with money. The Reagan administration sent the Atlanta mayor almost $1 million in grants—primarily for education and mental-health programs associated with the ongoing tragedy. And on March 13, in a joint White House appearance with Bush, Reagan announced that he was releasing another $1.5 million in federal emergency funds to the city. The FBI, he said, had been instructed to assign more agents to Atlanta. Reagan described the unsolved murders and disappearances as "one of the most tragic situations" ever to confront an American community.

The next day, George Bush flew into Atlanta. He and his wife, Barbara, met with Mayor Jackson, city and state law enforcement officials, and relatives of five of the slain children. At a news conference, the vice president told reporters that he was sensitive to implications that he and Reagan were responding to political pressures and that they were seeking to capitalize politically from events in Atlanta. He had "made sure" to call former president Jimmy Carter en route to Atlanta, Bush said. And Carter, who had just returned to live in his native Georgia after leaving the White House, felt Bush's visit was "appropriate." Mayor Jackson described the Bush visit as a "shaft of light heralding a better day."

Shortly thereafter, committees in both the House of Representatives and the Senate passed bills requesting $1.8 million to assist Atlanta in starting a variety of youth programs. The bills had bipartisan support. More funds would flow into the investigations from the gala concert given by Sammy Davis Jr. and Frank Sinatra on March 10—at which mothers of the slain children were royally feted.

Theresa Swindall taught a special education class at Dean Rusk School in Atlanta. One of her students was thirteen-year-old Timothy Lyndale Hill, a boy with severe emotional problems, including a "violent streak." Timothy usually called Swindall every day after school, "just to talk." She, in turn, doted on him.

Swindall had been out of town on the weekend of March 14, 1981. Returning home on Monday night, she received a telephone call at about 10:30. She was convinced that she was speaking with Timothy. But he was crying. The call lasted about thirty minutes, with Swindall doing most of the talking. At one point she said, "Timmy!" sharply, and the caller said, "What?" After Timmy hung up, several unrelated calls came in. In the meantime, a friend of Swindall's rushed to a neighbor's home and called the police.

Timmy called back. He sobbed into the phone for another fifteen minutes, Ms. Swindall told the police. Then he hung up, she said, and she never heard from him again.

Timothy had been missing from his southwest Atlanta home for nearly six days—since the Wednesday before he called his teacher. He had been playing that Wednesday in his backyard with his two-year-old niece, Najoma. He reportedly spent Thursday and part of Friday evening at a rundown house on downtown Gray Street, an alleged spot for frequent group homosexual activity. Atlanta police thus initially concluded Timothy had merely run away from home, and so they delayed in turning his case over to the task force. Timothy's older sister, Brenda, insisted that her brother was no runaway.

The last time anybody saw Timothy alive was Sunday, March 15, when several people reported spotting him at a rally for the missing and murdered children on the grounds of Morehouse College.

The closest police were able to trace the point of origin of Timothy's telephone call to his teacher was to a broad wedge of northern DeKalb County. Timothy Hill was never heard from again.

Funds received from the federal government, while helpful in keeping the Atlanta investigations going, did little to reduce levels of growing polarization. By the middle of March, a series of alignments in the ordering of racial forces had emerged, both in and outside Atlanta.

First was the alignment of mainline black civil rights leadership with Atlanta's black political elite. The touchstone for this alignment was the newly formed Black Leadership Forum, which had been organized, coincidentally, in Atlanta around the time that the string of disappearances and slayings began. Forum members included Benjamin Hooks, executive director of the NAACP, SCLC president Joseph Lowery, and representatives from the National Urban League and Congressional Black Caucus.

The forum concluded that, yes, a climate of hatred in America was indirectly responsible for the crimes. But they were not the work of organized white racists. Forum leaders thus urged the black masses "not to despair" or turn to hate. Instead, they should trust elected black authority to solve "this thing" for them.

After a private March 1981 meeting, forum leaders issued a statement calling for prayer and nonviolent efforts to "fight despair and desperation" and a "circus atmosphere" growing out of the Atlanta tragedy. They also condemned a type of vigilante activity that had sprung up in a few Atlanta neighborhoods in response to the killings and disappearances.

The second alignment was between Atlanta's white business elites and the city's black elected authority. Black political power in Atlanta, though at times filled with racial attitudinizing, had been very good for the city's white business and commercial elites. Black Atlanta therefore expected white business leaders—particularly from among a new class of transplanted economic elites—to show some concern for the people whose political representatives had in part made them wealthy.

But the new white economic elites had very little to say. Their reticence was not, however, simply a manifestation of their own racism. Rather, it reflected political pragmatism. Having few cultural or historical roots in Atlanta, they resisted gratuitously offending the city's black leaders or causing unnecessary trouble. Their most expedient route, then, was to align themselves with the city's black political directorate on the matter of the tragedy.

This much was acknowledged by Michael Trotter, convener of the Atlanta Action Forum, a post-1960s parallel power structure amalgam, in an interview with a reporter for the *New York Times* (1981e). According to Trotter, the people he represented had not spoken in public about the murders and disappearances because, if they expressed concern about "the problem," they would be viewed as "criticizing black leadership." But, he added, "if you don't speak out, you're considered not caring. So you somehow try to find a middle ground where you try to express concern about the situation without being critical."

The third alignment occurred inside the poor black communities from which the youngsters were being abducted and then slain. This was essentially an *oppositionist* alignment whose driving force was the Committee to Stop Children's Murders (STOP). Aligned with STOP in opposition to the Atlanta establishment were several grassroots organizations within the Atlanta inner city—including Atlanta Women Against Crime, Atlanta Youth Against Crime, and the publishers of the *Atlanta Voice*. Select members of the black intelligentsia, notably students and some faculty from the Atlanta University Center (more so from the solidly working-class Morris Brown College), also affiliated themselves ideologically with this broad oppositionist movement. The alignment was held together primarily by all parties voicing the contention that official Atlanta, black and white, was more concerned with image than with what was happening to the children of Atlanta's black poor.

The fourth and final alignment was among more extreme militant community elements. Within this ultraist configuration were vanguard sectors of the black working class who lived mostly in the city's public housing projects. They were aligned (at least sometimes) with elements of the white Marxian far left—

the Revolutionary Communist Party, among others. The alignment was based on both groups articulating a shared oppositionist *worldview* of the tragedy and their publicized willingness to use "any means necessary" to defend poor black neighborhoods against this type of "racist attack." The situation that developed in one housing project, Techwood Homes, showed up the volatile nature of this particular alignment. (Techwood Homes, the city's largest housing project, was located literally around the corner from the corporate world headquarters of Coca-Cola.)

In early March, residents organized what they called "citizens' patrols"—later referred to by the news media as "bat patrols." Small groups of men armed with baseball bats and legal firearms took up patrol posts in their neighborhoods.[2] The men said they wanted to guard neighborhood children against the "crazed racist killer," whom the Atlanta authorities seemed incapable of apprehending or even stopping. Besides, the men said, they had seen graffiti warning residents that the next abduction of a black youth would take place in Techwood. "We're only here to protect our community," Israel Green, retired postal worker and president of the Techwood Homes Tenants' Association, told reporters (*WP* 1981g).

The Atlanta authorities refused to accept this development. Residents of other housing projects across town were beginning to take a cue from the militant Techwood Homes residents. The specter of Atlanta's poor black communities uniting and turning public housing projects into armed camps gave nightmares to Public Safety Commissioner Lee Brown. He declared, "There will be only one police force in Atlanta."

On Friday, March 20, the commissioner's men, clad in full riot gear, went into Techwood Homes and seized two patrol leaders, Gene Ferguson and Chimurenga Jenga. Jenga, who lived across town, was a known political activist of years past. Both men were packing illegal firearms—Ferguson a handgun and Jenga an M1 rifle. They were arrested under an old anti-Ku Klux Klan law: "displaying a deadly weapon at a public gathering."

The police action disbanded the patrols and effectively eliminated any future possibility of radical organizing around the issue of the mysterious Atlanta youth murders. Rather eerily, though, during the furor over the bat patrols, on March 20, probably while police were searching Techwood Homes for patrol organizers, one Techwood resident, a retarded young black male, disappeared.

Twenty-one-year-old Eddie Lamar "Bubba" Duncan lived on Hunnicutt Street with his divorced mother. He had a speech impediment, twisting muscular movement in his hands, "poor judgment," and a sometimes volatile temper. He walked with a limp and had "the mind of a child," according to one neighbor.

Eddie seldom strayed far from Techwood Homes, except to visit his grandmother in Cascade Heights. His impressionable nature and the promise of easy money led him, neighbors said, to his only brush with the law, back in 1978. He was stopped by police as he walked along Techwood Drive, carrying two boxes of merchandise stolen from a nearby hardware store. Eddie told the officers that a man had given him the boxes to hold with the promise of fifty dollars if he did a good job.

Two reports recorded Eddie Duncan as last seen sometime between 11:30 P.M. and around midnight, Friday, March 20. But the reports differed on exactly where he had been seen. Atlanta police recorded him as last seen near a game room at the corner of Techwood Drive and Mills Street. But one woman claimed she saw Eddie at Techwood and North Avenue shortly after midnight getting into a car with a light-skinned black man.

Earlier that day, Eddie was running errands and telling neighbors he was on his way to South Carolina to help someone move. He took four pairs of pants to a Mitchell Street cleaners at about 6:00 P.M. and was seen back at Techwood at about 7:00 P.M. and again three hours later. He did not go home for either lunch or dinner. And he never came back to the cleaners.

When Eddie Duncan disappeared, several neighbors believed that a killer was reacting to the challenge posed by the citizens' bat patrol. The killer wanted to snatch someone from under the noses of patrol organizers, and Eddie, with his limp and childlike mind, was an easy target. Others saw it differently. The killer had merely fulfilled the "promise" made in a graffiti: that the next victim would be from the Techwood area.

Twenty-year-old Larry Eugene Rogers vanished from his near northwest Atlanta neighborhood on the rainy afternoon of March 30, 1981. "Little Larry" was a short, slender, retarded youth who had lived quietly on Ezra Church Drive with his foster father, seventy-nine-year-old George Hood, since he was fifteen months old.

A neighbor, Thomas Reid, told investigators that he saw Larry getting into a faded green Chevrolet station wagon with a light-skinned older black man on the afternoon of March 30. The man, Reid said, had long, stringy hair, wore eyeglasses, and had heavy eyebrows and a thick mustache. Larry seemed "stiff," the eyewitness said. And as the car passed three times along Ezra Church Drive, Larry never waved to his neighbor.

Sometime during that same week, another black man was reported missing.

Twenty-three-year-old Michael Cameron McIntosh grew up in the Windsor Street neighborhood in southwest Atlanta. Michael inherited the Windsor Street house in which he lived in 1978, when his adoptive mother died. Her death came a month before Michael was paroled from the Clarke County Correctional Institute, where he served sixteen months on burglary and armed robbery charges. It had been Michael McIntosh's third trip to prison.

Michael had a severe drinking problem, but he never seemed to let that stop him from seeking work. On some days he would check in with the transient "Add-a-Man" labor pool at 708 Northwest Spring Street. Other times he would stop by West Quick Shop to ask about work. "He said he'd mop floors, do anything," said owner Connie Taylor, who always declined Michael's offer. "I told him if he could straighten himself up and stop drinking, I'd give him a job. He was quiet, a loner, and he was depressed because he couldn't get a job" (WP 1981i).

Earlier in the year Michael had pleaded for a welding job at the Milton Avenue Foundry, where he had worked for three weeks in the fall of 1980, after finishing a welding course funded by the Comprehensive Employment and Training Act (CETA). Then he dropped out of sight. Friends said Michael was in the habit of doing things like that. He would disappear for weeks at a time, only to turn up and brag that he had been out of town working.

The foundry boss relented and hired Michael back. Michael went to work with his torch on Tuesday, March 24. He was quiet and kept to himself that morning, fellow workers recalled. He ate his lunch alone. At 3:30 P.M. the next day, Michael punched his time card out and left. He had earned $34.35, but he never came back to pick up his paycheck.

Michael did not live with relatives, and so no one noticed whether he had returned home on Wednesday. The police could therefore only guess that Michael was last seen near his Windsor Street home sometime between March 25 and April 1—sometime after he vanished from his job. They also noted that the diminutive young man had sometimes boxed in a rear parking lot with Jo-Jo Bell, who was now missing. However, because Michael was some seven years older than Jo-Jo, investigating authorities were cautious about linking the two cases.

Michael McIntosh was the fifth black male to disappear between March 1 and April 1, 1981. At twenty-three, he was the oldest of the five. He was now also the oldest of the twenty or twenty-one young blacks who had been murdered or abducted since July 1979.

Eddie Duncan, Larry Rogers, and Michael McIntosh were considerably older than the other cases on the task force list. But in piecing together the cases, investigators learned that the three exhibited childlike characteristics which could have attracted a killer preying on young male victims. In addition, Eddie, Larry, and Michael were mentally slow. And because they had small, slender bodies, they could have given the appearance of being physically nonthreatening.

The number of FBI agents assigned to the "Atlanta situation" now dramatically increased, and the bureau became the de facto lead agency in the investigations. So, following George Bush's trip to Atlanta, all physical evidence gathered from each new crime scene would routinely be sent to the bureau's crime lab in Washington—the cutting-edge science shop peopled by experts able to dazzle the ordinary person with amazing feats of detection through microscopic analysis of hair, fiber, paint, metal, and chemical residues.

Based on their lab results, FBI agents in Atlanta concluded that the Atlanta murders were the work of a lone killer who was probably acting with an accomplice. The agents would go on to request, in early April 1981, that the bureau's behavioral science unit travel to Atlanta to update an earlier draft of a psychological profile of the person responsible for the Atlanta killings: a killer who sought out children or childlike victims. The killer—a male serial killer— was mobile and knew the Atlanta metropolitan area rather well. He also knew a lot about what investigators knew about him.

10

A Dead Body Every Week

I don't know who's doing it. It's somebody that these children trust and somebody that's in authority that's doing this to these kids that they continue to go to without anybody seeing them, without struggle.

—Willie Mae Mathis

At midspring 1981, law enforcement in Atlanta had made a complete about-face and was now doggedly pursuing investigations into the Atlanta youth murders under the theory that the city was being besieged by a single serial killer. Local political authorities, notably Fulton County district attorney Lewis Slaton, were publicly speculating that at least seven of the twenty Atlanta murders could be tied to a "gentle killer." FBI authorities went further. Based on accumulations of what they believed were consistent sets of physical evidence left on victims' bodies, they were convinced that practically all the Atlanta murders involved a lone perpetrator.

FBI Director William Webster and an FBI special agent, Michael Twibell, kept saying, however, that two or three had been committed by a parent or close relative, who had killed the children because they saw them as "nuisances." As might be expected, mothers of the missing or murdered children were infuriated by the remarks. At least ten mothers met with spotlight-hunting attorney Mark Lane—whose list of clients included cult leader Jim Jones and James Earl Ray, the convicted killer of Martin Luther King Jr.—to discuss suing the FBI for defamation.

A number of folks on the city's black side were equally incensed. So were Mayor Maynard Jackson and his commissioner of public safety, Lee Brown. Both men were particularly mad at the FBI director for implying that the Atlanta police bureau was shying away from the racially difficult task of arresting black people for having murdered their own children. "Your statements about Atlanta's tragic child murders are starting to hurt," Jackson wrote Webster. "We need Washington's help, not more problems. . . . I do not wish to be indelicate, but I respectfully urge you to consider the impact of your casual statements on our local situation here" (*NYT* 1981f). The mayor insisted that the full text of his reprimand be printed in the Atlanta newspapers.

Not viewing things quite the same way, representatives of the city's white ruling elite held that "the Jackson-Brown assault on the feds is hardly conducive to encouraging federal cooperation in the case" (Shipp 1981c).

Despite this and other distractions, the serial murderer theme held. But, as Commissioner Brown kept telling reporters, none of three related essentials had as yet surfaced or seemed in the offing: a confession, an eyewitness, or a thoroughly controlled crime scene (preferably the scene of the actual crime, not merely the place where a dead body was found). The admission was tinged with irony, since Brown often made the statement while ensconced in the high-tech surroundings of the special police task force's command center, with its banks of expensive computer equipment processing thousands of tips, and its walls lined with maps, charts, graphs, and composite drawings of possible suspects.

According to criminologists Ronald Holmes and James De Burger (1988, 18–19), serial slayings involve the following elements:

- The serial murderer kills again and again and will continue to kill if not prevented.

- Murders may span months or years.

- The murders are committed one-on-one.

- The relationship between victim and killer is usually that of a stranger or slight acquaintance.

- The serial killer is primarily motivated by the act of killing. "These are not crimes of passion in the conventional sense, nor do they stem from victim precipitation."

- Clear-cut motives (other than killing) are typically lacking, "due to frequent stranger-perpetration of this crime."

- "But there are *intrinsic* motive systems . . . that originate within the individual; they govern and structure the serial killer's homicidal behavior. These motive systems ordinarily reflect neither passion nor personal gain nor profit tendencies."

In 1979, when the first four or so in the string of Atlanta murders were first reported, the FBI was perfecting techniques that would enable law enforcement to benefit more concretely from the general outlines of the above typology. The techniques were being developed at the Behavioral Sciences Unit of the FBI's Training Academy. The assumption was that, through "psychological profiling," investigators could identify specific predictable behavior patterns of an elusive serial killer. A profile could be constructed from reviews of crime-scene photos, autopsy reports, and a trail of evidentiary material. When examined in combination, these items would give some indication of the offender's age, sex, race, sexual habits, and family situation.

After four months, FBI authorities ruled out possibilities of the Atlanta killer being someone who was "mentally deranged." Agents had checked out area mental institutions for the criminally insane and obtained lists of persons who had been released into the Atlanta vicinity since 1978. Finding nothing useful in this approach, they, along with GBI crime lab experts, decided to concentrate exclusively on laboratory analyses of the physical evidence they had been recovering from the Atlanta victims: the bloodstains, fingerprints, and sets of slender, threadlike particles—mostly yarns and fibers—found on the victims' bodies, hair, and clothing.

Crime lab technicians had in fact identified a number of yellowish-green nylon fibers and some violet acetate fibers on the bodies and clothing of at least six slaying victims. The yellowish-green nylon fibers were generally similar in appearance and microscopic properties; they also seemed to have originated from a single source. The same was true of the violet acetate fibers. "Although there were many other similarities that would link these murders together," wrote FBI microanalyst and special agent Harold Deadman (1984b, 10), "the fiber linkage was notable since the possibility existed that a source of these fibers might be located in the future."

On March 26, 1981, the FBI recorded the following technical details relative to a set of fibers that technicians had removed from three corpses: "FBI laboratory examination discloses all fibers to be synthetic. . . . Specimen Q32 is a rug-type yellow lobal fiber. The remaining fibers are lustrous, fluted synthetic fibers."

Mounting physical evidence of this sort, FBI investigators reasoned, would further enable profiling of, say, the killer's personal habits and mode of operation. Once psychological experts were able to tie together all the baffling pieces in his persona, he would be caught. In fact, on several occasions local law enforcement officials seemed to dare the killer to kill again, because "if he continues to kill, he will get caught."

Investigating authorities still worried, though, that the killer could apparently stalk victims and abduct them, often in broad daylight—and he continued to do so in a city that had become highly vigilant. Medical examiners pointed out that bodies of children showed little signs of resistance, suggesting they had been caught by surprise, possibly by someone seated in a car.

Investigators further noted that the killer not only knew his way around the city but seemed to be playing games with them. He seemed, for instance, to have responded to DeKalb County public safety commissioner Dick Hand's taunt that his men would have solved the crimes had they taken place in his jurisdiction. Shortly after Hand spoke, the bodies of two victims, Patrick Baltazar and Curtis Walker, showed up in DeKalb County. Was the killer, then, some sort of professional, a trained assassin? Or, as some FBI officials secretly worried, was he a disgruntled former Atlanta police officer with a grudge?

A canoeist plying the Chattahoochee River about a mile south of the Campbellton Road bridge on Monday, March 30, 1981, stumbled onto a by-then familiar but still unsettling sight. Snagged on a tree limb stretched across the surface of the water was the sparsely clothed body of a black boy. Investigators from the now 108-member special Atlanta police task force rushed to the scene. After a brief examination of the site, they had the body removed to the Douglas County morgue.

The next day, Fulton County's associate medical examiner, Dr. John Feegel, performed the required autopsy. Although partially decomposed, the body had been preserved "rather well" by the cold river. From matching dental records and photographs, Feegel positively identified Timothy Hill, the thirteen-year-old who had last been seen two weeks earlier on the grounds of Morehouse College during a mass rally protesting the string of Atlanta murders.

As he had done so many times before, Police Chief George Napper went to deliver sad news to an Atlanta family. Timothy's eighteen-year-old sister, Brenda, became hysterical and collapsed on the crowded living-room floor. The police chief politely asked the throng of news photographers to stop taking pictures of her. Family members rushed Brenda off by ambulance to Grady Hospital.

For Brenda, the news of her brother's death was sad, vexing vindication. She had been insisting all along to the Atlanta authorities that Timothy was not a runaway. Atlanta police just couldn't accept the fact, she said, "that someone came and snatched" her brother. Public reaction to the blunder resulted in Atlanta police implementing the rule that a case of a missing person not found within seventy-two hours be reviewed for inclusion in the task force's investigation.

Medical experts attributed Hill's death to "probable suffocation." On his body and underwear—the only piece of clothing he had on when his body was removed from the river—investigators found fibrous material similar to that found on the bodies of other victims. Theresa Swindall, Timothy's teacher, figured her "Timmy" must have gone off with someone he knew, "someone he felt comfortable with." Someone who killed him.

Late Tuesday, March 31, one day after Hill's body was discovered, another canoeist traversing the Chattahoochee River came across a body. It was floating near the Georgia Highway 92 bridge, exactly two miles from where Timothy's body had hung from a tree limb.

This body also was lodged in a tree limb on the Douglas County side of the river. And it, too, was clad only in underwear: boxer shorts, which were bunched up around the waist. The body had apparently drifted downriver on a flood tide. Medical examiners later identified the body as Eddie Lamar Duncan, the slightly retarded, speech-impaired youth whom neighbors believed was snatched from his Techwood residence on March 20, the day Commissioner Brown's officers came into Techwood Homes to dismantle the citizens' patrols.

Again, Napper went to deliver bad news. Eddie's relatives, friends, and neighbors sobbed in anger and disbelief. Napper then told the crowd of reporters gathered outside the dingy redbrick apartment building that housed Eddie's family: "There are some similarities between the situation of Eddie Duncan and Timothy Hill. We are assuming there is some relationship in spite of the fact that he is twenty-one years old and falls somewhere out of the prototype of the other youngsters" (*WP* 1981h). After this mouthful, Napper abruptly left the sprawling shantytown in his shiny, black sedan.

Medical examiners never conclusively determined the cause of Eddie Duncan's death. They could not rule out drowning, since one autopsy finding revealed that Eddie was probably alive when his body hit the water. Also, examiners from the Georgia crime lab said they found "no obvious traumatic injuries" to his body. "All we know," the chief medical examiner said, "is that he wasn't shot, stabbed, or cracked over the head" (*WP* 1981h). The cause of Eddie Duncan's death was officially listed as "unknown," although investigators believed he was asphyxiated and that his body ended up in the Chattahoochee at a moment he neared death. From Eddie's body technicians recovered several minute fibers that the unforgiving river had somehow not washed away.

On April 9, an Atlanta police officer checking out an abandoned car at the bottom of a hill on Temple Street sensed a strong odor coming from an apartment in a nearby block of deserted buildings. The officer entered the apartment. On the kitchen floor he found the decomposing body of Larry Rogers, the twenty-year-old retarded youth who lived with his foster father on Ezra Church Drive, a dead-end street in the shadows of downtown Atlanta's skyline of glass and steel. Larry had been missing for well over a week. His body was found about two miles from the place he called home.

When Larry's body was found, investigators thought they had a "contained crime scene," that is, the place where the murder was actually committed. They eventually discarded that notion and instead concluded that Larry had been killed elsewhere and his body brought to the abandoned building. Bruises on his throat indicated he had been choked, presumably by the killer's forearm. From Larry's body, state crime lab investigators recovered some dog hairs and some yellow, violet, and green fibers.

Investigators intensified their questioning of anyone they believed resembled a composite sketch of the man an eyewitness said he had seen Larry with the day he disappeared. Larry, the eyewitness had said, got into a faded green Chevrolet station wagon driven by a light-skinned, middle-aged black man with long, stringy hair, glasses, heavy eyebrows, and a thick mustache.

Three days later, on April 12, Atlanta police were drawn to the death of another black man. The body of twenty-eight-year-old John Harold Porter was found dumped in a vacant lot at 796 Northwest Bender Street, four blocks from where the body of nine-year-old Anthony Carter was found in July 1980. Porter had been murdered in almost the same way as was Anthony: multiple stab wounds to his chest and abdomen.

Atlanta authorities decided at the time, however, that Porter's death lacked sufficient "pattern elements" to justify including it in their list of murders, even though technicians had recovered from his body fibers that they deemed similar in microscopic qualities to those recovered from the bodies of several listed victims. But, they reasoned, Porter was much older than those victims, and he would have been able to defend himself against a killer preying on weak, defenseless youngsters. Porter's name was therefore not added to the official list of Atlanta's missing and murdered. However, crime lab technicians kept specimens of his blood.

Early on the afternoon of April 19, a couple trying out their new trail bikes off Klondike Road in Rockdale County spotted a decomposed body lying in a dry area where the South River had receded along the boundary between DeKalb and Rockdale Counties.

Medical examiners identified the body as Joseph "Jo-Jo" Bell, the fifteen-year-old who was last seen more than a month earlier at Cap'n Peg's, a Georgia Avenue fried-fish restaurant. Jo-Jo's body showed signs of "having floated down river" and bore injury marks usually seen on "bodies that get snagged and come over rocks and things like that," the chief medical examiner said. Only a tiny amount of physical evidence was recovered from Jo-Jo's body, which, like four of the last five discovered bodies, was clad only in underwear. Investigators did find fibers, which they later determined were similar to those recovered from the bodies of at least eleven other slaying victims. Jo-Jo Bell died of asphyxiation, the medical examiners concluded. And like Curtis Walker, he suffered an injury to his upper spine.

The next day, a Fulton County farmer came across a nude, decomposing body floating in the Chattahoochee River below the Campbellton Road bridge. The spot was no more than a few miles from where the bodies of Timothy Hill and Eddie Duncan were discovered one day apart a month earlier. After the usual investigative protocol, the authorities determined that this was Michael McIntosh, listed as missing since April 1, 1981.

The authorities decided that McIntosh's death warranted task force investigation. At twenty-three, he would be the oldest on their list. But, according to the Fulton County police chief, Clinton Chafin, "When you look at where [McIntosh's] body was found, the cause of death, the area of town where he came from—these factors lead you to believe there's got to be some kind of connection" (WP 1981i).

McIntosh fell into a category of two other recent adult victims—Eddie Duncan and Larry Rogers—who, apparently unlike twenty-eight-year-old John Porter, were mentally slow or retarded. Eddie and Larry also were trusting of strangers, making them even more vulnerable to the unfriendly ways of the street. Although not retarded, Michael McIntosh appeared "slow in the mind," a childhood friend recalled. He was especially slow, his friend said, when he drank. And Michael drank a lot. Another common characteristic between his and the other victims was that Michael died of asphyxiation, making him the fourteenth black youth to die this way in less than a year.

Between March 2 and April 1, 1981, five black Atlanta youths had disappeared. Between March 30 and April 20, the murdered bodies of the five—and John Porter's—were discovered all over metropolitan Atlanta. The task force now listed twenty-five slayings. (Darron Glass they still listed as missing, and they had not added John Porter's murder to their list.) If indeed a single serial killer was operating on the streets of Atlanta, as FBI authorities now firmly believed, he had dramatically increased his pace. He was quite possibly going berserk!

Two notable features of four of the five latest listed killings were that the bodies were found in area rivers and they were practically nude when found. The killer, investigators reasoned, was methodically disposing of victims in a manner that would destroy the fibers which the news media had been unwisely reporting as continuous links in the string of slayings. But the killer seemed bent on playing an additional game: he was disposing of bodies mostly in the Chattahoochee River, but he was doing so on different sides of the river and at different points downstream. Investigators took this to mean that he wanted to further confuse them and at the same time involve several different law enforcement jurisdictions.

But why the apparent turn to older victims? The view among investigators was that the various curfew measures the city had implemented were keeping boys off the city's streets, leaving the killer with available childlike adults. Several parents maintained, however, that the many awareness sessions put on in schools and at parent-teacher meetings by groups like STOP had caused parents to either keep children off the streets or at least monitor them properly. Whichever was true, investigators held that the pattern toward vulnerable adult victims had been established.

Forty-six special FBI agents were assigned full-time to the Atlanta cases by April 1981—up from thirty-two. The agents interviewed school children about any strange solicitations, questioned operators of businesses that did customizing work for recreational vehicles, and examined buildings and automobiles for carpet matches with the fibers that crime lab technicians kept recovering from the bodies of the Atlanta victims.

To get their man, FBI brass eventually decided on a "proactive investigative course." They proposed to Atlanta authorities that a bridge surveillance program be instituted under FBI coordination (Glover and Witham 1989). On April 24, 1981, four days after investigators had found the body of Michael McIntosh, the bureau embarked on its bridge surveillance program for a thirty-day "trial period."

Expecting the killer to stay with his established pattern of dumping bodies in area rivers, teams of Atlanta police officers and FBI agents targeted fourteen bridges for dusk-to-dawn surveillance. The bridges connected sparsely traveled roads passing over the Chattahoochee and South Rivers.

Black Atlantans had an eerie feeling about the racial and historical contexts of the strategy. The FBI's immersion in the Atlanta drama was in itself troubling. Folks sensed, however, something that was reminiscently evil in a story involving black male bodies turning up in southern rivers. Was it not too long ago, folks kept reminding each other, that in a somewhat similar story—the search for missing civil rights workers with the Mississippi Freedom Summer project of 1964 (James Chaney, Michael Schwerner, and Andrew Goodman)—federal authorities had ordered massive dragging of Mississippi's rivers? And didn't divers retrieve the bodies of black men and boys who had been missing for months and even years? These victims of yesteryear did not die at the hands of some "psycho" serial killer. Rather, they had been systematically snatched and murdered by vengeful whites.

And even though most folks believed that the FBI was committed to solving the Atlanta murders, they kept asking: What really was their angle? Why was the agency suddenly so enthusiastic about the Atlanta cases, to the point where they were now "running things"? Speakers at community meetings kept reminding folks that the FBI's track record on matters relating to the rights, safety, and protection of black people couldn't stand the light of day. Was the FBI, with a "brother" (black SAC John Glover) running the Atlanta office, now trying to save face and correct history by being overly aggressive in finding a killer of black people?

Truth was, the federal government was spending lots of money on the crisis in Atlanta. Between February and early April, $3 million in direct federal assistance had either been spent or appropriated for Atlanta—a sum which did not include salaries for FBI agents brought in from outlying jurisdictions and reassigned to Atlanta, nor monies for other directly associated FBI costs, including cars and surveillance equipment. Moreover, the Atlanta mayor had been up to Washington demanding millions more for targeted "safe summer" youth programs.

Officials in Washington, then, wanted nothing more than a termination to this run on the federal purse. And what surer way was there for this to happen than to have the federal government's own reliable people—namely, its unimpeachable FBI agents—firmly in control of things in Atlanta?

Added to their concerns over money, Reagan administration officials were increasingly worried by plans for a solidarity march on Washington. The march was set for Memorial Day, May 25, 1981. Its goal, organizers were publicly stating, was to call national and worldwide attention not just to the ongoing tragedy in Atlanta but also to the plight of black and poor children all across America. The march would mark the first time that grassroots groups and mainline civil rights organizations had come together to rally around racial themes that emerged from the Atlanta murders.

For conservative Republicans, such spectacles as solidarity marches in the nation's capital and city officials shaking down the federal government for money to fund inner-city child safety programs simply had to end—the sooner the better.

11

A Loud Splash

The unsolved killings in this normally upbeat Sun Belt city are phenomena the city's public relations experts can't even mention, let alone solve.

—*Wall Street Journal*, June 2, 1981

Three more black youths would disappear from the city's streets. And more bodies would be discovered. But this dread routine would be interrupted by a "splash" that was said to have come from the darkness of the impenetrable Chattahoochee River early one morning in May 1981.

The case of Atlanta's missing and murdered youths began to visibly hurt the city's economy. Promotional experts were admitting that booster slogans selling a city tainted by news of mysterious murders was in poor taste. For this reason, the issue of the tragedy could not be ignored in the ongoing mayoral campaign.

The negative effect of the tragedy on the business of Atlanta was felt most acutely in the twin area of tourism and conventioneering. Analysts reported an 8 percent decline in tourism in the first months of 1981, most of which they attributed to adverse publicity. Particularly reluctant to travel to Atlanta were tour groups of children (*WSJ* 1981).

Between April and May, the Atlanta Convention and Visitors Bureau received some thirty calls per week from concerned convention planners who had read about the murders and wanted to know the "tone" of the city. Potential visitors began responding by going elsewhere. European tour operators canceled thousands of reservations at Peachtree Plaza Hotel. Six hundred reservations—for Dutch and West German tour groups—were canceled in a two-week period. The tour operators all cited the string of murders as the reason, saying the guests, who had planned to attend a two-day jazz festival at Piedmont Park, were put off by the publicity.

Not canceling their convention and travel plans to the city, however, were all-black professional organizations. The National Medical Association, an organization of black doctors, still planned to hold its annual meeting in Atlanta in the summer of 1981.

The tragedy had a continuing effect on the contest to decide who would succeed Maynard Jackson as mayor of the heavily Democrat city. The contest was in high gear by mid-April. Andrew Young, former ambassador to the United Nations, two-term congressman from an integrated Atlanta district, and veteran of the civil rights movement, had come home to compete for a job many thought was rather pedestrian for a man of his galactic stature. Young was one of eight candidates in a race in which the tragedy was the city's most explosive issue. Yet candidates seldom mentioned it.

Young's reasoning why the issue of the youth murders was kept "within bounds" is instructive. "The alternative [i.e., talking publicly about them] would be to put the police and the city on trial," he said. "Our objective is to put the killer or killers on trial. No one can profit by second-guessing and drugstore quarter backing" (Harris 1981).

Others within the city's black political elite quietly worried, though. All the murder victims came from the impoverished neighborhoods that any black mayoral candidate would need to win an election. The unsolved slayings "could turn poor blacks against those in power, or anyone associated with them, and make the race a free-for-all," as *Washington Post* writer Art Harris observed (1981). A situation like that would make it possible for anyone, *including a white minority candidate,* to win the election.

The topic of the murdered youngsters came up at a NAACP-sponsored forum. Fifty black residents from the DeKalb County portion of the city (where at least six of the dead children had lived) turned out to grill Police Chief George Napper—Jackson's "ivory tower cop." NAACP lawyer Dwight Thomas asked, "If the number of dead children reaches fifty or seventy-five, will you consider resigning?" Napper snapped, "That question is too horrible to contemplate." He refused to elaborate, leaving the audience to wonder what their police chief found "horrible": more murdered children or the prospect of resigning?

But the question about more youngsters being murdered persisted in the minds of many black voters. If the killings and disappearances continued, then the least voters expected would be heads to roll in the Jackson administration, particularly if Jackson wanted his handpicked candidate, Andrew Young, to win. If the cases weren't solved, and the other candidates in the race were able to make Young "defend" Jackson on the issue of the tragedy, Young would lose, predicted Dwight Thomas.

Young's principal opponent in the mayoral contest was A. Reginald Eaves, who continued to enjoy strong support among the city's black poor. He did so, observers believed, because he was the only one in the race giving voice to the deep-seated frustrations, fears, and anger of the community at risk.

In one of his columns for the *Atlanta Voice*, which became his favorite medium for launching political broadsides at his opponents, Eaves presented a thoughtful, coherent analysis of what to him was the tragedy's profound meaning. The police investigation into the murders, he wrote, "cannot in any way deal with the social aspect of the crimes being perpetrated on our children. Catching the killer(s) will not see an end to the conditions that rendered these kids vulnerable to the traps set by poverty and other oppressive circumstances" (Eaves 1981, 5).

Most white Atlantans backed the other principal contestant, Sidney Marcus, a liberal white state legislator. Several analysts were predicting that, if issues surrounding the tragedy were exploited for political gains, it could divide the black vote between Young and Eaves come election day, giving neither the absolute majority needed for victory. That would set the stage for a white-black showdown—between Marcus and either Eaves or Young—in the runoff.

Young scoffed at the scenario. "I don't feel [the tragedy] will split the black community," he said to reporters. But, he added, "some hope that it will." Pushed for a comment on the way the probe was going, Young would only say that he would take a "serious look" at the cases, and the police brass he would inherit, if he were elected mayor. Understandably, police heads would roll, he said, only if the cases remain unsolved after his inauguration.

Racial strains were indeed heightened whenever the conversation about who should be mayor of Atlanta included discussion of the unsolved murders. Mayoral politics and the politics of class could not be separated from what was "happening to these children," STOP's Camille Bell insisted. "These killings wouldn't have gone on so long without nothing being done if it was not for black people with a little something not caring about black people who ain't got nothing," she said to the *Washington Post*'s Juan Williams (1981).

On April 21, 1981, Roy Innis, the in again, out again executive director of the New York-based Congress of Racial Equality (CORE), held a news conference on the steps of Atlanta's city hall. He told reporters, "We are very convinced we have broken this case, and we can prove it" (*AC* 1981g).

Innis was referring, of course, to the unsolved Atlanta murders. He produced a sealed envelope, which he said contained the photograph of the individual he knew had killed at least six of the Atlanta victims. He declined to reveal the culprit's identity. He did say, however, that volunteer "investigators" from CORE working with bereaved parents over the previous six weeks had found a "secret informant." The informant was one Shirley McGill from Liberty City in Miami, Florida. Innis said he passed on to law enforcement officials the information he had obtained from Ms. McGill.

Investigating authorities admitted that they had interviewed Shirley McGill and that the story she gave about an ex-boyfriend being involved in a ritualistic slaying of the Atlanta youngsters was "plausible." They had even checked out some of the leads she had given them. They still could not "prove" the overall validity of her story, however.

But the authorities' bigger problem was with Innis's own credibility. CORE officials in New York said Innis was in Atlanta "acting on his own." The *Washington Post* (1981j) quoted CORE chairman Waverly Yates as saying, "What we are concerned about is that the organization is not embarrassed nationally" by Innis's Atlanta escapade. Yates was one of Innis's opponents within CORE. Innis's handling of CORE finances was the subject of an ongoing, contentious dispute between the two. Innis had in fact come under scrutiny by New York State's legal authorities for his dealings. Atlanta officials thus figured that the embattled one-time civil rights luminary was in Atlanta on a quest for heroic publicity.

Atlanta authorities ended up treating the information that Roy Innis and his "witness" gave them as part of the "investigatory process." Nothing useful came out of their story. Innis eventually returned to New York and to his troubles with CORE. He steadfastly held to a ritualistic or cult angle to the Atlanta murders, though. Weeks after his fruitless meeting with FBI and Atlanta authorities, he came back to Atlanta claiming he had "discovered" new evidence related to the killings at a site on Roswell Road in predominantly white far northwest Atlanta. The "evidence" included a cross and other signs of what Innis claimed were white-cult activities. A local satanic group was responsible for the Atlanta murders, Innis insisted, obviously determined not to step out of the Atlanta spotlight. While he was hogging newspaper headlines and TV cameras, however, another black youngster quietly disappeared from the Atlanta streets.

On Wednesday morning, April 22, 1981, following his routine, Jimmy Ray Payne walked his girlfriend to the Vine City MARTA rail station, then returned to his home two blocks away in the Vine City Terrace Apartments on Magnolia Street, where he lived with his sister and stepfather. The apartment building was a block from Foundry Street, where twelve-year-old Patrick Baltazar had lived.

Jimmy left his home again at about 10:30 A.M. He told his sister he was going to the Omni to sell some coins. After he failed to meet his girlfriend at the MARTA station that night, his sister called the police the next day. She feared something terrible had happened. Her brother was small in stature. At twenty-one, he weighed only 137 pounds and was not much more than five feet tall. He could easily have been mistaken for a teenager, as apparently was the case with the three most recent Atlanta slaying victims.

But Atlanta police held off for almost five full days before assigning Jimmy Payne's case to the special task force. His case remained instead with the ABPS's missing persons unit; this despite Commissioner Lee Brown's ruling two weeks earlier that any missing persons case not solved within seventy-two hours would be reviewed for inclusion in the task force's investigations. Jimmy Payne's case was not turned over to the special police task force within the allotted time because an eyewitness claimed he had seen Jimmy over the previous weekend. (The person sighted turned out to be Jimmy's cousin.)

Moreover, reports had been circulating that Jimmy wanted to change his identity. Friends told investigators that a few days before he vanished, Jimmy had tried to get a new identification card in another name. Jimmy had spent two years in prison for burglary and shoplifting, and as a result he was having a tough time finding a job. He thought his chances would improve if he changed his name. So at first when no one could find him, friends and family—along with the police—figured Jimmy disappeared on purpose as a way to enhance his new identity.

The theory seemed borne out on Monday, April 27, 1981, five days after Jimmy had disappeared. An Atlanta police officer arrested a man for slapping a woman outside Cap'n Peg's Seafood on Georgia Avenue. Asked to produce some identification, the man pulled out a wallet; in it was Jimmy Payne's prison identification card. The man, a known scavenger, could not explain how he had come across the card. But one of the last places that Jimmy Payne could have been en route to his new identity was in the vicinity of Cap'n Peg's, where he might have tossed his old I.D. card into the nearest trash bin.

Late that Monday afternoon, within hours of the incident outside Cap'n Peg's, a couple fishing on the Chattahoochee River spotted a body floating face-down in the river, just before it became entangled in some branches. The spot was near the Fulton-Cobb County line, where Bankhead Highway crossed the river. Like the five other bodies found in a waterway within the previous three months, this body, too, was clad only in undershorts. Medical authorities eventually identified Jimmy Payne. His body had been in the river for five days and was substantially decomposed.

Fulton County medical examiners' initial findings relative to cause of death were inconclusive. Dr. Saleh Zaki, who performed the autopsy, ruled that Payne's death was a "case of probable asphyxiation." Zaki also told reporters that he could not rule out drowning as the cause of death. In filling out the death certificate, Zaki listed the cause of death as "undetermined," not homicide. However, because investigators had recovered several familiar carpetlike fibers, they decided to treat Payne's death as a homicide. They also placed his name on the Atlanta police special task force list.

One problem with Jimmy Payne's "probable homicide," though, was that, unlike slaying victims Eddie Duncan, Larry Rogers, and Michael McIntosh—to whom Jimmy could be likened in terms of age and size—Jimmy was not "slow." Friends said Jimmy was too smart to have become a victim of a serial killer of unsuspecting youths; Jimmy had an IQ of 104. So, if indeed Jimmy Payne was a victim of the Atlanta killer, investigators figured that size was a key. The killer was choosing victims based on their race, sex, and size.

Jimmy Ray Payne was twenty-sixth on the list of kidnapped and murdered black Atlanta youngsters. His would not be the last name on that list, however.

"Billy Star" is what they called seventeen-year-old William Barrett on the streets of east Atlanta. The nickname had a certain poignancy to it, because it was somewhat like an ill-fated *starbwai*—the bold-hearted guy in a grade B Western who never recovers from his wounds—that the brief course of the short, slightly built youth's life ran.

William was released from Milledgeville Youth Development Center, a state juvenile correctional facility, on March 10, 1981. His little life of never-ending brushes with the law seemed on the mend. Billy went to live with his mother at 396 Second Avenue in Decatur, and started attending counseling sessions at a nearby state-run community treatment center on Columbia Drive near Glenwood Avenue. He hung around his mother's home most of the time. But he also tried to find a job.

On the morning of May 11, 1981, Billy's mother asked him to go across town to the McDaniel-Glenn housing project to "pay some money she owed to a man" (Dettlinger and Prugh 1983, 302). Billy apparently rode a MARTA bus on the errand and later returned to the general vicinity of his home; he was scheduled for a counseling session late that afternoon. But his counselor became ill, and no one noticed that Billy never showed up. A neighbor recalled seeing Billy a few blocks from his home as late as 6:00 P.M. that May 11. Then he vanished. Investigators figured he could have left his neighborhood again later that evening taking either a bus or a train toward downtown Atlanta. After that, the trail got cold.

Shortly after midnight on May 12, 1981, less than seven hours after he was last seen, federal lawmen found William Barrett's fully clothed body in a wooded area near Interstate 20 and Glenwood Road, along dead-end Winthrop Drive in DeKalb County. The body, FBI authorities noted, "was in no way hidden," indicating that the killer "intended quick discovery." Like Terry Pue and Patrick Baltazar, medical examiners ruled that William Barrett had been strangled, probably with a soft cord or cloth.

But unlike any of the other listed victims, Billy had been stabbed in the abdomen *after* he died. Anthony Carter and still-unlisted John Porter, whose bodies also showed stab wounds, had died *of* their wounds. The wounds on Barrett's body, made with a small knife with upward motions toward the chest, baffled investigators, since the killer they thought they knew had never shown a penchant for abusing victims' bodies.

Because Barrett's body was found within hours after he was last seen alive, FBI investigators were able to recover a number of trace items from his body, including several green carpet fibers, violet fibers, and white undercoat animal hairs. Beyond that, the search for William Barrett's killer turned up precious little.

Twenty-seven-year-old Nathaniel Cater was a muscular man who stood five-feet ten-inches tall. He had only recently moved out of his father's Verbena Street apartment in the Dixie Hills housing project (in near northwest Atlanta) in May 1981. In Dixie Hills, Nathaniel and his family lived upstairs from slaying victim Latonya Wilson. When the girl turned up missing in June 1980, the first place her mother went in search of her was the Cater apartment.

Nathaniel's new address was the Falcon Hotel, a rundown single room occupancy (SRO) abode at 180 Northwest Luckie Street, near the Greyhound bus station in downtown Atlanta's transient section.

Nathaniel was smart enough to have skipped a grade in grammar school, but he never was able to successfully meet life's later challenges. His father, a sanitation worker for the city for more than twenty years and a member of the work crew which had gone on strike in 1977, had done just about all he could for his son. Nathaniel somehow managed to sustain himself, but just barely, by picking up odd jobs through the "Add-a-Man" labor pool. There he probably would have run into another ne'er-do-well, Michael McIntosh, who ended up as murder victim number twenty-five on Atlanta's special police task force list.

On days when checking in with the labor pool proved futile—which was more often than not—Nathaniel would hang around the Silver Dollar Saloon or the Cameo Lounge, two seedy downtown sporting houses. At either place, he would hustle suckers, male and female—many of them white, well-dressed out-of-towners—seeking cheap sexual thrills. But despite his ready engagement in the darker methods of urban-cowboy survival, Nathaniel lived unobtrusively with his SRO roommate at the Falcon, whose manager came to see him as not much more than a "slick hustler." Nathaniel usually paid his rent on time, and he "never tried to steal anything or cause trouble," the hotel manager later would tell reporters.

Nathaniel Cater's real trouble was with the bottle. He was a chronic alcoholic whose binges often landed him in the city jail's drunk tank. Still, he was a quiet drunk making the rounds at the bars near the downtown bus station. His drinking would often leave him helpless, however. "After he was drinking for an hour, there was no way he could protect himself," the manager of the Falcon Hotel recalled.

The hotel manager and Nathaniel's roommate were among the last to see the young man on the afternoon of May 21, when Nathaniel left the hotel. The manager waited for Nathaniel to show up the next day, Friday, to renew his rent. But he never did. Nathaniel apparently vanished near the bus station—right after he had paid his last visit to the bar at the Cameo Lounge.

Nathaniel Cater had been missing for some twelve hours when a final scene in the long Atlanta drama began to unfold. It happened in the vicinity of the James Jackson Parkway bridge, which crossed the Chattahoochee River at the Atlanta city limits.

The FBI-initiated stakeout over area bridges was into its third uneventful week. The bureau's strategy had called for positioning officers at or near these likely crime scenes, where they could nab anyone attempting to dispose of a body by tossing it into the river. By mid-May, five bodies had been pulled from the Chattahoochee.

The story, as related in Atlanta newspapers, FBI records, and prosecution testimony, was that Atlanta police cadet Robert Campbell had resumed his surveillance position on the west bank of the river about thirty feet downstream from the towering Jackson Parkway bridge. He was still trying to settle into the scrub brush and weeds for his midnight-to-morning shift when, at about 2:50 A.M., his solitude was shattered by what he would later describe as a "loud splash" in the river. The splash was louder than, and different from, the swishing sound of a live animal hitting the water. That particular sound the rookie officer said he had grown accustomed to, after hearing them repeatedly over the many nights that he had been close to the water's edge.

Glancing up at the bridge, Campbell said he saw a slowly moving car with its headlights on. No other cars were on the bridge. Campbell used his radio to call fellow cadet Freddy Jacobs, who was hunkering between concrete rails atop the bridge's eastern end. Campbell asked Jacobs if anyone was "up there" because he had heard "a loud splash down here."

Jacobs leaned out to peer into the gloom. He told Campbell that a car was indeed on the bridge, but it was "really close to the edge of the bridge." He was able to see only one headlight and could not determine whether the car had actually *stopped* on the bridge, but he could see that it was "going really slow," as if "coming from a parked position."

The car, a white 1970 Chevrolet Concourse station wagon, slowly rolled past Jacobs; it was headed southeast, in the direction of downtown Atlanta. The car cleared the bridge, then pulled into the parking lot of a small liquor store. Then, suddenly, it turned around and headed back to the bridge.

Patrolman Carl Holden, a seven-year veteran of the Atlanta police force and leader of the bridge surveillance team, was sitting in his unmarked silver Ford Granada at the edge of the woods behind the liquor store. Holden and FBI agent Gregg Gilliland had been keenly listening to the radio conversations between Campbell and Jacobs. Holden observed the station wagon as it went through its U-turn and pulled back onto Jackson Parkway, heading northwest toward Cobb County. He started his car engine and set out behind the station wagon, now gunning its way back over the bridge. As the two cars swept past the western end of the bridge, Gilliland fell in line behind Holden.

The lawmen tailed their quarry onto an expressway ramp off Cobb Drive leading to Interstate 285. They turned on their flashing blue lights and pulled the station wagon off the highway.

A swarm of FBI agents descended on the scene. Firmly taking charge, the FBI's Gilliland approached the vehicle, aiming his flashlight into the face of the driver, a bespectacled young black man with a medium "Afro." The man seemed sunk down deep behind the steering wheel. Gilliland asked him to step outside and produce his driver's license, vehicle registration, and proof of insurance.

The driver shuffled out of the car, revealing his portly frame. "What this all about?" he inquired presumptively.

Gilliland, ignoring for the moment his question, pressed him for some identification. The man produced a driver's license, which stated that he was Wayne Bertram Williams. He was twenty-three years old, and he lived at 1817 Northwest Penelope Road in Atlanta. The car was his uncle's, but his father was using it, Williams explained.

Again Williams asked, "What this . . . all about?" Gilliland responded, "I can't tell at this time."

After a pause, Williams turned to Gilliland and glibly offered, "I know this must be about those boys."

Holden had returned to the bridge. He, Jacobs, Campbell, and two other Atlanta policemen set up portable lights along its edges. They used the lights to scan the river. But, finding nothing peculiar or unusual on the surface of the water, they gave up searching after about fifteen minutes. Holden went back to the row of cars along the interstate, taking Jacobs with him. He asked the cadet if the stopped station wagon was the same vehicle he had seen driving slowly over the bridge. Jacobs said it was.

Williams, according to FBI records, then "voluntarily consented" to a routine search of his station wagon. On the front passenger seat were a flashlight, a pair of dirty gloves, and a two-foot nylon cord. On the floor of the right front side of the car was a knapsack of what appeared to be men's clothing. And in the gate area were two cardboard boxes, a large open bag of women's clothing, and a white bedspread with black and green design.

Williams told the officers that he had worn the clothing in the knapsack earlier that day at a gym in Ben Hill, just outside Atlanta, where he had been trying out for a basketball team. The other clothing belonged to his mother, and he was supposed to have thrown it away.

Gilliland instructed Williams to empty the contents of the knapsack onto the car's front seat. A pair of dark colored slacks, black shoes, white jockey shorts, and a red (or red and black) striped tank top tumbled out.

Gilliland commented to Williams that the car was "a mess" and that it looked as if it had been carrying animals. Williams said he had been carrying a dog in the car. Gilliland asked, "What kind of dog?" Williams answered that the dog was his parents' fourteen-year-old German Shepherd, which had been in the car "any number of times."

After spending about an hour and a half questioning him and listening to his story—that he was a musical talent scout with an early morning appointment to see a woman at an unfamiliar address in the nearby town of Smyrna, Georgia, so the reason for him being in the vicinity of the bridge was to do a "trial run"—the federal agents released the oddly assured young man, sending him on his way. They had no reason to detain or further impede him, since, at the very least, he said he didn't know any of the Atlanta victims, and he denied ever stopping on the bridge or tossing anything into the river (although one version of the sequence of events, reported by the Atlanta police, is that Williams responded, "Garbage," when asked if he had thrown anything, or anyone, off the bridge).

Neither was it necessary, the FBI agents figured, for them to seize or take a formal inventory of the contents of Williams's car or to ask him to submit a written account of his activities that night.

Hours later, Atlanta police officers dragged the Chattahoochee River in the vicinity of the Jackson Parkway bridge. They came up with nothing. Later that day FBI agents would nonetheless go to the Atlanta address indicated on the driver's license of the man they had stopped: a redbrick bungalow on Northwest Penelope Road in the Dixie Hills section of the city. For two hours they questioned the cocky young man, who seemed not to have had a good reason for his bizarre driving earlier that morning or for being on the highway—apparently headed for no particular place—at that late, dark hour of the Georgia night.

Neighbors would recall that, soon after he returned from his "trial run," and again the next day, they saw Wayne removing several boxes from his dwelling. They also couldn't help noticing the huge bonfire he had going a few days later in the family's backyard barbecue pit.

12

A Man with Big Dreams and Peculiar Activities

He told us to get ready. That we were going to Chattanooga for a show, and that the first ten rows would be nothing but producers.

—Would-be Atlanta entertainer Joe Bailey

We deal with hype.

—Willie Hunter, Atlanta music man and Svengali to Wayne Williams

When Atlantans awoke on Friday, May 22, 1981, they knew nothing about the "loud splash" an Atlanta rookie police officer said he had heard in the Chattahoochee River just before dawn. Nor, as the day progressed, did folks hear about the visit by FBI agents to the home of one Wayne Williams. Folks knew nothing about these developments because the news media was not yet onto them.

Neither had folks heard of Nathaniel Cater, whose name was not on the official list of Atlanta's missing and murdered. Two and a half days would pass before anyone other than Nathaniel's roommate and the manager of the SRO hotel where Nathaniel stayed had even noticed that he had disappeared. Atlanta police would not have been interested in connecting the missing drifter with the string of slayings and disappearances, anyway, since at twenty-seven Nathaniel would have been much older than the youths whose deaths they were investigating. But the discovery of the body of yet another black male in—where else?—the Chattahoochee River would once more challenge unreconstructed notions about age in the string of mysterious Atlanta murders.

On Sunday, May 24, at about 11:30 A.M., two boys who had paddled down the Chattahoochee on a fishing trip hurried back upstream. Scared and out of breath, the boys blurted out something to two adults standing nearby—something about having just seen a dead man in the water.

Cobb County police and rescue workers arrived within minutes. They found the nude body of a black male, face-down in shallow water on the Atlanta side of the river, about two hundred yards south of the I-285 bridge overpass near South Cobb Drive. The body had apparently floated downstream before coming to rest in a pile of wood at approximately the same spot where less than a month earlier the body of Jimmy Ray Payne had been discovered. Atlanta police had dragged this same vicinity two mornings earlier—shortly after FBI and Atlanta special police task force investigators had stopped and questioned Wayne Williams.

The man appeared to have been murdered. In his autopsy report, Chief Medical Examiner Robert Stivers described the body as belonging to a 150-pound, five-foot ten-inch, fairly muscular man between twenty-five and thirty years of age. No visible marks were found on the corpse, Stivers told reporters, but the autopsy showed "neck trauma." He concluded that the man died of asphyxiation, which could have resulted from a choke hold, a forearm across the throat, or a pillow pressed down against the neck area. There was no evidence of sexual molestation, major injuries, or "appreciable scratches or abrasions," Stivers said. He believed, however, that the victim may have put up a brief struggle.

The body had been in the water for days, probably more than two but not more than a week. But, the medical examiner cautioned, there was no way of knowing how long the victim had been dead before being dumped in the river. Autopsy findings were nonetheless consistent with immersion "sometime soon after death" (*AC* 1981h).

Investigators at first figured that this latest victim could have been twenty-two-year-old Ronald Crawford, a mentally retarded youth reported missing since mid-May. Before investigators could establish the possible connection, however, Ronald Crawford called his family—after he had heard news of his death. Ronald told his mother he had been away picking peaches in the Augusta, Georgia, area.

Eventually, through additional analysis of medical records and fingerprints, experts determined that the dead man was Nathaniel Cater, whom practically no one knew was missing.

The authorities delayed releasing this information for several hours. They wanted to buy time to trace Nathaniel's path from the point when he vanished to his ending in the muddy waters of the Chattahoochee. He was the sixth black Atlanta male to end up exactly this way in less than six months. But could this muscular man have been a victim of a child killer? Investigators believed he was. Toxicology reports showed that Nathaniel was intoxicated when he was killed. Even a muscular man could be made helpless while under the influence of too much alcohol, investigators figured. They concluded that, like all the other victims on the special police task force list—including the four adults (Eddie Duncan, Larry Rogers, Michael McIntosh, and Jimmy Payne) who were deemed "childlike"—Nathaniel Cater, because of his drunken state, was easily subdued and murdered without too much trouble.

Georgia crime lab technicians recorded that, from the hair on Nathaniel's head, they recovered a yellowish-green nylon carpet-type fiber, which was similar in microscopic qualities to fibers already recovered from the bodies of other slaying victims. Fulton County district attorney Lewis Slaton said he was connecting Nathaniel Cater's death to the other unsolved Atlanta slayings because of the way the body had been discarded, "the fact that he was nude, and the way he was killed."

Nathaniel's body seemed to have floated downstream from the vicinity of the James Jackson Parkway bridge, on which surveillance officers said they saw a car being driven in a suspicious manner early on the morning of May 22 by Wayne Williams. And the body was found less than a half mile from the spot where an Atlanta police cadet said he had heard a loud splash in the river *at the same time that Williams's car was on the bridge.*

FBI authorities in particular figured that the chain of events was more than coincidental. They decided to take a closer look at Williams. They needed to scrutinize his movements and to check into his background. This FBI-led targeting of Wayne Williams would commence against the backdrop of a significant demonstration in the nation's capital.

On Memorial Day, five to six thousand demonstrators came to Washington. They came, many with protest signs, in part to embarrass but also to call on the national powers that be to give yet greater attention to Atlanta's tragedy and the plight of poor black children in America. The rally had been organized primarily by the Atlanta-based Committee to Stop Children's Murders (STOP). It was endorsed, however, by a broad coalition representing more than a dozen causes: from organized labor and civil rights to child advocacy. Several celebrity activists, including Dick Gregory and Stevie Wonder, also showed up for the event.

At the Lincoln Memorial, an interracial gathering heard speeches railing against the "sickness," "chaos," and "physical and psychological destruction" of American society. Perhaps the most militant of these speeches came from Victor Goode of the National Conference of Black Lawyers, Bernice Krawczwk of the United Automobile Workers, and Michael Amon-Ra of the National Black United Front (NBUF).

Picking up on the day's "Save Our Children" theme, Goode said, "Let us save the children who are about to be drafted in imperialist wars; let us save the children who roam city streets without jobs; let us save the children who are questing for an education while school systems are about to close down because of a lack of funds."

Krawczwk reminded the audience that "no change comes without struggle." He added, "Our friends, neighborhoods, coworkers in the labor movement have to understand that sitting at home shaking our heads in disbelief while child after child is murdered in Atlanta will not change anything. That calmly sitting at home while the racists in our society come once again to terrorize and turn back the clock on hard fought gains won't stop them. We have to take back this country."

And Amon-Ra called on the crowd to employ "a number of tactics," including armed self defense and a national boycott of corporations, to stop the Atlanta murders and to protect black communities in distress. People "who are constantly the victims of brutal assault cannot eliminate any options from their struggle," he warned. "We have to defend our children, our lives, our people, by any means necessary" (*Guardian* 1981).

The Reverend Jesse Jackson, representing People United to Save Humanity (PUSH), was probably the most conciliatory speaker that day. Jackson urged people of goodwill to "fight" against all forms of death—including genocide, homicide, and fratricide. The Atlanta murders, he said, had made the nation more sensitive. "Our children cry out from their graves, 'Stop the killing and start the healing'" (*WP* 1981k).

But it was skeptic William Raspberry, columnist for the *Washington Post*, who perhaps had the last poignant word on the day's activities.

> Too many children live in needless poverty. . . . Too many children are having their hopes and aspirations snuffed out by hopelessly inadequate education. Too many children know racism firsthand. But they are not disproportionately in Atlanta, and nothing said or done at the rally will create a single job [or] educate a single child. . . .
>
> "Halt the genocide," the ralliers demanded, as though it is easier to believe that the killings are part of a conspiracy to wipe out a race than to see them for what they apparently are: the frustrating, mind-bending, infuriating madness of one or more maniacs. . . .
>
> For those who believe the conspiracy theory, who believe that the government is party to some murderous plot, or who believe that societal sickness is the culprit, the rally might have seemed logical: Expose the plot or bring the society to repentance, and the killings will stop.
>
> But surely most of the crowd must have recognized the truth of what [STOP's] Camille Bell told them: that a rally is no substitute for dogged, determined police work. . . .

It is fair to assume that most of the demonstrators were there out of deep concern. They are people who, like most of us, would like to do something to end the slaughter but who, like the rest of us, cannot think of anything useful to do. (Raspberry 1981)

At the end of the day, Reagan administration officials must have heard the anger, even if they did not exactly "feel the pain." No one needed to remind them, though, of Atlanta's trauma, since what was happening in Atlanta was proving quite costly to the national treasury. Congress had only recently approved Vice President George Bush's task force recommendation that huge sums of money for a "Safe Summer" program be sent to Atlanta. *Time* (1981a) would bill the program "the most comprehensive children's summer program in urban history."

The funds were to go toward providing supervised recreation or jobs for all of the city's 69,000 public school children for up to twelve hours a day. The program would begin the Monday (in June 1981) after school was out for the summer, and continue until classes resumed in September.

Washington's "Safe Summer '81" program for Atlanta was expected to add $1.5 million to the city's revenue. Among other things, it would pay for children's lunches and for police and civilian patrols assigned to observe children at pickup and delivery points. Political folks in Washington did not need, then, big demonstrations to call their attention to Atlanta. The city already had their full attention. What the feds desperately needed was a "break."

That break suddenly occurred, embodied in the young black man whom the FBI and Atlanta lawmen had stopped near the Jackson Parkway bridge two days prior to the Memorial Day event. In the weeks to come, FBI agents and Atlanta police would interview some four hundred people who knew, knew of, or associated with Wayne Bertram Williams.

At five-feet seven-and-one-half inches and a bit more than 160 pounds, twenty-three-year-old Wayne Williams could be considered stocky. Wayne was never sloppy, but neither was he ever well-dressed. His "Afro" and thick, horn-rimmed glasses—he had been wearing them since puberty—set against a rotund, pockmarked face, gave him the appearance of a 1960s-ish militant college student majoring in black studies.

But, as it turned out, Wayne's intellectualist facade came not so much from a cultivated approach to the rigorous steadfastness of academia as from the ephemeralness of being thought of as "smart" and being lauded as a "genius." He may have been a science wizard while a student at Atlanta's Anderson Park

Elementary School, but he dropped out of college at Georgia State University after less than a year.

Wayne was the only child born to Faye and Homer Williams, both former Atlanta teachers who waited until their late forties to start a family. The result of this "late start" was a relationship in which Wayne was everything to his parents. Wayne, in turn, became driven to pull himself and his parents up out of their lower-middle-class life. He strove to do so in a hurry, relying as much on ingenuity and craft as on show-business hype—an approach to life that was light years away from his parents' humble, hardworking bungalow existence.

When he was fourteen years old, Wayne started his own micro radio station at home. He did so using funds his father had secured from a second mortgage on the family home. Run by high school friends Wayne hired, the station was little more than a whimsical child-prodigy project whose listening radius extended no more than a few blocks beyond the Williams's address. Still, this bold effort in youthful black entrepreneurship did not go unnoticed in influential black circles. While campaigning in 1974 for a congressional seat, Andrew Young stopped briefly at the Williams home for some friendly banter on Wayne's unlicensed WRAZ-AM. And in July 1974, Chicago-based *Jet Magazine* ran a picture of Wayne seated at his station's control board. He was being admiringly observed in the picture by former FCC commissioner Benjamin Hooks.

Growing up, Wayne immersed himself in Atlanta's budding black music industry and in freelance news photography. For the photography end of his "business," he created—on paper, that is—Metro News Production Company, for which he acquired expensive photographic equipment. Most of the pictures he took were of incidents on the Atlanta police beat: fires, wrecks, shootings, stabbings. Along the way, he managed to obtain official credentials from the city's fire bureau, although no records existed to show that he ever received a paycheck from the city.

Perhaps because he spent so much of his time around city emergency workers, Wayne came to nurture a curious interest in police work. He became a "scanner freak"—someone who regularly listened to police conversations with state-of-the art multichannel police scanner radios. Using emergency information acquired this way, Wayne would dart from one police scene to another, often arriving there well ahead of the police.

Wayne's other major interest was recruiting musically inclined—but not musically *talented*—black boys. He seemed bent on producing and recording their efforts at singing and songwriting through his imaginary Nova Entertainment

Corporation. A select group he said he would someday use to form a musical group, Gemini.

Wayne's efforts at turning his youngsters into musical stars made him a rather well known "entity" to executives at local recording studios. Wayne would pay them anywhere from fifty to a hundred dollars or more for an hour of studio time (Wayne himself meticulously at the controls) to record youngsters he had picked up off the city's streets, most of them having little or no apparent musical or artistic bent. The youths were nonetheless impressed and excited.

Wayne would hire top area rhythm-and-blues musicians, even horns and strings, to provide backup. Wayne did things like this, the recording executives believed, to strengthen the youngsters' faith in what he had promised them out there on the mean streets of the city: that he would catapult them to wealth and stardom.

Studio executives at first thought they were seeing in Wayne Williams someone committed to putting together another Jackson Five or a black version of the Donny and Marie Osmond singing duo. Part of his style with the youngsters was to just sit and talk. One executive recalled that once Wayne booked an hour of studio time and brought in some teenagers. He then spent the entire hour simply talking about what would be expected of them in the recording industry. Even though Wayne did not record a single note, he paid for the studio time.

This way Wayne had of spending money puzzled studio executives. He clearly was not generating any returns on the huge sums he had been investing in recording time. Moreover, deals and recording contracts with major recording companies (the likes of Motown and Capitol Records) that he was always speaking excitedly about never materialized. The executives soon found that Wayne was being financed, to the tune of thousands of dollars, from his retired parents' nest egg.

Wayne would often combine his search for young, impressionable "talent" with a thing or two he had picked up along the way from being close to Atlanta police operations. He had acquired, for instance, an uncanny ability to impersonate a police officer. The practice got him into trouble back in 1976, when he was arrested in the city (but never convicted) for "impersonating a police officer and unauthorized use of vehicle." The vehicle had been illegally equipped with red lights beneath the grille and flashing blue dashboard lights.

Wayne learned from this undesired run-in with the law that he would have to throw more panache into his impersonation. Late one night in the spring of 1980, driving one of his father's cars, Wayne and an aspiring black entertainer, twenty-year-old Joe Bailey, were speeding down Interstate 20 near downtown Atlanta. As the car raced past 80 mph, an unmarked Atlanta police patrol car pulled alongside. Wayne, Joe Bailey recalled, calmly switched on the ceiling light of his car. He turned to the officer with a smile and waved at him. The officer drove on. The officer, like wide-eyed Joe Bailey, apparently thought that Wayne was a plainclothes policeman.

Several aspiring entertainers who came under Wayne Williams's influence did in fact believe that Wayne was a detective who dabbled in the music world, an image Wayne enhanced by owning several used, unmarked police cars.

But imagery was really all there was to Wayne Williams's life. In 1976 he told an employee she would be losing her job at his radio station because a Chicago company was buying the station. Truth was, Wayne's parents had gone broke and were filing for bankruptcy as a result of their son's misadventures.

Wayne seemed to thrive on being well connected, on knowing people, on knowing who was doing what rather than in getting anything of substance accomplished. The business deals and recording contracts were empty boasts. Record company executives with whom he claimed he had major deals "going down" had never heard of him—although, according to one account, Wayne did contact independent record promoter Wade Marcus in Los Angeles practically every week.

The last time Joe Bailey heard from Wayne Williams was when a big music show was supposedly in the works for Joe's band sometime in 1981. "He told us to get ready. That we were going to Chattanooga for a show and that [in] the first ten rows would be nothing but producers," Joe recalled Wayne telling him (AC 1981t). Joe never heard from him again.

Wayne didn't seem to have any close friends other than one Willie Hunter, a shadowy persona who became Wayne's guru and mentor in the music business. Some of the folks he dealt with, other than the music executives, believed Wayne had a hidden evil side. An associate of four years, nineteen-year-old Carla Bailey, characterized Wayne as "fascinating" as he was "mysterious." No one was sure, for one, of his sexual orientation. This gave rise to speculation that Wayne's abiding interest in young boys had a dark homosexual subtext that was laden with predatory, criminal intentions.

Wayne often expressed negative feelings toward blacks; he frequently did so to the white emergency workers around whom he freelanced. He seemed "resentful of being black," recalled one white police officer. White ambulance driver Bobby Toland said it was "common knowledge that Wayne was not crazy about the black race." Another emergency worker said Wayne often would portray black people as a "sorry lot—the way they lived, the way they acted, leeching off the government" (*AC* 19810).

Once when the entire nation seemed genuinely affected by the mysterious youth slayings and disappearances, an associate of Wayne's recalled him "putting down the idea" of people raising money for victims' families. Wade Marcus would remember mentioning to Wayne in January or February 1981 that he was considering sending money to assist in the investigation of the Atlanta murders. Wayne, Marcus recalled, told him not to waste his money because the kids were "just prostitutes hanging around all night long" (*AC* 19810).

Of such were the dreadful musings, FBI agents had learned, of the young man they had stopped on May 22, after a rookie Atlanta police officer said he had heard "a loud splash" in the night. That splash, FBI agents now firmly believed, was the body of Nathaniel Cater being dumped without ceremony—and without witnesses.

Stepped-up measures for discreetly monitoring Williams's activities would be necessary. But these measures should go beyond Atlanta detectives and/or FBI agents physically following him around. In other words, Williams would have to be monitored via sophisticated, state-of-the-art electronic surveillance devices. But with whose devices? The feds' or Georgia's? And, more important, which government agency would conduct the surveillance?

The matter of putting anyone under electronic surveillance was particularly problematic for the lead investigative agency in the Atlanta cases, which was now clearly the FBI. A recent history, dating back twenty years, of contemptible eavesdropping on civil rights leaders (notably Martin Luther King Jr.) and antiwar protesters had prompted enactment in the 1970s of numerous state laws curtailing FBI authority to conduct surveillance operations within local jurisdictions. Georgia was one of those states; its laws allowed only "peace officers," and only under carefully prescribed conditions, to "install and monitor electronic surveillances" of someone suspected of engaging in dangerous activities.

Congress also had pressured the U.S. Department of Justice (DOJ) to curtail unwarranted surveillance operations. In April 1980, DOJ responded by issuing Executive Order No. 890-80. The order strictly limited FBI involvement in electronic surveillance operations in local jurisdictional matters.

But Atlanta authorities had maintained since the fall of 1980 that solving the Atlanta cases would require all-out, maximum FBI involvement. They now resolutely agreed that no minor, arcane technicality relating to something as dubious as "state's rights"—with all its terrible racialist implications known so well in this part of the country—should impede federal investigation into as serious a matter as that taking place in the city. Thus began a series of legal and bureaucratic maneuvers to give the FBI "cover" to monitor every move and action of a presumed dangerous and slippery Wayne Williams.

In the end, legal experts in the FBI's Atlanta office, in conjunction with the U.S. attorney's office for Atlanta and the attorney general's office for the state of Georgia, succeeded in convincing Fulton County Superior Court judge John Langford to allow the FBI to electronically monitor Wayne Williams. The plaintiff (in this case federal and state authorities) had argued that, given the "crisis situation" in Atlanta, FBI agents should indeed be considered "peace officers," as state law required (FBI, n.d.).

On May 29, FBI agents, *qua* "peace officers," began round-the-clock surveillance of Williams's comings and goings. Among other things, they surreptitiously installed an automobile tracking device on the vehicle he was driving the night he was stopped and which he seemed to use most often: the 1970 white Chevrolet Concourse station wagon. They also attempted to install a "listening device" *in* the car, but gave up trying because of "logistical difficulties" in gaining undetected access. The surveillance plan called for a fully integrated operation consisting of backup "ground units" and aerial/aircraft support, including "a surveillance team of six experienced special agents, six surveillance vehicles, one fixed wing surveillance aircraft, two special agent pilots, and twelve secure radios with antennae for Bu[reau]cars" (FBI, n.d.).

Federal authorities had obviously decided to spare no expense in pursuing what they saw as the most promising development in the Atlanta situation. According to FBI documents, "As of daylight hours of May 22, 1981, the fixed surveillance at 14 targeted bridges [was] discontinued." The feds in Atlanta were firmly convinced they had found the man whom the entire bridge-surveillance operation had been designed to apprehend. All they needed to do now was make him "sweat." Within days, FBI Director William Webster would say on PBS's *MacNeil/Lehrer Report* that he had never been so "optimistic" about progress in the Atlanta case. In fact, his men had in effect "solved" the case.

13

Pursuit and an FBI "Interview"

They said, "You killed Nathaniel Cater. And you know it and you're lying to us."
—Wayne Williams

Investigative interest in Wayne Williams increased after Nathaniel Cater's body was discovered. Soon the FBI was watching the self-proclaimed talent scout twenty-four hours a day. A convoy of lawmen followed Williams in unmarked police cars wherever he drove. The mission of keeping their man under close scrutiny, FBI authorities in Atlanta reported to their superiors in Washington, would continue "until logically resolved" (FBI, n.d.).

Their subject was rather "active," agents reported, especially between the hours of 6:00 P.M. and 3:00 A.M. Of greater concern to FBI agents, though, was that he became aware of this tight surveillance from the outset. They reported him being "very 'tail conscious' as evidenced by frequent cleaning moves." (Williams was often able to elude the out-of-town agents assigned to tail him, sometimes causing major traffic snarls as the agents tried to pursue him in the wrong direction on one-way city streets.)

The FBI pulled back from this heavy-handed watch for a while, perhaps to see whether their subject would "slip" and abduct a youngster. This would provide the kind of evidence they needed to make an arrest. They would need more than an isolated attempt at either murder or kidnapping, though, if they were to make a convincing case that Wayne Williams was Atlanta's serial killer. Such evidence might come from being able to observe from a more discreet distance the young man's total routine.

But Wayne seemed to be doing nothing out of the ordinary. All he did was drive around the city, making brief but frequent stops at various bars. FBI investigators worried that behind this seemingly aimless activity, their quarry might be discarding or destroying incriminating physical evidence that could link him to the murders, evidence he could be removing from his home and/or cars. It was time, they figured, to confront him.

On Wednesday, June 3, 1981, Judge John Langford of the Fulton County Superior Court responded to an FBI request by authorizing search warrants "for the person of Wayne Williams," the 1970 Chevrolet Concourse station wagon he was driving the night he was stopped by federal and Atlanta lawmen, and his residence at 1817 Northwest Penelope Road.

Later that day, Wayne was standing in a telephone booth when FBI agents approached him and, he would later say, "insisted" he come downtown with them. The agents wanted to ask him a few questions. They escorted him, without fuss or fanfare, to their Atlanta office where, according to the FBI, Williams "voluntarily submitted" to an "interview."

Other FBI agents, along with Atlanta police officers and technicians from the Georgia State Crime Laboratory, then searched his home and station wagon. The rationale for the search was, if there was a probable connection between Williams and the two-year string of slayings, to hold forth in a court of law, evidence of that connection would have to be stronger than Williams's sudden appearance on an Atlanta-area bridge after a police cadet said he had heard a splash in the river below, even if that splash was followed two days later by the discovery of the murdered body of yet another black male.

Moreover, as things stood, prosecuting authorities would have been unable to make a case around any specific suspicious thing they had seen Williams do since he had been put under constant surveillance. A strong case could be made, however, if results of lab tests demonstrated that Williams's environment— namely, his home and his car—was *the most likely* source of all those mysterious fibers that kept turning up on victims' bodies.

Upon entering the Williams home, FBI agents noticed that "most of the furniture had been rearranged" since their visit of two weeks earlier (i.e., following the bridge incident) and that new carpeting had been installed in some areas. Lab experts dusted the house for fingerprints, taking several lifts from areas occupied by Wayne. After spending hours ripping the house apart, they also seized and removed the following:

- Wayne's "business papers"—that is, assorted documents, some of which had attached to them photographs (some charred) of young black males;

- carpet samples—including a swatch of green carpet stained with what appeared to be blood;

- numerous fibers and debris—including animal hair—taken or scoured from a purple throw rug, a yellow rug, yellow and green carpets, a blue toilet rug, a green rug, a red bathrobe, pink, yellow, and blue blankets, a blue-green drapery, pink and green bedspreads, and a purple toilet seat cover;
- "unknown [blunt] object wrapped in adhesive tape" (subsequently identified as a slapjack).

All the items came from Wayne's living area and a rear portion of the house and backyard mostly controlled by him.

Before leaving, agents had Wayne's father pluck for them a few hairs from the family's aging German Shepherd. They searched, then decided to impound for an additional search, the 1970 Chevrolet station wagon, after finding in it what appeared to be dried bloodstains and other "questioned material" on the rear seat.

Meantime, down at FBI headquarters, agents once more grilled Williams—this time more aggressively, if not threateningly, than they did the morning of the bridge incident and subsequently in his home. Two U.S. attorneys were on hand to advise the agents during their twelve-hour questioning. Agents wanted to hear more about Wayne's activities leading up to the moment they and Atlanta police officers stopped and questioned him after he had crossed the James Jackson Parkway bridge twice in quick succession. Without an attorney present to look out for *his* best interests, Wayne told the feds a lot.

On Thursday, May 21, at approximately 1 P.M., he was in the vicinity of Fairburn and Campbellton Roads in southwest Atlanta looking for one Thomas Johnson, Wayne said. He never found Johnson. He ended up, he said, playing basketball at the Ben Hill Recreation Center. After that, he came home.

At about 4 P.M., he received a telephone call from a woman who identified herself as Cheryl Johnson. She was interested in auditioning for a singing job with him and wondered if they could meet for an interview. He took her telephone number and address. The address was an apartment number at the Spanish Trace Apartments off South Cobb Drive and Church Street in Smyrna, Georgia, northwest of downtown Atlanta. She told him she would prefer to do the interview at her home the next morning at around seven o'clock. They agreed on that.

He stayed home the rest of the evening. He had dinner with his mother at about 6 P.M., then slept for a brief time. His parents had gone out and had taken the station wagon. Sometime during the course of the evening, while at his home, he held a phone conversation with his sidekick and trusted wise man, Willie Hunter.

At approximately 1 A.M., he drove to the Sans Souci Lounge at 760 West Peachtree Street in downtown Atlanta. He went there to see the manager about getting back a tape recorder he had lent him. He talked to the "girl at the door." She told him that the manager was "tied up," whereupon Williams left the lounge.

He then decided he would try to locate Cheryl Johnson's apartment. He couldn't recall the exact address, but he believed it was F4 or some such two-digit number. He drove around in the Smyrna area looking for the Spanish Trace Apartments but couldn't find them. He stopped at a liquor store on Cobb Drive and tried to call the telephone number he had for Cheryl Johnson. He got a busy signal. After he hung up, he noticed some empty boxes in the liquor store. He picked up two of them for his mother. A short time later, while on Cobb Drive, he stopped and made another call to Cheryl Johnson. This time the phone rang, but no one answered.

He then drove south on Cobb Drive, headed toward Jackson Parkway, as the thoroughfare was called on the Atlanta side of the Chattahoochee River, after crossing the Jackson Parkway bridge. And here, as expected, Williams's recall of what happened in the next few minutes markedly differed from the version reported by Atlanta and FBI authorities.

Four vehicles, including his, Williams said, crossed the bridge roughly within the same time span. One of them was an El Camino with a camper in tow; a white male was at the wheel. Another vehicle was a small white Purolator delivery/pickup truck that had blue writing on it.

After crossing the bridge, without ever stopping or appreciably slowing down, he pulled off the road onto a graveled parking lot. He wanted to use the background lighting of area stores to double-check the phone number he had just called. He proceeded to a Starvin' Marvin store near the intersection of Bolton Road and Jackson Parkway, and once again called the number he had for Cheryl Johnson. Someone answered and said, "There's nobody here by that name," and hung up. He picked up some more cardboard boxes, this time for himself. He needed them "to pack some items."

He drove back onto Jackson Parkway, headed northwest, back in the direction of the bridge he had just crossed, toward Cobb County. As he passed the same graveled parking area where he had stopped to check the telephone number, he noticed a vehicle pulling out from the general area of the store with its lights on. He looked in his rearview mirror and saw that the vehicle began to follow him. The total time it took him to drive from the graveled parking lot to the Starvin' Marvin to make his futile telephone call and then return to his car was two minutes, Williams said. Anyway, he proceeded to cross the bridge for a second time. He exited at the intersection of I-285. He was about to take the interstate toward Atlanta when he was stopped by federal and Atlanta officers.

At no time during his travels that early morning did he have occasion to stop on the Jackson Parkway bridge. He may have slowed down to about 25 miles per hour, he said, because of bumps in the road near the bridge. He did not immediately turn around after he crossed the bridge and head back in the opposite direction. He did not throw anything off the bridge. Neither did he know Nathaniel Cater or any of the Atlanta victims. And in no way was he involved in anyone's death.

The 1970 Chevrolet station wagon he was driving the night he was stopped was not the only car he had driven in the past two years, Williams told his FBI interrogators. His parents also had owned a 1979 Ford LTD, which was repossessed. And he had owned a 1978 Plymouth Fury, which also was repossessed, in late 1979.

According to FBI records, after this detailed account "Williams was asked if he would consent to a polygraph examination conducted by an Agent of the FBI." The purpose of the polygraph was explained to him, "and he voluntarily consented. . . . He was advised by Supervisory Special Agent that the results of this polygraph could not be used against him in a court of law, nor could it be used in his favor."

The results of three separate polygraph examinations showed, according to the FBI, that Williams's responses were "deceptive." Before they were through with him, the agents took samples of his head and pubic hairs.

With Williams still in FBI custody, sometime around 2 A.M., June 4, Atlanta police commissioner Lee Brown, police chief George Napper, deputy police director (and task force head) Morris Redding, and Fulton County assistant district attorney Gordon Miller came down to the Atlanta FBI office.

The federal agents briefed them. The local lawmen in turn communicated their view of this latest FBI-initiated episode by phone to Fulton County district attorney Lewis Slaton.

Much to the chagrin of the feds (who thought Williams's story was "full of holes"), Slaton decided that he, and by implication the state of Georgia, did not have sufficient probable cause for the feds to arrest or further detain Williams. Shortly thereafter, the federal authorities released Williams—after, officials would later say, he indicated he wished to go home. Deputy Director Redding offered to provide Williams with protective custody, which he refused. Wayne left the FBI office with his father, who had come downtown after another set of lawmen finished digging up his house. Homer Williams was allowed to speak with his son in the last few minutes of Wayne's nightlong ordeal. The two had spoken in hushed tones, off in a corner and away from the authorities.

By this time word had already leaked to the media that someone, a black male, had been taken into FBI custody and subjected to prolonged questioning in connection with the Atlanta murders. Reporters quibbled, though, about the ethics of reporting to the public the name of someone whom they had no indication was being officially considered a suspect. But in relating the previous night's development, newspapers from around the nation sought to play up the story's unexpected racial denouement.

Completely disregarding any lingering protocol that might have existed between the news media and the agencies of officialdom, and paying scant attention to the complicating little matter that no one had been charged, the *New York Post* went straight for the racial hot button. Emblazoned on the front page of its early edition on June 4, 1981, was this damning headline: "Atlanta Monster Seized; Police Nab Black Suspect."

14

The Media Blitzkrieg and Developing Evidence

Numerous violet acetate fibers were located.... [They] exhibit the same
microscopic characteristics ... as fibers removed from a bedspread on the
bed of Wayne Bertram Williams.

    —FBI's "ATKID" file

As expected, law enforcement officials in Atlanta were irritated with the *New
York Post*'s "tabloidization" of the turn of events. They were equally unhappy
that, to get a head start on the competition, editors of the respected *Atlanta
Constitution* chose to name the man FBI agents had interrogated the previous
day. Any further hope of concealing investigative interest in Wayne Williams
became moot later that morning, however, when Williams called reporters into
his home for a "news conference."

The unusual event started with Wayne handing reporters a five-page résumé
of himself. He wanted folks to know, he said, that he was being harassed by the
FBI for no reason whatsoever—although he acknowledged he was a "prime suspect" in the string of murders. He characterized his twelve hours of questioning
as nothing but "accusations and threats the whole time." The FBI was "trying to
pin the murders on someone as soon as possible," he said. "It's just a matter of
time before we get you," he quoted one agent as forewarning him—after the agent
had attempted to get him to sign a statement confessing to "twenty-some deaths."

Williams did have an opinion, though, about the victims and their situations.
"Some of these kids are in places they don't have no business being at certain
times of the day and night," he said to the pool of overwhelmingly white reporters. "Some of them don't have no kind of home supervision, and just running around in the streets wild. I just feel some of the parents just need to
tighten up and get strict on the kids." Williams ended his news conference by
warning, in a "curious subjunctive formulation," to use *Time* magazine's

phraseology, "If all this boils out to be nothing, I have been slandered by the police and the news media" (*Time* 1981b).

The young Atlanta man seemed at first to relish the attention. He basked in a limelight that he had craved but that had been denied all those heady, child-genius years. But it didn't take long for the frenzy of the media to overwhelm, if not consume, him and his family—and the pleasant little neighborhood of shuttered brick and frame houses where the family lived.

In the first two weeks of June 1981, the 1800 block of Northwest Penelope Road became a continuous stakeout, with police cameras secretly recording the family's comings and goings. Several black Atlanta notables—ministers, politicians, and civil rights leaders—were recorded visiting the home. Police cars, marked and unmarked, shuttled in and out. Each time Wayne drove out, a bevy of black police sedans would take off behind him.

Penelope Road was transformed into a "media carnival, with television vans constantly going on, or returning from, assignments and Coca-Cola runs to nearby fast-food joints, and taxis delivering reporters to relieve other reporters in shift changes" (Montgomery 1981). Reporters pestered neighbors for interviews and the use of their telephones.

Day and night, television camera crews, photographers, and reporters filled the street in front of the Williams home. Long-range lenses on tripods were "trained like field artillery on the building," wrote the *Atlanta Journal and Constitution*'s Bill Montgomery. "Plainclothes police and FBI agents . . . sat in silence on the hoods of their unmarked cars in a church parking lot across the street. Everyone, police and reporters, craned for a sight of Wayne B. Williams." Three times in one day, Homer Williams, himself a freelance photographer, "trained his camera and shot pictures of the news people, their vehicles and the license plates. . . . [F]amiliar faces from the local TV news urgently demanded: 'Mr. Williams, why are you taking our pictures?'" (Montgomery 1981).

The parking lot of the True Light Baptist Church became a command center for vans from Atlanta television stations and the networks and for radio stations and newspaper cars. The church's pastor eventually yielded to complaints from neighbors about the congestion and banned the vehicles from the lot.

This type of "vulgar" news coverage was just too much for former Atlanta city solicitor Mary Welcome, whom Faye and Homer Williams retained as counsel for their son. At a crowded news conference, Welcome criticized the media and threatened reporters with legal action. She would subsequently ask law enforcement officials to restrict release of information concerning developments in the case and file a legal petition charging that Wayne Williams was the victim of a "blitzkrieg of media harassment." The petition asked a federal judge to limit publicity about Williams. The Atlanta Chapter of the Society of Professional Journalists/Sigma Delta Chi responded, saying its members would "reject and oppose any judicial action that would impede our ability to report news developments [and] which might interfere with the public's right to be informed" (AC 1981k).

The matter of exactly how the news media should cover Williams was never finally resolved by the courts, as other developments quickly superseded it.

Firmly convinced that Wayne Williams was their man, FBI and Georgia state crime lab experts zeroed in on a high-tech project of building a chain of circumstantial and scientific evidence that would link the self-proclaimed talent scout to the life, and ultimately the death, of the Atlanta victims. FBI agents theorized that Williams's unlikely presence on the Jackson Parkway bridge in the early morning hours of May 22 more than likely meant that he was connected with the death of *at least* those victims whose bodies were found in area rivers: six in the Chattahoochee and three in the South River.

The mission of the lab experts was serious business; their methods would have to be rigorous, leaving little room for error. Their main task consisted of comparison tests of not only standard criminalistic items such as fingerprints and blood samples but also the fibrous particles recovered from the victims' bodies and surrounding crime scenes. And so while Wayne Williams went on with whatever was his business in and around town—under, of course, the watchful glare of law enforcement and worldwide media—experts with the Georgia and FBI crime labs poured over slides of two sets of material, searching for matchups.

One set of slides consisted of the trace items investigators had recovered or taken from victims' bodies—fingerprints, bloodstains, and various fibrous materials. The other was of the items FBI agents had seized and removed from Williams's home, his 1970 Chevrolet station wagon, and his body—sweepings, carpet swatches, carpet fibers, bloodstains, and hairs. The objective was to look for matchups in molecular properties (color, size, and shape) within each set and from one set to the other.

Within a matter of days, sources were leaking word that the tests—particularly the fiber matches—were proving "productive." Fibers collected from Wayne Williams's environment were similar to, or "not significantly different from," those found on the bodies of several slaying victims. "It is my understanding that several of the fibers are matching up," one high-ranking special police task force official was quoted as saying less than two days after the swatches and offscourings of the Williams home had come under microscopic scrutiny. "The more you find that match up, the better you are," he gleefully pointed out (*AC* 1981k).

In the weeks ahead, lab experts would indeed claim that they were finding, within a range of scientific certainty, increasing numbers of reliable fiber matches. Particularly compelling were the sharp, angular matches between a set of unusual fibers recovered from two of the most recently discovered victims and fibers that had been vacuumed from Williams's car and home.

One of the victims was Jimmy Ray Payne; he was the twenty-one-year-old man who apparently tried to change his name and whose body was found in the Chattahoochee River on April 27, 1981. The other was Nathaniel Cater, the twenty-seven-year-old drifter who never made it back to renew his rent at the Falcon Hotel and whose body was discovered in the Chattahoochee two days after federal and Atlanta lawmen had pulled Williams over because a rookie officer said he had heard a "loud splash" in the river.

Lab experts were discovering, according to FBI microanalyst Harold Deadman (1984b, 16), that "all of the fiber types removed from Payne and Cater . . . were present in debris removed by vacuuming" the Williams family station wagon. Fiber types found on Jimmy Payne's body included what the lab experts determined were some violet and green bedspread fibers, some yellowish-green nylon carpet-type fibers, some yellow blanket fibers, some blue rayon fibers, and automobile carpet fibers. Crime-scene investigators also had recovered from Jimmy Payne's body particles that the lab experts determined were dog hairs.

Fiber types found in Nathaniel Cater's head hair included *all* fiber types found on Jimmy Payne, except the blue rayon fibers and the automobile carpet fibers.

The yellowish-green nylon carpet-type fibers found on the bodies of both men were of particular interest to the lab experts. They were "very coarse" and had an unusual lobed cross-sectional shape. This unique quality, the experts believed, would improve the chance of successfully tracing the fibers' exact origins.

On the basis of several more tests, the experts were soon certain, within a narrow range of probability, that the violet and green bedspread fibers found on the bodies of Payne and Cater were consistent with fibers taken from a bedspread in Wayne Williams's bedroom. The yellowish-green nylon carpet-type fibers were consistent with fibers from a carpet in his bedroom. The dog hairs on Jimmy Payne's body were consistent with hairs plucked from the family's German Shepherd and with those sucked up in debris from behind the Williams house. The yellow blanket fibers were consistent with fibers from a blanket found in Wayne's bedroom. The blue rayon fibers (found only on Jimmy Payne) were consistent with fibers found in debris from behind the Williams home. And automobile carpet fibers found on Jimmy Payne's body were consistent with carpet fibers from the 1970 Chevrolet station wagon that Wayne regularly drove.

FBI authorities saw in these findings a narrow arrangement of deducible facts as to just what could have happened to Jimmy Ray Payne and Nathaniel Cater. The most "elementary" was that the victims had shared a common venue, either shortly before or after their deaths. And that venue was the source of several identical fibers found on their bodies. Another was that Jimmy Payne, either shortly before or after his death, had been in Williams's station wagon. It also was plausible that Cater had been in Williams's car. But his corpse had been washed clean by the river of any automobile carpet fibers. (Cater's body, unlike Payne's, was completely nude when discovered in the Chattahoochee.)

Additional microscopic analyses over the next several days were unraveling even more details. The FBI recorded the following:

- Numerous violet acetate fibers were located on seventeen glass microscope slides. [They] were recovered from seventeen of the victims in this case. These violet acetate fibers exhibit the same microscopic characteristics as violet acetate fibers present in the composition of yarns removed from a bedspread on the bed of Wayne Bertram Williams.

- Light green cotton fibers were located on several of the glass microscope slides which contained fibers removed from the bodies of victims. . . . These light green cotton fibers exhibit the same microscopic characteristics as green cotton fibers present in the composition of yarns removed from the bedspread of Wayne Bertram Williams.

- Green nylon fibers were located on fourteen glass microscope slides. [They] were recovered from fourteen of the victims in this case. These green nylon fibers exhibit the same microscopic characteristics as green nylon fibers obtained from the carpet located in the bedroom of Wayne Bertram Williams.

- Dog hairs were located on approximately five glass microscope slides. [They] were recovered from five of the victims in this case. [They] were white and white to dark brown in color and exhibit the same microscopic characteristics as dog hairs . . . obtained from the dog located at the home of Wayne Bertram Williams.

Sometime into the lab-testing process, FBI analysts detected a problem with the task force list. Local authorities had not added John Porter's stabbing death. Lab technicians discovered, though, that light violet acetate and coarse, yellowish-green nylon fibers recovered from Porter's body were identical to fibers recovered from the bodies of several list victims. This prompted FBI authorities to launch an independent investigation into Porter's death and to connect it to Wayne Williams.[1]

By the second week of June 1981, lab experts had determined that each of the trace objects recovered from the bodies of the Atlanta victims probably originated from a source in Williams's environment. According to the FBI, it would have been "virtually impossible for the numerous victims in the Atlanta killings . . . to have picked up the fibrous debris recovered from their clothing and bodies" without them having been "in contact with items from the home and/or vehicle of Wayne Bertram Williams."

But skeptics wanted to know the likelihood of the objects coming from a source, or sources, *other than* Williams's environment. Wasn't it possible that another residence and another automobile could have had similar carpets? Was it not also possible that the Atlanta victims could have been in those other environments? And, assuming that the answer to each of these questions was no or highly improbable, did any of this prove that Wayne Williams murdered these men and boys?

Answers would come with more analyses, the crime technicians responded. But, to be sure, questions of this sort had long been an Achilles' heel in homicide cases relying exclusively on circumstantial scientific evidence. However, as others directly familiar with the criminalistic elements of the Atlanta murders argued (e.g., Bisbing 1985; Tierney 1981; Deadman 1984a, 1984b), and as defenders of the use of science in criminal cases pointed out, reasonable people are called upon every day to make plausible inferences from a fact, or conjunction of facts, about the existence of an ultimate fact.[2]

The clustering of a number of scientifically demonstrated collateral facts in the Atlanta cases allowed for inference of *one* ultimate fact, scientific experts working on the cases contended. Minute objects in Wayne Williams's environment reciprocated, at a high level of statistical significance, with minute objects found on the bodies of at least two of the Atlanta victims: Jimmy Ray Payne and

Nathaniel Cater. This justified the conclusion that Wayne Williams, or some-one in the Williams household, had murdered the two men.

So plausible was this inference in the reasoning of federal authorities that, in the ensuing days, they aggressively pushed local law enforcement officials—particularly Fulton County district attorney Lewis Slaton—to promptly arrest Wayne Williams and charge him with the murder of Jimmy Ray Payne and Nathaniel Cater.

15

The D.A. Makes a Highly Political Arrest

More than fiber evidence is needed.

  —District Attorney Lewis Slaton

Fulton County district attorney Lewis Slaton was not a man easily swayed. Nor was he easily impressed. Two big-picture issues in the case the FBI wanted to bring against Wayne Williams bothered the hard-nosed, "notoriously finicky" prosecutor (as he was described by the *Atlanta Constitution*'s Frederick Allen).

First, for months federal authorities had come into Atlanta and taken control of the investigations into the string of murders, the city's black political directorate having effectively conceded jurisdiction in them. For reasons embedded in regional history, the unapologetically southern-bred Slaton didn't share the same enthusiasm or trust in Washington—or in the abilities of federal office-holders to solve problems—as did Atlanta's black political elites, who, as far as the Slaton people were concerned, had practically ridden into political prominence on the backs of federal judicial and enforcement agencies.

The second big-picture issue was not quite as politically or ideologically complex. Would local prosecutors be able to convince an Atlanta jury that, based on esoteric scientific evidence, Wayne Williams had murdered anybody, let alone that he was responsible for the string of slayings?

Lewis Slaton's people—as well as several top professionals on the special Atlanta police task force—resented the FBI's got-it-alone approach. And as far as they were concerned, the FBI had mishandled key aspects of the case against Williams. Local authorities were *only now* being brought in to prosecute the feds' badly flawed, and probably bungled, case.

The FBI started mishandling the case from the night they stopped Williams, fumed the district attorney's staff. Despite their expensive bridge-surveillance operation, the best the FBI could come up with was a tenuous, highly circumstantial link between a splash heard in the Chattahoochee, a body found in the river two days later, and the man they had stopped right after hearing the splash.

Moreover, FBI agents did not ask the man they had stopped to provide them with a statement of his activities that night. Only hours later did agents go traipsing out to his house—after the man had had more than enough time to concoct a story and destroy evidence. Neither did agents on the night of the stop take an inventory of items they saw—or claimed to have seen—in the man's car. Because they had not done so, much confusion prevailed in the ranks—between Atlanta police, task force officers, and the FBI—as to just what items were in Wayne Williams's car that night.

Why didn't the FBI detain Williams after they had stopped and questioned him? Rather curious, Slaton's people kept pointing out, that FBI authorities were saying to them, well after the fact, that they did indeed have sufficient probable cause to have held Williams that night. Yet they allowed him to go back to his home, from which neighbors would recall seeing him, early that same morning, removing several boxes.

But all that aside, what really troubled Lewis Slaton was that he liked to build his homicide cases the old-fashioned way: around solid, direct evidence. He didn't put much stock in inferential, heavily scientific evidence. He preferred developing his cases around a murder weapon, names, eyewitnesses, motive, opportunity, and (if but rarely) a confession. If, Heaven forbid, he had to go the treacherous route of indirect evidence, then it would have to be of the tried and true kind; it would have to be along lines of, say, fingerprint identification or firearms evidence.

Slaton didn't see how any responsible prosecutor, let alone one of his legendary stature, could hope to build a homicide case around vacuum sweepings, fiber types, consistencies, molecular properties, and statistical probabilities. So up until late June 1981, three weeks after FBI and Georgia crime lab experts had announced matchups between fibers found on the Atlanta victims' bodies and in Williams's environment, the "country prosecutor" still had not decided to take away the young Atlanta man's freedom.

An arrest is "not imminent," Slaton would tell reporters, after another top-flight meeting with federal and Georgia state officials who had tried to bring him around. "We're looking toward discovering the truth, whatever it might be. At this point the evidence has not been shored up enough to where we can make an arrest," he testily declared after another combat meeting. "More than fiber evidence is needed. Fibers generally won't lead you to a suspect; they are important for the shoring up of evidence" (AC 1981j).

Slaton held his ground even after a panel of fourteen fiber specialists and crime lab experts—from as far away as Frankfurt, Germany—came to Atlanta and agreed with FBI and Georgia crime lab technicians' findings. The district attorney's insistent defiance so infuriated the federal command structure that the U.S. attorney for Atlanta and the Georgia state attorney general discussed an "alternative strategy to the opposition of Lewis Slaton to proceeding in a legal manner regarding Wayne Williams" (FBI memorandum, n.d.).

The feds, in other words, wanted to do an end run around the county prosecutor. They considered hiring a special state prosecutor—"Someone with more courage, who was not a coward," as one federal official leaked it. On another occasion they proposed pressing federal civil rights and kidnapping charges against Williams, thus entirely removing the case from local jurisdiction. Neither proposal got very far, however.

Of pressing importance to the well-seasoned Slaton was whether a jury of plain Atlanta folks would understand purely circumstantial evidence built around probabilities and approximations of microscopic particles—and then be willing to convict someone of possibly capital murder based on that evidence. Wouldn't a good defense attorney be asking, over and over, How many blankets, carpets, bathrobes, and bedspreads bearing the critical fibers in question have been made? Ten thousand? (*AC* 1981j). Without significant corroborating evidence (albeit also scientific) such as blood or fingerprint matches, *and reliable eyewitness accounts*, the Slaton people held it would be fruitless to arrest and charge Wayne Williams with anything.

The feds had a response to Slaton. Even though the strongest evidence they had pointing to Williams was their fiber matches, they pointed out that these made up only one set of items within a larger whole. Lab experts were scrutinizing numerous fingerprint items; early results seemed "promising." Enzyme analysis of the stained area on the rear seat of the Williams 1970 Chevrolet station wagon conducted by the Georgia crime lab in June 1981 determined that the stains, which were less than ninety days old, were of two types of human blood. Results of further serological tests revealed consistencies with the blood type of two slaying victims: William Barrett and John Harold Porter. Barrett was the young man whose badly knifed body was discovered on May 12, 1981. John Porter's knifed body was discovered on April 12, 1981. Up to the time of the blood analysis, however, the Atlanta authorities had still not included his death on their list of Atlanta's missing and murdered.

But the case for arresting and charging Wayne Williams also was strengthened, FBI investigators held, when they proved Williams's exculpatory statements to be false. Unbeknownst to him, the abundance of apparently unforced information Wayne had offered without benefit of counsel in his June 3 FBI "interview" created an opening for investigating authorities to challenge, and ultimately impeach, his story. Working backwards, from the Thursday evening into the early Friday morning hours of May 22, when he first came to the attention of the authorities, a number of things Wayne had told the FBI about his activities during those hours just didn't add up.

FBI agents learned from the manager of the Sans Souci Lounge that Wayne had called him at his home Friday afternoon to tell him to bring Williams's tape deck to the lounge later that evening. The manager was "absolutely certain" of this. Wayne stopped by the lounge on Friday night, not Thursday, as he had told the FBI. The manager spoke briefly with Wayne when he came by the lounge Friday night, then returned Wayne's tape deck.

The reason Williams gave for being in the vicinity of the Jackson Parkway bridge—to locate the address of a prospective client—didn't check out, either. He had given his FBI interrogators two possible telephone numbers, either of which, he said, could have been the number a Cheryl Johnson had given him as her home number. He had tried calling one, or both, of those numbers on the night that federal and Atlanta authorities stopped him. Investigators who checked the phone numbers found that one of them was listed to the Southern Bell Telephone Company of Tucker, Georgia, as an "assignment number," which the company used for in-house operations. The other had a recording advising that it had been changed; the new number was for a cosmetic studio in College Park, Georgia—several miles away from where Wayne's intended client was supposed to have lived. Individuals who answered at both Southern Bell and the cosmetics company told investigators they were "unfamiliar with the name Cheryl Johnson as an employee or a customer."

And the closest that investigators could come to finding Wayne's Spanish Trace Apartments—where Cheryl Johnson was supposed to have lived—was the Center View Terrace Apartments, off South Cobb Drive in Smyrna. No one, the manager of the Center View complex told them, had rented an apartment there using the name Cheryl Johnson. Neither was she aware of any person with the last name Johnson sharing an apartment with a tenant.

Wayne also had recalled seeing vehicles besides his crossing the Jackson Parkway bridge at roughly the same time investigators claimed he was on the bridge dumping the body of Nathaniel Cater. Two vehicles he said he saw were a white Purolator truck and a Chevrolet El Camino. After checking his records, the chief dispatcher for the East Point office of the Purolator Courier Corporation told investigators that the company had "no route near the Jackson Parkway bridge during the time period 2:00 A.M. through 3:00 A.M." and that no company vehicle had been out on any type of delivery or pickup during those hours on May 22.

FBI and Atlanta special police task force investigators were unable to locate either the El Camino or its driver.

Then, in police interviews with teenagers who knew a number of the Atlanta victims, several said victims had told them that they knew, or knew of, Wayne Williams. Several witnesses told investigators that they and slaying victims on the task force list had been to Williams's "house studio" for auditioning. Wayne had taken them there in his car. One boy told investigators that once in Wayne's bathroom he saw a "huge pile" of what appeared to be children's clothing on the floor. Other eyewitnesses recalled seeing Wayne with a boy who would shortly be reported missing.

Some witnesses recalled seeing Wayne with Michael McIntosh and Eddie Lamar Duncan within days of their disappearance. Another recalled, after viewing FBI photographs, that Wayne was seated in the car in which his frail-looking neighbor, Larry Rogers, was riding the day Larry disappeared. Another identified Wayne as someone she had seen "hanging around" the K-Mart on Bankhead Highway moments before victim Curtis Walker disappeared from the area. And residents of the Thomasville Heights housing project identified Wayne as the young man who had been in their neighborhood distributing fliers for a talent show one week before Patrick Rogers disappeared.

John Laster—who, according to Wayne's seized appointment book, Wayne had recently interviewed and auditioned—told investigators he was well acquainted with slaying victim Joseph "Jo-Jo" Bell. Laster also knew Timothy Hill and Darron Glass. John and Jo-Jo were good friends. They played ball together, and on one occasion John said he spent a night at Jo-Jo's house. He told Jo-Jo about his interview and audition with Wayne Williams. Jo-Jo responded, "Yeah, I know that dude." Jo-Jo then told him that he also had auditioned for Wayne Williams—as a dancer.

Jo-Jo's other friends and associates said he used to talk with them a lot about his association with Wayne Williams. John Laster's brother, Lugene, vividly recalled the series of events that transpired the last time he saw Jo-Jo. Lugene had played basketball with Jo-Jo on the afternoon of March 2, 1981, on a court at Agnes Jones School, in the Westview area, the place Jo-Jo apparently ended up after leaving Cap'n Peg's restaurant, saying he was going up the street to "shoot some ball."

Jo-Jo had brought his own ball, but he lent it to some girls who wanted to play in an adjacent court. Jo-Jo was ready to leave before Lugene; he went over and collected his ball from the girls, then walked toward Westview Drive. At exactly that moment, Lugene Laster said, he had to chase a stray ball. He happened to look up and saw Jo-Jo getting into a station wagon.

Lugene said he decided shortly after getting back to the court that he, too, would quit playing. As he was getting into his car, he again saw the station wagon. Jo-Jo was in it. He was still wearing his dark baseball cap and holding his brand-new basketball in his lap. The station wagon pulled into an apartment building driveway, then backed out and turned onto Westview Drive. Lugene Laster told investigators he had a good look at the car and its driver: a 1970 or 1972 Chevrolet station wagon being driven by a light-skinned black man wearing a silklike shirt. From photographs handed to him by FBI agents, Lugene Laster identified the man as Wayne Williams.

Then, from all accounts, Wayne had turned up at the site where Terry Pue's body was discovered on the morning of January 23, 1981; he was there as a freelance photographer. The Rockdale County sheriff's office recorded that a man claiming to have done photographic work for other police departments presented himself to them. They had no reason to doubt his claims, since the man appeared "very businesslike and professional" and was loaded to the hilt with "an extensive amount of camera equipment." The Rockdale officials asked him to "photograph the crowd that appeared at the roadblock area." The description given by the Rockdale police of the freelance photographer matched Wayne Williams.

The act of returning to the scene of their crimes, FBI behavioral consultants pointed out, was consistent with the known behavior patterns of serial killers. Both Wayne and his father, it turned out, had been regularly photographing victims' funerals—although Homer Williams may have been doing so solely in connection with his retirement job as chief freelance photographer for the black-owned *Atlanta Daily World*.

Federal authorities wondered whether Slaton and his people knew or fully understood that Wayne bore on his body the marks of his crimes. His dying victims had not let their last gasps of breath leave their fragile little bodies without putting up a fight. They had clutched, clawed, and tugged at their unfathomable slayer. One studio executive with whom Wayne regularly did business told investigators that in the weeks leading up to May 1981, Wayne "came in with some very severe scratches on both his arms." The wounds appeared to him to have been inflicted "possibly by a knife or fingernail scratches." When the executive asked Wayne what happened, Wayne said that he had fallen.

A female studio assistant likewise recalled seeing cuts and scratches on Wayne's arm in April 1981. She, too, asked Wayne what had happened. She received the same answer he had given the studio executive. The studio assistant did not believe that the marks could have come from a fall. She told FBI and task force investigators that "the marks went the whole length of both [Williams's] arms and were very ugly." She further stated that "they looked like they had bled a lot and were very swollen. . . . That the marks were up and down," not across Williams's arms" (FBI, n.d.).

Those marks, investigators theorized, could only have come from youngsters struggling to free themselves from an attacker whose powerful arm was wrapped around—and was ready to snap—their necks. They were marks that came from brave but delicate shorties trying desperately not to die.

While analysts continued to pour over their slides and the folks in the Fulton County district attorney's office fumed, Wayne Williams was free to roam the streets of metropolitan Atlanta. And roam he did—but not without a trail of plain black police sedans with federal and Atlanta lawmen always obtrusively in tow.

But how long could this go on? Wayne seemed to enjoy taking his procession of undercover lawmen on 80 mph drives in the wrong direction on one-way city streets. He mostly did that sort of thing not because he was trying to get away but just for the heck of it. A time or two, though, he did actually elude the officers—once by leaving his home in the trunk of a rented car driven by his father.

Investigators learned that Wayne was making plans to travel to California "on business." If he were to make that trip, it would complicate even more, if not doom, a case in which the feds had invested significant amounts of valuable resources. (In banter on the street outside his house, Williams did, however, "advise" FBI agents watching over him that his trip to California was "probably off" because of an expected air traffic controllers' strike.)

It was time to end this silliness. Fully convinced that *his* special police task force, under *his* commissioner of public safety, working *with* the FBI, had effectively solved the Atlanta crimes, Mayor Maynard Jackson went to see Governor George Busbee on Thursday, June 18. Busbee agreed that it was time to force an ending to the spectacle.

Political writer Frederick Allen (1981b) described significant moves that, simultaneous with Jackson's maneuvering, also came into play. On that same

Thursday, "armed with a thick briefing book," acting U.S. Attorney Dorothy Kirkley and FBI Special Agent-in-Charge for Atlanta John Glover flew to Washington to "explain to members of the U.S. Department of Justice's Criminal Division the FBI's case against Williams."

The briefing was repeated for the DOJ's second-ranking official, Deputy U.S. Attorney General Edward C. Schmults. The thrust of the meeting was that "the FBI had nailed Williams dead to his rights," but a "coward" local district attorney was "diddling around."

Convinced by the briefing that Williams should be prosecuted, the folks at DOJ decided, like the Atlanta mayor, to enlist Busbee in "pushing Slaton forward." Schmults called the governor that Thursday afternoon and asked him to give Glover and Kirkley a hearing. "Busbee, who is nobody's fool, understood what was happening. The feds were trying to use him. He told the Justice officials that he would listen to the briefing only if Slaton, Georgia Attorney General Arthur Bolton and several other state and local officials were on hand" (Allen 1981b).

A meeting of these top state and federal officials was arranged for the following morning at the governor's mansion, magnificently situated between the dogwoods and majestic Georgia pines in upper northwest Atlanta. The meeting began at 10:30 A.M. in an "extremely unpleasant atmosphere." Allen described aspects of its peculiar dynamics:

> No one had failed to grasp the message that the meeting had been set up by a request from the highest levels of the Reagan administration. Busbee even gave several of the participants the impression that Vice President George Bush had arranged it.
>
> Slaton scowled as Ms. Kirkley argued adamantly that a prosecution should be undertaken immediately. Glover and Ms. Kirkley returned the scowls as Slaton shot back that he'd have a much better case if the FBI hadn't goofed things up. . . . Glover . . . argued that Williams was a growing threat. . . .
>
> At this point, Busbee took over. . . . [He] was anxious for some type of resolution—he was tired of the nine-ring circus surrounding Williams—but he also understood that he couldn't order Slaton to begin prosecution. . . . [I]nstead of direct pressure [on Slaton], Busbee used psychology. . . . Much to the surprise and discomfort of the feds, he championed Slaton's right to make the decisions in the Williams case.
>
> One participant in the meeting describes seeing a look of physical relief pass across Slaton's face as he listened to Busbee lecture Glover and Ms. Kirkley. Then, however, Busbee took Slaton aside for a private chat. His message, ba-

sically, was that the Williams case had to come to some sort of resolution. The timing was up to Slaton—but the sooner the better.

The meeting ended on a polite note, although Slaton left without making any commitment to begin prosecuting Williams. The strongest aftertaste of the meeting, however, was a general agreement that an arrest ought to be made if Williams gives any further indication he might flee Atlanta. (Allen 1981b)

The night after the meeting at the governor's mansion, Wayne took the covey of undercover officers assigned to watch him on another of his high-speed cavalcades around the city. Two of the places he took them were the homes of Mayor Jackson and Commissioner Lee Brown. Sometime, too, that evening, FBI and Atlanta authorities learned that Homer Williams had been out to Hartsfield Airport talking to a private airline pilot about hiring him for a flight to South America. Whether it was this particular set of events or the meeting at the governor's mansion the day before that finally pushed Lewis Slaton over the edge, no one knew for sure.

But at 5:05 P.M. Sunday, June 21, two Fulton County detectives (Slaton's men), accompanied by defense attorney Mary Welcome, arrived at the Williams home. They informed the FBI agents keeping watch outside the house that they had come for Wayne Williams. The county lawmen had a warrant signed by Deputy Police Chief Morris Redding for Williams's arrest. The detectives went inside, informed Wayne of his rights, and told him he was being taken into custody for the murder of Nathaniel Cater. They took him in handcuffs downtown to the Fulton County jail, where he would be held without bail in an isolation cell.

This last set of details was exactly the way Lewis Slaton had planned them. His decision to have his men make the arrest meant that he wanted the case handled in the Fulton County Superior Court rather than in the Municipal Court (Allen 1981b). The Municipal Court was located in the same Decatur Street building that housed the ABPS, headed by the mayor's folks, with whom the venerable Slaton did not share the same optimistic beliefs in federal interventionism.

The day after Williams's arrest, FBI and Atlanta lawmen made one final, exhaustive search of the Williams home. They were unable to find a number of items they had taken mental note of, but did not seize, in their June 3 search: a yellow blanket under Wayne's bed and textbooks on fingerprinting and scientific criminal investigations, for example.

But not to worry. FBI authorities immediately notified law enforcement agencies around the nation to "discontinue coverage of leads in this matter except as they relate to subject Williams." Three days after Williams's arrest, Mayor Jackson flew to Washington to brief President Reagan.

On July 17, a Fulton County grand jury returned a "true bill" indictment charging Wayne Williams with *two* counts of homicide: that of Nathaniel Cater and Jimmy Ray Payne. The addition of Payne was an early, promising result of the prosecution's bid to pursue a "litigation strategy." A litigation or joint trial strategy would give the prosecution an advantage, because circumstantial evidence in one case could strengthen the circumstantial evidence in another. The strategy was permissible under state law, if the prosecution could show that more than one murder was committed under the "same scheme or design."

If accepted by the presiding judge at Williams's trial, the strategy would allow the state to introduce evidence common to more than one victim. For starters, Payne's body was found in the Chattahoochee River about one hundred yards from where Cater's body was found. But more important, the state intended to show that the murders of the two men, and of several of the other listed Atlanta victims, were linked by identical fibrous material found on their bodies.

The state, Miller said, could be ready for a "speedy trial"—within thirty days—if Williams's lawyers requested it. He gave no indication that the prosecution would seek the death penalty.[1]

No group outside the city's black political directorate was as thankful to the feds for their "mission accomplished" as Atlanta's white business elite. The morning after Williams's arrest, an *Atlanta Constitution* lead editorial effusively proclaimed: "With the arrest of a prime suspect now, the FBI may well be reducing the number of agents in Atlanta. . . . Before anyone leaves, let's make our feelings clear again: Thanks, FBI" (*AC* 1981q).

As might be expected, poor black Atlantans were not equally enthralled. They remained guarded at news of the arrest and indictment of Wayne Williams. Camille Bell perhaps voiced best the mood at the grassroots. The arrest of Wayne Williams, she said, "has left the community in a position of wait and see" (*AC* 1981p).

16

Pretrial Activity

I hope that they [the prosecution] have more than fibers and that he [Williams] was on a bridge at one o'clock in the morning.

  —Defense attorney Mary Welcome

Atlanta's "Safe Summer '81" program had gotten under way just days before Wayne Williams was arrested. The program, which had been conceived in response to the string of slayings and disappearances, offered five thousand summer jobs to disadvantaged city youths. Some $5 million had been earmarked for both the mammoth summer program and the Atlanta investigations, according to Vice President George Bush's office, which was in charge of coordinating federal help to Atlanta (*AC* 1981l).

Despite the program's apparent success, parents and children on the poorer side of town were saying they were still afraid—this after the presumed Atlanta killer was behind bars. Confident that they had the right man, local law enforcement authorities shifted their attention back to solving "ordinary" crimes. No new incidents fitting the pattern of the past two years had occurred since Lewis Slaton's men took Wayne Williams into custody.

One significant development during the hiatus between Williams's arrest and his eventual trial was the eruption of a feud that had been simmering for months between Georgia state authorities and the Committee to Stop Children's Murders—the fuse for which had been lit by local black politicians' loud and insistent charges of irregularity in STOP's fund-raising activities.

In the spring of 1981, STOP leaders had filed (under threat of subpoena) documents with state authorities registering the group as a charity organization. Throughout the summer and early fall, with Wayne Williams tucked away in jail, making for slow news days, Tim Ryles, the ambitious white-knight head of the governor's office of consumer affairs, aggressively took on the organization of poor, bereaved mothers.[1]

Ryles was not convinced that contributions STOP had indicated in disclosure statements (amounting to about $40,000 between October 1980 and March 1981) went entirely into what state officials considered "charitable causes" (e.g., summer camps). STOP's documents suggested to Ryles that most of the group's funds had gone directly to the mothers; he wanted to know exactly how the money was spent.

What apparently mattered least to Ryles and his backers in the corporate Atlanta media was that STOP had never claimed in its incorporation documents that donations would be spent only on summer camp activities for at-risk children. A story in the conservative black-owned *Atlanta Daily World* on July 3, 1981, reported that those documents specifically stated that the group's organizational activities would *not* be limited "to fund-raising for summer camps." In the story, STOP attorney Don Keenan pointed out that founding members also had set as goals "'child awareness and family purposes,' which would include donations to victims' families."

STOP spokespersons admitted that, since the group's inception, some $16,000 had been paid out in burial expenses, and "several dollars more" had been used to purchase flowers and needed clothes for mothers to attend their children's funerals. State authorities and the elite Atlanta media nonetheless kept up a relentless campaign against STOP. Within months—in October 1981—the organization of ghetto mothers would quietly disband.

The city's black political class, in the meantime, took credit for holding Atlanta together during a crisis. In a speech to the Resurgence Club (a biracial group of fifty white and fifty black professionals) in July 1981, Ozell Sutton, regional director of the U.S. Community Relations Service, said a black mayor and strong black political power had enabled Atlanta to weather the strains caused by the "terrible" tragedy. "I don't know of a single city that could have held itself together as well as this city has. It is a credit to this city that it kept its eyes on the problem rather than getting sidetracked" (*AC* 1981s).

Faye and Homer Williams entrusted the fate of their only child, Wayne, before the Fulton County Superior Court to a thirty-seven-year-old attorney of known Atlanta black bourgeoisie respectability. Mary Welcome was the city's first black city solicitor—a position to which she had been named by Mayor Maynard Jackson early in his first term.

As city solicitor, Welcome led Jackson's much-reported, and much-praised, assault on Peachtree Street's notorious porn row. During her crusade to shut down the bathhouses, which city authorities had claimed harbored nothing but prostitutes, she earned the nickname "Wild Mary." News photographers were alerted night after night to raids on the establishments; they would show up with cameras flashing. Eventually, bolstered by strong public support (generated in part by the publicity), Welcome's office managed to close down fifteen bathhouses deemed "public nuisances" (*Atlanta* 1977; *Black Enterprise* 1981).

Mary Welcome quit her job as city solicitor in 1978 because, she had said, a private law firm offered her more money than she could make in government. But it was "no secret," as the *Atlanta Constitution* (1981p) reported, that Jackson had been "displeased that she openly sided" with former public safety commissioner Reginald Eaves, whom Jackson had fired because of Eaves's alleged involvement in a police promotion scandal.

Everyone in town knew that Mary Welcome loved public attention and that she was not one to shy away from cultivating the media for causes she deemed worthwhile, including her own political ambitions.[2]

To assist her in defending Williams against his double murder charge, Mary Welcome called on a black Atlanta attorney whose strengths would balance hers. She recruited Tony Axam, a meticulous, quiet man who shunned interviews and cameras and relished the role of "lawyer technician." Axam was no stranger to high-profile criminal cases, however. He had begun his career in Detroit. He was part of renowned civil rights lawyer Millard Farmer's legal team, which defended the "Dawson Five" in Georgia's Terrell County in 1977. In that case, five black men were accused of killing a white grocery store clerk during a robbery. The charges were based on the confession of one of the accused. The defense contended that white police officers had intimidated the confessor, a mentally slow, vulnerable black man. Axam and Farmer succeeded in getting the confession thrown out and the charges against the "Dawson Five" dropped.

Mary Welcome and Tony Axam had successfully teamed up in the past. In December 1980 they worked with lead counsel Louis Polonsky to defend three Morris Brown College football players against charges of raping a coed in their dormitory. Despite an admission by the players that they did indeed have intercourse with the young woman, the jury convicted them only of simple battery. Polonsky credited Welcome with creating a "feeling of compassion for her clients" as the reason why the men were not convicted of more serious charges. At the close of the trial, Polonsky told reporters, Mary Welcome approached the jury from the "woman's point of view," telling them: "When I was growing up we were more cautious about getting into those kinds of situations, but times are different now. I'll tell you that my little girl would have known different" (*AC* 1981n).

Axam's contribution to the Morris Brown case was that he "really knew the law," while shunning the publicity that the case had generated. He was supposed to play a similar role in the Wayne Williams trial, mostly testing prosecution experts and the limits of the law.

The man who would be making the critical calls in Axam's "tests" would be Judge Clarence Cooper, the first black elected countywide to the Fulton County Superior Court bench. In late July 1981 a computer program "randomly selected" (according to news reports) the thirty-eight-year-old Cooper to preside over the Wayne Williams trial.

Cooper's selection came about in the normal way that judges were assigned cases, according to state officials. An administrator for the Fulton County Superior Court told reporters that judges in the system were assigned cases randomly by a computer twice each week, based on when indictments from grand jury sessions were received. The purpose of the random computer drawing was to prevent either the defense or the prosecution from "judge shopping," that is, seeking the assignment of a judge whose judicial demeanor was considered pro-defendant or pro-prosecution.

But Cooper may well have been the defense's first choice. Although the case against their client could not rightly have been considered political or racial in the populist sense—like, for example, the case against the "Dawson Five"— it was nonetheless a case loaded with racial themes and implications. Guilty or not, Wayne Williams had become yet another young black male who was hopelessly caught within the "oppressive" tentacles of the American criminal justice system.

Clarence Cooper's rise to judicial eminence was rooted, precisely, in the perception among black Atlantans that his experience as a black man in America would make him a judge that any black male accused of a crime could trust. Cooper's earlier appointment, in 1976, as a municipal court judge was widely hailed by Atlanta blacks. And his election in August 1980 to the Fulton County Superior Court was regarded by white opinion makers as an "upset": in a runoff he defeated a well-financed white opponent who enjoyed extensive backing from the city's white legal establishment.[3]

Cooper won his seat largely as the result of organized black grassroots support. The black-nationalist *Atlanta Voice* had heartily endorsed his candidacy. One month before the election, the paper's editorial board made their position absolutely clear. "Clarence Cooper is the man of the hour. He is for judicial reform in this city and this is enough in itself for us to give him our unqualified support." The editorial continued:

> Black people dominate the criminal justice system. More of us are charged with crimes. More of us have to stand trial. More of us are found guilty and more of us are incarcerated. This means we have an interest in the criminal justice system that should exceed all other ethnic groups. . . .
>
> We do not believe that white judges can be equitable, even if they wanted to be. They do not understand our culture. They do not possess the background to empathize with our plight. This is if they wanted to. Many do not even have the desire. They look down at us from the bench. . . .
>
> We need judges with Clarence Cooper's sensibilities and understanding. He will not be overly lenient as he has proven in his position with municipal court. But he will be fair. This is all that we can ask and require.
>
> He is now offering for superior court judge. Right thinking Blacks should do more than consider him—they should support his effort with their contributions, they should enkourage [*sic*] others (Blacks and whites) to do so. They should vote overwhelmingly for him. (*AV* 1980a)

This ringing endorsement of Cooper as someone more likely to understand black defendants' side of things deliberately overlooked an important item in the judge's past. After law school, he spent eight years working as an assistant district attorney; his boss was none other than Lewis Slaton. Not many viewed this as a major handicap, however—including Williams's defense lawyers. The potential for a previous working relationship between Slaton and Cooper being detrimental to their client's best interest would be minimized not only by the judge being a fair and decent man but also by the force of informal racial solidarity. The judge circulated freely in the same social circles bounded by race as did lead defense attorney Mary Welcome. Besides, as an assistant district attorney, Cooper had worked with Welcome when she was waging her *jihad* against Peachtree Street's smut merchants.

In the month that Wayne Williams was to be arraigned for murder, state authorities were expressing a serious concern over one of the two murders for which he had been indicted: the unclear nature of Jimmy Payne's death certificate could make it harder for prosecutors to argue that he was actually slain.

So the Fulton County medical examiner, Dr. Saleh Zaki, amended Jimmy Payne's death certificate. In a corrective letter to the Vital Records Section of Fulton County's Health Department, he wrote that back in April 1981, when Payne's body was removed from the Chattahoochee River, he had "inadvertently" written under "manner of death" on official state forms the word *un-*

determined. What he should have written was *homicide.* "This amendment is necessary," Zaki's letter continued, "to reflect my original findings and to correspond with my official report on file in this office" (Epstein 1981a).

At 9:00 A.M., August 17, 1981, one week after Zaki's amendment was officially entered, Wayne Williams was arraigned before Judge Clarence Cooper in Fulton County Superior Court. Williams pleaded "not guilty" to the indictment charging him with the murder of Nathaniel Cater and Jimmy Ray Payne. Cooper set September 4 as the date he would hear defense motions to suppress statements that Williams had made to federal lawmen the night he was stopped[4] and to have him tried separately on the two murder charges. He set October 5 as a tentative trial date and ruled that no open cameras would be allowed during the trial. The judge dismissed court admonishing both the prosecution and the defense to cease leaking information about the case to the media.

Both sides kept talking, however, as each continued to hold mini news conferences in the manner that had become de rigueur in high-profile trials. Always available for a comment or two was the telegenic Mary Welcome, who seemed to be disregarding her own earlier concerns about her client being "blitzkrieged" by the media. Ten days after Williams's arraignment, Judge Cooper issued a judicial "gag" order prohibiting all persons involved in the Williams case—"prosecution, counsel for the defense, potential witnesses, court personnel, members of the Special Police Task Force; including Commissioner of Public Safety, the Director of the Bureau of Police Services and/or persons affiliated therewith"—from making any extrajudicial statements or comments to the media "relating to any matters having to do with Wayne B. Williams." Certainly in this case Cooper was going to be a no-nonsense judge.

The September 4 hearing was carried over to September 10. At that time Cooper heard major defense motions for suppression of evidence and for separate trials. Mary Welcome argued that authorities did not have sufficient probable cause that a crime had been committed on the morning of May 22. Thus her client had been stopped and searched illegally. Williams was not advised that he was being arrested, so anything he said then—specifically that "This must be about those boys"—ought not to be held against him. She further argued that the Cater and Payne murders showed no convincing evidence that they were connected to the "same scheme." Williams should therefore be given two separate trials.[5]

Cooper took under advisement the two major motions but ruled on several less weighty ones. He denied defense motions requesting public funds to pay for a private investigator and another seeking the same for a poll of prospective jurors. Welcome had argued that, although her client was not indigent, he did not have the money necessary to adequately prepare his defense. The investigator was needed to help find defense witnesses, and the poll of community attitudes was necessary to determine whether the defense should try to move the trial outside Fulton County. But Cooper noted that Williams was represented by counsel from two law firms and had shown at previous hearings that he had several other attorneys and research personnel already working for him. And, the judge said, the defendant could obtain information on public attitudes toward him through the *voire dire* process (i.e., the questioning of potential jurors at the start of the trial).

On September 21, Cooper ruled on the two major defense motions: to suppress Williams's statements and to have him tried separately. He denied both. All would not be lost to the prosecution, though. The state was dealt a setback of sorts when Cooper granted a defense motion asking him to broaden his examination of investigative files to all twenty-eight slayings then listed. (Cooper had previously limited his review to the two cases for which Williams was indicted.) The purpose of the review was to determine whether any favorable or exculpatory evidence existed in any of the twenty-eight cases that should be turned over to Williams's defense team.

If, after examining the records, as astute *Atlanta Constitution* staff writer Gail Epstein (1981b) pointed out, the judge allowed Williams's defense attorneys "access to evidence concerning the other cases," the defense would "gain information about motives or patterns possibly crucial to the state's case." Primarily, though, state attorneys opposed a wide review of the "thousands of pages of documents" pertinent to the other cases because the task would delay Williams's trial—as indeed it did.

On October 5, 1981 (the date originally set for the trial to begin), Cooper met with attorneys for both sides. Barely getting started with his review of the twenty-eight cases, and waist-deep in some forty-two defense motions—including a motion to throw out all fiber evidence because search warrants for the Williamses' home and car had been unjustifiably issued—the judge informed the attorneys that he was indefinitely postponing the starting date of the trial.

The defense attorneys, in the meantime, were having more than their share of troubles. Lacking both leadership and money, they were nowhere close to being ready for trial. They had interviewed very few of the prosecution's four hundred listed witnesses. And although they had consulted some forensic experts, none had been formally recruited to examine the mounds of technical evidence that the state had amassed. Lack of money, Mary Welcome was quietly saying, was frustrating efforts to hire defense experts.[6]

But underneath their money problems were ongoing disputes between the two attorneys over shared responsibilities. Mary Welcome found herself filling more than the public relations role she had designed for herself. Falling more and more to her was the detail work on legal and evidentiary issues for which she was less well prepared. She was doing, in short, Tony Axam's work.

Williams fired Axam, then rehired him. He fired him again. Eventually, at Welcome's urging, in late October 1981 the Williamses hired Alvin Binder, an experienced white Jackson, Mississippi, trial attorney. Described as a "shark" and a "winner," Binder had a national reputation as an expert in cross-examination. His manner was sarcastic and aggressive.

On October 21, Judge Cooper denied all defense motions seeking to either suppress or throw out evidence against Williams. He found, moreover, little exculpatory material in the twenty-eight cases he had examined that should be turned over to the defense. Jury selection would begin after the Thanksgiving and Christmas holidays—and after the big mayoral election.

On December 28, two months after Andrew Young beat white state representative Sidney Marcus in a runoff to become Atlanta's next black mayor, jury selection for Wayne Williams's trial began. Four panels, each consisting of forty-five potential jurors, were grilled by prosecution and defense attorneys and by the judge. After a relatively short five days into this challenge process—in which, according to news stories, "only a handful" of the presumed representative group of Atlanta citizens said they had formed an opinion about Williams's guilt or innocence—attorneys for both sides took twenty minutes to agree on the needed twelve jurors and four alternates. Of the twelve, nine were women, eight were black, and four were white. Judge Cooper ordered their immediate sequestration, which would last the duration of the trial. They should report to court, the judge instructed, Wednesday, January 6, 1982, to hear opening arguments.

17

The Trial No One Wanted to Miss

Our case is going to be to you like a jigsaw puzzle.
> —Fulton County district attorney Lewis Slaton

You don't get a killer from a boy that was raised like that boy was.
> —Defense attorney Alvin Binder

I really feel that Wayne Williams did kill somebody.
> —Prosecution witness Sharon Blakely

Six months after Lewis Slaton's men arrested Wayne Williams for murder, Atlanta and the nation were in for a court trial unlike any other. The scene was, as the *Atlanta Constitution*'s Bob Dart (1982) put it, "a circus of humanity." "Private eyes, prophetesses, cops and commies, suburban housewives and big-time journalists, the curious and the curiosities," all found their way to the fourth floor of the Fulton County courthouse during the nine-week trial.

The courtroom pews were split down the middle between journalists and the public. Courtroom artists sat in the first row on one side. The defendant's family and friends sat directly across the aisle. Two closed-circuit television cameras recorded all from overhead.

Down the hall from the courtroom was the press viewing room. Side-by-side screens showed closeups of the witness stand. Another press room held telephones, typewriters, and portable computer terminals. A bulletin board there carried messages from editors, a list of missing press badges, and solicitations for bridge games. It was there that folks could order T-shirts with the logo "Woven with Fibers from the Wayne Williams Trial."

Public curiosity waned during days of technical testimony about fibers. It peaked during Williams's days on the witness stand, when some four hundred eager beavers showed up each day—as early as 4:00 A.M.—for the 9:00 A.M. start of court. Only about eighty-five would manage to get inside and be able to hold a required seat in Judge Clarence Cooper's courtroom.

The prosecution laid out its case against Wayne Williams in nineteen days of testimony. In his opening statement, District Attorney Lewis Slaton—now fully, and personally, into his job as chief prosecutor—likened the case to a jigsaw puzzle. To help put the pieces together for the jury, Slaton and his team presented testimony from 120 witnesses: police officers, FBI agents, crime lab technicians, medical examiners, fiber experts, and a host of character and eyewitnesses. For the better part of five weeks, the twelve jurors and four alternates viewed dozens of maps, charts, aerial photographs, and elaborate exhibits furnished by the FBI's special projects division.

The state painted a profile of a "mad-dog" killer with a "Manichean personality." The defendant, prosecutors argued, was "intelligent, literate, and quite possibly talented." But he also was "a pathological liar, frustrated dreamer, and contemptuous failure" (*Time* 1982).

The state won approval from Judge Cooper to pursue their "litigation strategy" as regards nine other listed killings and one previously unlisted murder (John Porter's). The judge thereby allowed the prosecution to introduce, in open court, evidence pointing to Williams as the culprit in at least *ten* other slayings (i.e., plus Cater's and Payne's) for which he was not formally charged. As reason for doing so, Cooper cited Georgia law permitting introduction of normally excluded evidence if the prosecution can demonstrate a pattern of criminality, vis-à-vis the similarities among various criminal acts that a defendant may have committed.

As Williams's trial got under way, Atlanta authorities had on their special police task force list a total of twenty-nine murders and one still-missing case.

The state argued that the chain of circumstantial and scientific evidence linking Williams to the murder of the Atlanta victims was strongest in the twelve cases in question (see table 3). He was narrowly tied to the murders of Nathaniel Cater, William Barrett, Jimmy Payne, John Porter, Larry Rogers, Joseph "Jo-Jo" Bell, Patrick Baltazar, Terry Pue, Lubie Geter, Charles Stephens, Eric Middlebrooks, and Alfred Evans.

Throughout the trial, the prosecution kept intimating, however, that they had equally significant—though perhaps less substantial—evidence linking the defendant to practically all the Atlanta murders. Based on the available evidence, Williams *could not* be ruled out in any of the twenty-seven murders of young black Atlanta males on the task force list (see table 4), including the two cases for which investigators had "no recoverable evidence." Prosecution testimony basically fell into the following "pieces":

- The bridge incident
- The defendant's credibility
- Blood, hair, and fiber comparisons
- Eyewitness identification
- The defendant's habits, lifestyle, and attitude

We discuss the state's presentation of each of these pieces below.

Everything in the case brought against Wayne Williams started with the series of events that transpired in the predawn hours of May 22, 1981, in the vicinity of the James Jackson Parkway bridge, and with the discovery, two days later, of the body of Nathaniel Cater.

Atlanta police officer Robert Campbell testified about hearing a loud splash in the river beneath the bridge at same time that his partner above him saw a car moving slowly across the bridge. Veteran Atlanta police officer Carl Holden testified that he observed the white station wagon drive off the bridge, then immediately make a U-turn in the parking lot where he was positioned. The station wagon proceeded back across the bridge, tailed by him and FBI Special Agent Gregg Gilliland. Gilliland testified to stopping and questioning the driver of the station wagon, Wayne Williams, who said in response to being stopped: "This must be about those boys."

Ben Kittle, a civil engineer with the Army Corps of Engineers, testified that his men had conducted a study of the conditions of the Chattahoochee River. It was his expert opinion that the most logical place that Nathaniel Cater's and Jimmy Payne's bodies could have been placed in the water was either off the Jackson Parkway bridge or under the I-285 overpass. Neither spot would have been far from where the bodies were discovered.

Decatur jewelry store owner Eustis Blakely testified that he and his wife, Sharon, were friends of Wayne Williams. They got to know Williams in the summer of 1980 because they and Wayne had been pouring money into promoting young black Atlanta musicians. The articulate witness, a businessman immaculately dressed in a navy-blue suit and necktie and wearing wire-rimmed glasses, appeared relaxed and comfortable on the stand; he frequently chuckled at the tragicomic stories he related under friendly prodding from Slaton. Eustis Blakely looked the part: he was the black success story that Wayne Williams probably wished he had been.

Blakely testified to Wayne's pattern of deception. Wayne once tried to impress him, he said, with his résumé. But it was obvious to him that Wayne's claims

Table 3. Prosecution's Hair and Fiber Evidence Linking Williams to Twelve Victims in Question

Probable source in Williams's environment	Nathaniel Cater	William Barrett	Jimmy Ray Payne	John Harold Porter	Larry Rogers	Joseph Bell	Patrick Baltazar	Terry Pue	Lubie Geter	Charles Stephens	Eric Middlebrooks	Alfred Evans
Violet and green bedspread	X	X	X	X	X	X	X	X	X	X	X	X
Green bedroom carpet	X	X	X	X	X		X	X	X	X		X
Pale green carpet squares in office/workroom area	X							X		X		
Yellow blanket found under bed	X	X	X	X	X		X					
Trunk liner from 1979 Ford LTD										X	X	
Red carpet from 1979 Ford LTD											X	
Dark carpet from 1970 Chevy station wagon		X	X	X	X		X		X			
Yellow toilet seat cover					X					X	X	
Gray glove found in station wagon							X					
Brown waist and collar from leather jacket							X					
Yellow kitchen rug									X			
Blue acrylic throw rug			X									
Trunk liner from 1978 Plymouth Fury												X
Fibers found in debris from station wagon (several colors)	X	X	X	X	X	X	X			X		
White polyester fibers found in debris from rug in station wagon cargo area							X	X		X		
Animal hairs consistent with Williams's dog	X	X	X	X	X		X	X	X	X	X	X
Bedspread hanging in carport area				X	X							

Source: Atlanta Journal, February 2, 1982.

Table 4. Purported Hair and Fiber Evidence Linking Williams to Nearly All the Atlanta Slaying Victims

Probable Source in Williams's Environment	Edward Smith	Alfred Evans	Milton Harvey	Yusef Bell	Angel Lanier	Jeffery Mathis	Eric Middlebrooks	Christopher Richardson	Latonya Wilson	Aaron Wyche	Anthony Carter	Earl Terrell	Clifford Jones	Darron Glass	Charles Stephens	Aaron Jackson	Patrick Rogers	Lubie Geter	Terry Pue	Patrick Baltazar	Curtis Walker	Joseph Bell	Timothy Hill	Eddie Duncan	Larry Rogers	Michael McIntosh	Jimmy Payne	William Barrett	Nathaniel Cater	John Porter
Violet and green bedspread	X	X		X	Apparently not connected	No recoverable evidence	X	No recoverable evidence	Apparently not connected	X	X	X	X		X	X	X	X	X	X	X	X	X	X	X	X	X	X	X	X
Green bedroom carpet		X		X						X			X		X	X		X	X	X			X		X		X	X	X	X
Green bedroom carpet squares in office/workroom area											X	X			X				X										X	
Yellow blanket found under bed							X			X	X	X			X					X				X	X		X	X	X	X
Trunk liner from 1979 Ford LTD							X								X															
Red carpet from 1979 Ford LTD							X																							X
Dark carpet from station wagon							X											X		X								X		X
Yellow toilet seat cover																				X		X								
Gray glove found in station wagon															X					X				X	X					
Brown waist and collar from leather jacket																				X										
Yellow kitchen rug																		X					X				X			
Blue acrylic throw rug																											X			
Trunk liner from 1978 Plymouth Fury		X	X												X				X	X					X		X	X	X	X
Fibers found in debris in station wagon (several colors)										X		X	X		X				X	X									X	
White polyester fibers found in debris from rug in station wagon cargo area							X					X	X		X			X	X	X					X		X	X	X	X
Animal hairs consistent with Williams's dog		X		X																									X	X
Bedspread hanging in carport area																								X						X

were wildly exaggerated. He said he asked Wayne what he did for a living, since Wayne didn't have a steady job listed on his rather lengthy résumé. Wayne's response was that he was a member of the air force and that he flew F-4 fighters at nearby Dobbins Air Force Base once a month.

"That struck a nerve with me," Blakely testified, because he happened to have been in the air force. Blakely said he once wanted to pilot an F-4 but was told he couldn't because he wore glasses (Willis 1982). He knew that Wayne, who also wore eyeglasses—with much thicker lenses than his—could not have been an F-4 pilot.

Then, according to Blakely, Wayne told him, "Well, I'll bet I know more about anatomy than you do." Blakely said he conceded that one to Wayne. It was an item the prosecution wanted mentioned, though. (Sharon Blakely would likewise testify that Wayne had tried unsuccessfully, on more than one occasion during the year before he was arrested, to engage her in conversation on the martial arts and other physiologically immobilizing techniques.) The chubby defendant, the prosecution wanted jurors to hear, had stored away in his pocketful of show-and-tell knowledge a thing or two he had picked up along the way on how the human body is held together—about which he had given hideous contemplation. Williams knew perfectly well the easiest and least physically demanding ways to deprive a body of life.

Additional witnesses helped the prosecution pinpoint numerous lies and discrepancies in the stories Williams had given investigators. The manager of the Sans Souci Lounge testified that he had known Wayne and his lying ways for more than three years. He further testified that Wayne came to see him at the Sans Souci to collect his tape deck on Friday evening, May 22, 1981—not Thursday, May 21, as Williams had told FBI agents. Annie Smith, the cashier at the Sans Souci, also testified that Williams was at the lounge on the evening of May 22, not May 21.

The manager of Ben Hill Recreation Center, where Williams said he had been in the early evening hours of Thursday, May 21, prior to his supposed arrival at the Sans Souci, testified that Williams was not at the recreation center that evening.

Highlighting these discrepancies was important to the "opportunity to commit the crime" component of the prosecution's theory. Williams had lied about his activities on May 21 because he was in downtown Atlanta with Nathaniel Cater. Sometime in the course of that Thursday night, Wayne had taken a drunken Cater for a deadly ride in his station wagon.

Blood, hair, and fiber particles have been essential trace items in scientific crime detection since the late eighteenth century. The nuts and bolts of the state's case against Wayne Williams rested on laboratory findings and analyses relative to all three.

Building on the science of serology (i.e., the study of blood fluids), the German scientist Paul Uhlenhuth discovered in 1901 how to distinguish between animal and human blood. The first "great" case with which criminal culpability was demonstrated using Uhlenhuth's precipitin test was that of Ludwig Tessnow, suspected of killing several youngsters in the German countryside between 1898 and 1901. Seventeen specimens of human blood with properties matching those of the victims were removed from the suspect's clothes, and as a result he had been convicted and sentenced to death (Marriner 1991). Since then, blood evidence and (much later) DNA testing have been used in hundreds of homicide trials in Europe and North America to both convict and exonerate defendants (see, e.g., Roberts and Willmore 1993).

The first treatise on hair analysis appeared in 1857 (Marriner 1991), and by the turn of the century scientists were able to microscopically distinguish between different species of animal hair and human hair and between human head, pubic, armpit, and facial hair. They also could tell the race and gender of the hair's owner.

Fiber analysis developed as the primary experimental technique that would demonstrate Edmond Locard's "exchange principle." One of the earliest cases involving its use was that of Lazare Tessier, a Frenchman accused in 1924 of murdering a seventy-year-old man by inflicting multiple blows to the victim's head. The man's body was found wrapped in a sheet and left on the street. The body was removed to the laboratory of the Judicial Police in Paris. The only lead that investigators had was that the dead man had been missing for nine days and that the motive for his killing appeared to have been robbery.

Investigations of the victim's associations led to Tessier. Investigators searched the cellar of Tessier's house, and from it lab technicians collected bags of sand, sawdust, wine casks, and pieces of wood. The technicians found traces of human blood on one piece of wood. But the most telling clues came from a jersey belonging to Tessier. Fibrous materials from the jersey were identical to fibers found on the murdered man's clothing. Tessier was found guilty of manslaughter—primarily so because the jury felt "uneasy about convicting him for a capital crime purely on evidence produced by the microscope" (Marriner 1991, 220).

But a more recent case that demonstrated, for the Atlanta experts, the usefulness of fiber evidence was a 1976 British homicide case. As recalled by E. J. Mitchell and D. Holland (1979), two of the forensic experts involved in the British case, at approximately 7:30 P.M. Thursday, November 11, 1976, an eleven-year-old boy dressed in scouts uniform left his Bradford home to walk one and one-quarter miles to attend the weekly meeting at the local scouts headquarters. When he failed to return home at the expected time, his parents called the headquarters and learned that the boy never arrived for the meeting. A search of the nearby vicinity turned up the boy's murdered body three days later.

The body was found "lying partly on its side in a crouched position." Semen was found in the boy's anus and inside the back of his trousers and underpants. "Superficial fibres were recovered by sellotaping the clothing and exposed body surfaces and taken for analysis at the Harrogate Forensic Science Laboratory." Among the recovered fibers were "200 man-made fibres which were similar in appearance." They were of uniform short length, broad diameters "and were present as three separate colours" (Mitchell and Holland 1979, 23).

The lab experts determined that the fibers in question were from a flock carpet. Because the fibers were of an unusual type and were present in "significantly large numbers," investigators were able to trace the carpet's manufacturer: a small French carpet spinner of a line of flock carpet known commercially as Flotex. The line had been discontinued, but a limited quantity had been sold in large consignments to contractors who in turn had sold odd lengths, or "off-cuts," to refurbishers of used cars.

By pursuing each of these purchases, investigators were led to a carpet-fitter who had used off-cuts of the Flotex carpet to recover the floor of his car. The carpet-fitter had sold the car to a student who was studying at Bradford College. The college was on the same street as the local scouts headquarters.

The Bradford College student was interviewed and his car examined. Still fitted to the car was the discontinued Flotex carpet. Yellow wool fibers recovered from the dead boy's body matched yellow wool fibers from a pair of trousers the student had in his closet. Moreover, "some two dozen red cotton viscose rayon fibres" recovered from the boy's body matched a towel in the student's possession.

Additional lab analyses indicated that the student was the likely source for the semen found on the dead boy's clothing. The student confessed to assaulting and killing the boy in his car. He was found guilty of manslaughter and imprisoned.

In Wayne Williams's trial, blood analysis experts stated that human blood-stains were found in a swatch of carpet taken from his house and on the rear seat of the 1970 Chevrolet station wagon. The stains on the station wagon were definitely consistent with the blood type of William Barrett and John Porter.

Lab experts also testified that dog hairs found on the bodies of six of the twelve Atlanta victims in question were consistent with that of the Williamses' German Shepherd. And two head hairs of "Negroid origin" recovered from Patrick Baltazar's body "were consistent with originating from the scalp of Wayne Williams."

FBI and Georgia crime lab experts testified that, in ways almost identical to the Bradford, England, case, they had accumulated abundant fiber evidence linking Williams—or certainly his immediate environment—to the bodies of the Atlanta victims. In two separate phases of the trial, fiber experts testified that more than twenty-eight different fiber types, from a total of more than seven hundred fibers, were used to link up to nineteen objects from Williams's environment to one or more of the twelve victims in question (tables 3 and 4). Prosecution experts said it was impossible for the victims to have picked up, or have transferred to them, so many fibers similar to those found in Williams's home and car without them having been in physical contact with him; this they concluded after conducting numerous scientific tests, including subjecting the fibers to high-intensity heat treatments.

Of the more than twenty-eight fiber types recovered from the defendant's environment, fourteen originated from a rug or carpet in his room. The FBI's Harold Deadman and Georgia crime lab's Larry Peterson, both microanalysts, were on the stand the longest of all experts in the trial. Deadman testified, and would later write (1984a, 1984b), that the green (or yellowish-green) nylon fibers found on the bodies of ten of the twelve victims in question (table 3) were so unusual in microscopic properties that they were able to trace their manufac-turer, the textile product(s) they had gone into, the wholesaler and retailer of the product(s), and ultimately the purchaser(s) of the product(s).

The fibers had been manufactured by the Wellman Corporation at its plant in Johnsonville, South Carolina. The company had assigned a batch number, #181B, to that particular fiber, and *that* batch they manufactured *only* from 1967 to 1974. The Wellman #181B fiber was sold to twelve companies, all carpet spinners.

FBI agents were able to determine, Deadman testified, that the West Point Pepperell Corporation of Dalton, Georgia (a short distance up the interstate from Atlanta), was one of the purchasers of Wellman fiber #181B. They further learned that West Point Pepperell had used its fiber #181B to manufacture a line of carpet in 1971 called "Luxaire," which was constructed in the same manner as the carpet in the Williams home. One of the colors offered in the Luxaire line was called "English Olive," the color of the carpet in the Williams home.

Prosecutors produced for the court sales records showing that, on December 7, 1971 (not in 1968, as she would later contend), Faye Williams had contracted for residential carpeting. The Luxaire carpet she bought had been constructed from the unique Wellman fiber #181B found on the Atlanta victims' bodies. The reason for this, the prosecution argued, was because portions of the Luxaire carpet had been installed in the area of the Williams home primarily occupied by Wayne. That Wellman fiber #181B was transferred onto the clothes, bodies, and hair of the Atlanta victims—whom Wayne had murdered.

Some of the youngsters Wayne had smothered to death right there in the back area of his parents' home, the prosecution contended. He did so after he had drugged them with chloroform. Witnesses testified that they had either seen chloroform in Wayne's possession or heard him discuss its possible lethal uses. One anesthetized victim, Eric Middlebrooks, Wayne had clubbed to death on the floor of his house, leaving the boy's bloodstains in the carpet. The ghastly deed Wayne had carried out using a "slapjack," the item FBI and Atlanta officers had removed from the Williams home wrapped in adhesive tape.

Wayne had strangled, stabbed, or snapped the necks of other victims in one of the three cars he had access to since the summer of 1979. He would bring some of the dead bodies back to his section of the little redbrick house on Penelope Road. And there, rather ghoulishly, he would strip the bodies—leaving them nude, seminude, or with the clothing rearranged—before dumping them in an area river or along a roadway or at a remote site.[1] Still clinging to areas of the youngsters' broken and bruised bodies, though, were microscopic particles of the indestructible Wellman fiber #181B.

But how many other homes in the Atlanta area had a carpet like the critical Williams carpet? Based on sales records they obtained from the West Point Pepperell Corporation (the only company to have manufactured the Luxaire line), prosecution experts testified that they estimated a "very low chance"—one in more than eight thousand—of finding such a carpet in *occupied* Atlanta-area residencies (Deadman 1984b).

Fibers recovered from victims' bodies that hadn't come from the Williams home were traced to the carpets in one of the three cars Wayne drove between July 1979 and May 1981. Three types of either automobile carpet fibers or trunk liner fibers were recovered from the bodies of eight of the twelve victims in question (table 3).

The experts testified that the fibers recovered from what the state claimed were Alfred Evans's remains[2] were traced to the trunk liner of the carpet in Wayne's repossessed 1978 Plymouth Fury. The fibers found on the body of Eric Middlebrooks were traced to Homer Williams's repossessed 1979 Ford LTD. And the fibers found on the bodies of Lubie Geter, Patrick Baltazar, Larry Rogers, John Porter, Jimmy Payne, William Barrett, and Nathaniel Cater were traced to the family's 1970 Chevrolet station wagon, which Wayne mostly controlled and was driving the night he was stopped.

The prosecution presented a stream of eyewitnesses, all ordinary citizens, who said they had seen Williams at least once with one of the twelve victims in question.

Margaret Carter lived on Northwest Verbena Street, where she was a neighbor to Nathaniel Cater's parents. She testified that, approximately a week before Cater's body was found, she saw him with Wayne on a park bench across the street from her apartment. In the immediate vicinity of where the two men were sitting, Ms. Carter said she saw a "frisky" German Shepherd dog and a white station wagon. (Williams's lawyers later would have Wayne's father bring to court the family's fourteen-year-old German Shepherd, whom they said was in such poor health, and with only "a few months to live," that the poor dog could hardly have been considered "frisky.")

Testimony by Robert Henry, a friend of Nathaniel Cater, also placed Williams in Nathaniel's company. Henry's testimony, moreover, helped the prosecution establish their timeline. Henry testified that, at about 9:30 P.M. Thursday, May 21, he saw Cater and Williams leaving the rear entrance of the downtown Rialto theater, situated in the heart of the city's tenderloin district at 84 Northwest Forsyth Street. The two men, Henry testified, were holding hands.

This account supported testimony from a nurse who said she saw Cater at an Atlanta blood plasma donor center earlier that Thursday. The state wanted to show that, based on testimony from the two eyewitnesses, Cater was alive on May 21 and that he was killed sometime later that evening—during the time about which Wayne Williams either had lied to investigators about his activities or was quite hazy about his whereabouts.

Lugene Laster restated under oath what he had earlier told investigators about the last time he and Jo-Jo Bell were together: that Jo-Jo left the basketball court on which they had finished playing in a Chevrolet station wagon driven by the person he identified as Wayne Williams.

Ruth Warren testified that, while taking her mother shopping at the Stewart-Lakewood Shopping Center on January 2, 1981, she saw a young man and a boy in front of the Sears outlet store on Stewart Avenue. She overheard the boy say,

"I'd like to go with you, but I've got to sell these." The youth then referred to a box. From photographs handed her, Ms. Warren identified the boy as Lubie Geter and pointed at Wayne Williams as the man to whom Lubie had been speaking.

Eighteen-year-old Anthony Barber testified that he was a member of Wayne's singing group in the making, Gemini. On one occasion, he said, he observed scratches on the right side of Wayne's face and arm. Wayne, he said, told him that his dog had bitten him. The youth further testified that, before leaving on a trip to South Carolina, Wayne had told him, "Don't get killed." He asked Wayne, "Why did you say that?" Wayne's reply was, "The last time I said that, I went to a funeral." (Just before he disappeared, mentally handicapped Eddie Duncan was telling folks in his Techwood neighborhood that he was on his way to South Carolina. And Wayne and his father, eyewitnesses had said, attended a number of the Atlanta victims' funerals.)

Wayne Williams led a curious life, the state contended. He presented himself as ambitious and always on the go. But underneath this favorable exterior was a "strange" person. Wayne, prosecutors argued, was an angry young man with fluttery goals and confused sexuality. He was a spoiled brat who, if he hadn't exactly failed at life, was certainly not serious about the music business. He grew into a flim-flam man with a hateful streak, which he was capable of displaying in the most violent way. He ruled his parents, once assaulting his father in a downtown parking lot for refusing to rent a car for Wayne's equally flim-flam mentor and Svengali, Willie Hunter; after the incident Wayne warned his father "not to come home that night."

At least two boys testified that Wayne made unwanted sexual advances to them. One of them, a fifteen-year-old, testified that Wayne outrightly sexually molested him in August 1980. Wayne picked him up in a car. During the ensuing ride, Wayne put his hand into the boy's pants pocket, asking, "Do you have any money?" But, rather than checking his pocket for money, the boy testified, Wayne was fondling the boy's penis. Wayne drove him to a wooded area, gave him two dollars, asked him to unzip his pants, and then went around to the trunk of the car. At that point, the boy said, he jumped out of the car and took off running.

Ambulance driver Bobby Toland testified that he got to know Wayne pretty well over the years Wayne was doing his freelance photography. Toland repeated under oath what he had already told investigators about Wayne's thoughts on race and how Wayne calculated for him that, by killing over time a given number of black boys, it wouldn't take long to wipe out a race of poor black people. (Eustis Blakely also had testified that Wayne often spoke hatefully about poor black children.)

But it was Sharon Blakely's chilling testimony that the prosecution wanted to leave ringing in jurors' ears. Like her spouse, Eustis, Sharon Blakely testified to a close association with Wayne Williams. Among other things she learned about her inscrutable friend, she said, was that, although pudgy and only five-feet seven-inches tall, Wayne was physically strong. On one visit to her jewelry store, she testified, Wayne picked up a "fairly bulky" jewelry display case with one arm and moved it to another part of the store. It had previously taken two women to move the awkwardly built case.

Ms. Blakely told the jury that after Wayne became a suspect he told her he would confess if the authorities obtained enough evidence to connect him with the string of murders. But then she asked him, "If they get enough evidence, will you confess before you get hurt?" And Wayne said yes.

She said she "respected" Wayne for his knowledge of the entertainment business. But when defense attorney Alvin Binder cross-examined her, he tried to suggest that Sharon Blakely harbored a resentment toward Williams—a sort of professional jealousy. Ms. Blakely said she did not.

"I don't think that people understand that Wayne is weird and he has a split personality. I think Wayne needs help." Binder then asked if she was therefore implying that Williams had killed someone. She replied, "You want me to answer that?"

Binder said, "If you feel that way, tell this jury." Then, apparently realizing that her answer could badly damage his client, Binder quickly reworded the question. "Do you know that he's killed somebody?"

"You know I don't," Ms. Blakely replied.

But on redirect Assistant District Attorney Jack Mallard quickly asked Blakely if she would like to answer Binder's earlier question. The court reporter read back the question: "Are you implying that [Wayne Williams] killed someone?"

A hushed courtroom waited for Sharon Blakely to answer. Looking firmly at the defendant, she responded, "Yes, I do. I really feel that Wayne Williams did kill somebody, and I'm sorry."

On that damning note, the state rested.

With expert trial attorney Tony Axam out of the picture, Wayne Williams's turn before Judge Cooper and the jury would be handled for the most part by

Alvin Binder, a white Mississippi trial lawyer. Mary Welcome still headed the defense team, but she mostly confined her courtroom work to leading friendly character witnesses through soft questioning.

One widely presumed "good" sign for the defense had come rather early in the trial process. It was the position taken by Camille Bell, mother of slain Yusef Bell and STOP leader. Ms. Bell decided to work in behalf of Williams's defense. Among other things, she helped his lawyers and private detectives develop exculpatory evidence. She later sat with them in court, every day, once the trial got under way. Her seemingly contradictory posture, which she characteristically assumed in a rather public and dramatic way, had the additional effect of indicating to the prosecution that, no matter how well they had done their job, a guilty verdict would not be unanimously hailed in the victim community.

But Camille Bell's unorthodox position was really more complicated than her appearing *not to believe* that Wayne Williams was guilty of the double murder charge—or that he had probably killed her own promising nine-year-old. The paradox begged explaining.

Of course, only Camille Bell knew what she truly believed at the time about Wayne Williams's guilt or innocence. Percipient as she was, she must have grasped the nature of the state's evidence against Williams. And she never really said that she fundamentally disagreed with the underlying epistemological assumptions in the state's case. She must have therefore discerned that, although her son's dead body also bore the state's incriminating hair and fiber evidence, the trail linking his murder to Wayne Williams was not as strong as for the twelve victims in question (table 4).

This still played only a minor role in determining her public posture at Williams's trial, however. Far more significant in influencing that posture were the racial, class, and ideological fault lines that had characterized the entire Atlanta episode. Camille Bell had defined herself and the movement she led as oppositionist forces. In opposition, that is, to both the Atlanta racial state and the larger established political-legal order that the racial status quo in Atlanta represented. That status quo had sought to marginalize her and her movement of bereaved ghetto mothers. The last thing anyone should therefore have expected was to find Camille Bell standing in support of the state in its resolution of the Atlanta crisis.

Her parading with Wayne Williams's defense team was thus symbolic representation of something apart from any implicit belief in either his guilt or innocence. Rather, it was an essentialist, visible continuation of a "war of position"—a war that did not stand Camille Bell apart from, or in opposition to, other mothers who didn't mind openly saying that they believed Wayne Williams had killed their sons.

The defense theory was that Wayne Williams was a good boy. He was raised well, probably too well, by overzealous parents. Therefore, he couldn't have committed the kind of terrible crimes for which he was charged. "You don't get a killer from a boy that was raised like that boy was," Binder had told the jury on opening day of the trial.

The defense offered two primary reasons why Wayne Williams was on trial:

1. He was in the wrong place at the wrong time. That is, he was on an Atlanta-area bridge which crossed a river from which bodies of several Atlanta victims had been fetched; he was there late at night and at a time when the FBI had the bridge under heavy surveillance.

2. The authorities, while not necessarily engaging in a frame-up, had nonetheless made a "rush to judgment," choosing to focus all their attention on one convenient suspect simply because they wanted to solve a case that had gone on for far too long.

But the defense claim of a good boy caught in the wrong place didn't exactly rest on solid, incontrovertible grounds. And the judge never allowed the jury to hear evidence the defense wanted to present as indicative of external political pressure to bring a hasty conclusion. The defense had subpoenaed Governor George Busbee and several high-level state and federal law enforcement officials who participated in the June 19, 1981, meeting that led to Williams's arrest. The lawyers' argument was that Williams's arrest was due to the machinations of federal, state, and local law enforcement officials. But testimony from the officials was never heard, as Judge Cooper quashed the subpoenas, ruling that anything they might have had to say would be irrelevant to the criminal facts of the case.

Defense attempts, then, to convince the jury of their client's innocence ultimately rested on doing the textbook thing: raising the element of "reasonable doubt," which the defense set about doing the usual way:

- Argue the defendant's good character

- Challenge prosecution expert testimony

- Challenge the credibility of eyewitnesses

- Let the defendant speak in his own defense

The character witnesses who came to the stand to support Alvin Binder's thesis that "You don't get a killer from a boy that was raised like that boy was" were

Wayne's retired schoolteacher parents; his "main man," Willie Hunter; and two young black women who testified about their knowledge of Wayne's sexual orientation. One of the women admitted that she once had sexual intercourse and a "romantic relationship" with Wayne—an indication, the defense contended, that prosecution hints of dark, predatory homosexuality in their client's background were pure prefabrication.

Homer Williams testified that his son was not a failure, even though Wayne's show business misadventures had driven him into bankruptcy. He spent "quite a bit of time" with his only child when he was growing up, playing games and going on fishing and hunting trips with him. On more than one hunting trip, the elder Williams testified, the two had taken a shotgun he had bought for the boy. But Wayne "lost interest" in hunting because "he didn't kill very much." Like every other parent, he, too, had occasional disagreements with his son. But the two had never fought.

Faye Williams declared from the witness stand, "They have drug my son's reputation through the mud; they have drug my husband's reputation through the mud; and they have drug my reputation through the mud. They have ruined the Williams family. They just lie and lie, but they have not produced evidence that my son is a killer."

The prima facie contention in the state's case was that the deaths of Jimmy Ray Payne and Nathaniel Cater—the only deaths for which Williams was formally charged—could not have resulted from anything other than murder. Williams's attorneys hired two experts whom they called to the stand to challenge that determination.

Dr. Daniel Stowens, a pathologist from Utica, New York, testified that he had read the autopsy reports on Payne and Cater. It was his opinion that Jimmy Payne's death was most likely due to drowning, an improvident conclusion earlier arrived at by the importuned Fulton County medical examiner, Dr. Saleh Zaki. The cause of Nathaniel Cater's death was unknown, with no evidence of foul play, Stowens stated. Stowens also testified that, in his opinion, Cater was dead for seven to ten days, and that if witnesses had testified that they had seen Cater three days before his body was found in the Chattahoochee—as eyewitnesses for the prosecution did—either they were mistaken or the body was not Cater's.

Stowens admitted under cross-examination to his professional inexperience with this sort of thing, however. He had performed only one autopsy on a homicide case in the past fourteen years.

Dr. Maurice Rogev, chief of the medical-legal bureau of the Israeli Army and onetime personal physician to Kenyan president Jomo Kenyatta, also testified that he could not exclude drowning as the cause of death for *both* Cater and Payne. Besides, he had "a feeling that Mr. Cater died of a state which [had] not been adequately explained: his state of an enlarged heart."

And to counter the core of the prosecution's case against their client—the fiber evidence—the defense called to the stand Randall Bresee. Bresee was an instructor of textile sciences at Kansas State University and held, according to Atlanta newspapers, "a doctorate in the study of clothing and textiles." A new member of the defense team, he conceded that he had examined the prosecution's hundreds of fiber slides for only five hours before coming to the witness stand.

Bresee nonetheless argued from the stand that the fiber tests done by the state were insufficient. He testified that he had examined, under a microscope, olive-green carpeting found around the office of defense attorney Mary Welcome. The carpet's fibers were similar to fibers in the green carpeting at the Williams house. He had also bought nine kinds of violet acetate fabric from an Atlanta store and found one type of fiber in each fabric similar to those in Williams's violet and green bedspread. He had even submerged a pillowcase in the Chattahoochee River at the Jackson Parkway bridge "to see if the river was a fiber source." His conclusion was that the river was "full of fibers." He found more than five hundred fibers on the pillowcase after thirty minutes in the river.

If he were comparing fibers to determine which fibers came from the same source, Bresee said, he would have conducted at least eight different lab tests, including use of a laser light technology he had himself been working on. Relying mostly on high-resolution microscope examinations, as was his sense of what the state had done, was not enough.

The prosecution was not the least bit impressed. Bresee was no expert, they contended. In fact, he wasn't even a "true" scientist, since he received his doctorate from a school of home economics. "I'm not going to ask you any questions about baking pies right now," prosecutor Gordon Miller remarked before cross-examining Bresee.

Defense lawyer Alvin Binder was known for the tough, unforgiving, and sarcastic cross-examinations he used in challenging the credibility of state witnesses. Early in the trial, Commissioner Lee Brown had given testimony concerning potential damage done to the case by the media's reporting, in February 1981, of fibers being recovered from victims' bodies. Binder asked

Brown if he was responsible for setting up "the little shacks or houses with little blue lights on top." Binder was referring to several mini stations that Atlanta police had set up downtown as part of their response to the upsurge in crime in 1979.

When Brown said he did not understand the question, Binder shot out, "You do understand English, don't you?"

"I have for a number of years," Brown shot back. The commissioner at least held his ground. But the white Mississippian's attack on the city's demure and highly regarded black official could hardly have won points with the mostly black jury.

The defense produced two witnesses whose testimony they thought would cast doubt on a key prosecution claim: that in the early morning hours of May 22, 1981, an Atlanta police recruit, Robert Campbell, heard the sound of Nathaniel Cater's body being dumped into the Chattahoochee River.

Two former Atlanta police recruits testified that during frequent bull sessions fellow recruit Freddie Jacobs (whom Campbell had radioed the moment he heard the alleged splash) had talked with them a lot about his bridge detail. Jacobs had told them that sometimes, especially after a couple of beers, while down on the riverbank, in the stillness of pitch-black Georgia nights, he and the other recruits often saw ghosts—"hazy white" figures dancing on top of the water.

So, not unlike his partner, Campbell could either have been "under the influence" or hallucinating when he heard, or thought he heard, a loud splash in the Chattahoochee River.

Williams's defense team figured that an effective way (more so than perhaps his parents' own testimony) to show that Wayne developed as a normal child was to have their client testify in his own defense. Reporters agreed that, throughout the almost two months of testimony, the defendant had done a flawless job of keeping his cool. He seemed engrossed in the trial, busily filling page after page of a yellow legal pad, tearing off small portions of what he had written and handing them to his attorneys, who would often use the items in cross-examination.

On Tuesday, February 22, it was Wayne's turn to convince the jury that he didn't have the temperament, background, or stomach to commit murder and that he couldn't possibly have hoisted dead bodies his size or larger and tossed them over shoulder-high bridge railings.

Under comfortable lead questioning from his attorney, Wayne seemed to be making the point. He followed his mother's four-hour testimony on the witness stand, spending several more hours portraying himself as a soft-spoken but confident man who was at peace with himself, despite his eight-month confinement in the county jail.

Defense attorney Alvin Binder asked him, "Have you ever taken your hands and put them around anybody's neck and choked them to death?"

"Never."

"Have you ever taken a rope and put that rope around somebody's neck and squeezed it until they were dead?"

"No, sir."

At one point, after asking the defendant if he knew karate, Binder had Williams walk over to the jury box. "Boy," Binder instructed, "show the jury your hands." Binder then invited the jurors, who were watching attentively, to inspect his client's hands. Two women and one man on the jury touched the defendant's hands while the others looked on.

After Williams made it back to his seat on the witness stand, Binder said to him: "Look at the jury, and you tell me whether or not you are a homosexual or have any sexual hangups."

"There ain't no way I'm no homosexual," Williams said, shaking his head. "I'll put it like this. I don't have no grudge against them, as long as they keep their hands to theirselves, stay away from me, I'm alright, but don't come near me."

Williams also denied making derogatory comments about fellow blacks, although he admitted to using the word *nigger*. "It isn't derogatory in some respects if a black person uses it to each other," he said, "but if a white person uses it to me, I take offense." He harbored no grudge against anybody, he said.

If Wayne had been acting according to script during lead questioning from his attorney, then he must have departed from the script during cross-examination from the assistant district attorney. Jack Mallard had earned a reputation for being one of the most effective criminal trial tacticians in the state. Nicknamed "Blood" by his associates, he was known to combine a steady, plodding style of questioning with down-home language (he was raised in rural Georgia) to appeal to jurors. A twenty-year veteran of the Fulton County district attorney's office, Mallard had "earned his spot at the head of the prosecution table" in the Williams case "through pure experience and skillful preparation," wrote the *Atlanta Constitution*'s Kevin Sack (1982).

Mallard's style contrasted sharply with the flamboyance of defense attorneys Mary Welcome and Alvin Binder. But, in his own toiling, insistent manner, Mallard seemed always to get the job done: that of tripping up the accused.

Under Mallard's cross-examination, Williams's composure weakened. What emerged, much to the prosecution's delight, was a belligerent, warring persona.

Mallard took Williams back over familiar ground, in a deliberate attempt to show inconsistencies in the defendant's stories. He went over with Williams his reason for being on the Jackson Parkway bridge, his explanation for what seemed to officers observing him that night as peculiar driving, the stories he had given the FBI under questioning at the FBI's Atlanta office, his views on race, and the "news conference" he had held in his home. When Williams indicated he was having trouble remembering details of what he had said in the past on these and other matters, Mallard suggested it was because he had made the whole thing up. He would have remembered the truth.

Mallard ended the first day of cross-examination by asking Williams if the scratches on his body were sustained as he choked the life out of his victims. "Isn't it true that, while you were choking them to death, with the last breath they were scratching your arms and face?"

"No."

"Did you experience any panic ... during the time you were killing these victims?"

"Sir, I'm about as guilty as you are," Williams shot back, adding a "challenge" to Mallard to find any scratches on his body in front of the jury.

On the second day of cross-examination, Williams became even testier. He snapped at Mallard, calling the assistant district attorney a "fool" and FBI agents who interviewed him "two of the main goons." He accused the prosecution of trying to make him fit an FBI profile of a killer, something he was not going to help them do. At one point, Williams's combativeness brought defense attorney Alvin Binder scurrying to the witness stand, apparently to try and calm his client—which suggested that Williams's behavior might have been a surprise to his lawyers.

Mallard recalled to Williams that while in jail he had called not only District Attorney Lewis Slaton and members of the media but also GBI Inspector Robbie Hamrick. Mallard asked Williams if he remembered making the calls.

"What's that got to do with anything?" asked Williams.

Mallard asked Williams again if he made the calls.

"Why don't you answer some of my questions?" Williams demanded, prompting Judge Cooper to instruct the defendant to answer the questions put to him.

Things went on like this the entire time Jack Mallard and Wayne Williams confronted each other. In the end, Mallard seemed pleased that he had accomplished his objective: to reveal that "other side" of Wayne Williams to the jury.

In redirect, and ultimately in their closing arguments, the defense sought to rehabilitate their client by reemphasizing that a boy raised the way Wayne was could not have gotten into the kind of trouble the state said he was in. Rather, their client was the misunderstood victim in the prosecution's chain of circumstances.

But in his summation to the jury, Jack Mallard painted a different picture of Wayne Williams. Beneath the defendant's entrepreneurial, whiz-kid veneer lurked a "mad-dog" killer with a dual personality. He compared Williams to Idi Amin, the Ugandan strongman who was hell-bent on annihilating his own people in the 1970s.

Ten minutes after convening, jurors chose Sandra W. Laney, a thirty-four-year-old cable market planner for the Atlanta office of Western Electric, to be jury forewoman. That first evening of deliberations—Friday, February 26, 1982—the jury concentrated on the "numerous lies and inconsistencies in Williams's story," four jurors would later tell reporters (*AJ* 1982). They doubted, most pointedly, Williams's account of the critical bridge incident and the existence of Cheryl Johnson, whose address Williams claimed he was looking for before he was stopped.

The next morning, jurors focused on the disparate evidence concerning the date of purchase for the critical carpet in the Williams home. Wayne's mother had testified that she purchased the carpet in 1968. Prosecution evidence showed that her Luxaire "English Olive" carpet was not manufactured until 1971—which perhaps was the single most important detail in identifying the source of the state's incriminating fibers.

Basing their discussions primarily on testimony of the prosecution's expert witnesses, whom they thought "credible," jurors said they then zeroed in on the fiber evidence presented by the FBI's Harold Deadman and the GBI's Larry Peterson. "We didn't consider the individual fibers, but the grouping of fibers," one juror later said. "The chances that someone else, other than Wayne Williams, would have had the same fibers were pretty slim" (*AJ* 1982).

Of the two murders for which Williams was formally charged, jurors said they dealt with Nathaniel Cater's first, "because there was more evidence on him, and Williams' story just didn't jell." By early afternoon their discussions on the Cater case were going smoothly, and a consensus seemed imminent. But the lack of believable *eyewitness* testimony in the other principal case—that of twenty-one-year-old Jimmy Payne—proved a sticking point and divided the jury at first. They agreed, however, that the prosecution had presented strong incriminating fiber evidence in the Payne case.

They decided to dismiss evidence concerning a motive or method in the killings. According to one juror: "If the prosecution couldn't answer those questions, we couldn't. We were more concerned with why Williams was lying." They also dismissed the body of evidence introduced in the ten other slayings for which Williams was not charged but officially implicated, and concentrated instead on the Cater and Payne cases.

After lunch, the jury devoted considerable attention to Williams's demeanor on the witness stand. Jurors later said they found his temper revealing and, according to one female juror, his "smart-aleck remarks" alienating. (For instance, when asked why he was on the Jackson Parkway bridge, he replied that he was trying "to get to the other side.") "I wanted to see his temper," one juror said. "The defense said he didn't have a temper. But when the prosecution badgered him, he showed his temper of violence" (*AJ* 1982).

After agreeing that since Wayne Williams's arrest no other murders resembling the string of disappearances and killings had occurred in Atlanta, the jury took the first vote. They were unanimous for conviction on the Cater case, because the combination of evidence in that case was "so strong." They spent another hour or so talking about the Payne case, then took a vote. They were split: six voted guilty, two voted not guilty, and four were undecided. A hung decision seemed in the offing. They sat for the next fifteen minutes and stared at each other. Forewoman Laney drafted a note to Judge Clarence Cooper. "We have a verdict on one case. We can't be unanimous on the second case," the note read (*AJ* 1982).

The jurors nonetheless continued to deliberate, always coming back to the credibility of the critical fiber evidence. As evening approached, the four undecided jurors agreed that Williams also was guilty of murdering Jimmy Ray Payne. And one of the two not-guilty holdouts switched to guilty. A written response from the judge, instructing them to "keep on," came just before the other not-guilty holdout changed her vote.

At 6:33 P.M. Saturday, February 27, 1982, Sandra Laney signed the verdicts declaring Wayne Williams guilty of two counts of murder. A court attendant took the document over to Judge Cooper. The jurors then filed out of the courtroom in which they had deliberated for eleven and one-half hours. Back in the jury room, they joined hands and prayed.

At 6:50 P.M. the court clerk read aloud the guilty verdict. Judge Cooper asked Williams if he had any last words before sentencing. "I maintained all along through this trial my innocence and still do so today," he told the judge. "I hold no malice against the jury, the prosecutors, or the court. I hope the person or persons who committed these crimes can be brought to justice. I wanted to see the terror ended. I did not do it."

Williams then stared silently as Judge Cooper sentenced him to two consecutive life sentences, to be served in the Georgia correctional system, for the murders of Nathaniel Cater and Jimmy Ray Payne.

At 7:20 P.M. the jurors filed out of the courtroom. Cooper went into the jury room to thank them and to tell them they had done a good job. He gave them the name of a deputy chief whom they could call if they were harassed and told them police protection would be increased in their neighborhood now that they were returning home.

Outside the courtroom Faye Williams was not as forgiving as her convicted son appeared to have been before Judge Cooper. She called Cooper an Uncle Tom and condemned the jury. "All they wanted to do was go home," she said of the jurors. "It was a setup from beginning to end" (*Time* 1982).

On Monday, March 1, 1982, two days after Williams's guilty verdict, at a news conference held in the converted auto dealership that served as the special Atlanta police task force's headquarters, law enforcement officials declared twenty-three of the twenty-nine listed murders solved.

The preponderance of incriminating forensic evidence, they said, showed that Wayne Williams was responsible for the murders of the following:

- Alfred Evans, thirteen

- Yusef Bell, nine

- Eric Middlebrooks, fourteen

- Christopher Richardson, twelve

- Aaron Wyche, ten

- Anthony Carter, nine

- Earl Terrell, ten

- Clifford Jones, twelve

- Charles Stephens, ten

- Aaron Jackson, nine

- Lubie Geter, fourteen

- Terry Pue, fifteen

- Patrick Baltazar, twelve
- Curtis Walker, thirteen
- Joseph "Jo-Jo" Bell, fifteen
- Timothy Hill, thirteen
- Eddie Duncan, twenty-one
- Larry Rogers, twenty
- Michael McIntosh, twenty-three
- John Porter, twenty-eight
- William Barrett, seventeen
- Jimmy Payne, twenty-one
- Nathaniel Cater, twenty-seven

Atlanta's commissioner of public safety, Lee Brown, announced that the special Atlanta police task force would be going out of business the following week, almost twenty months after it began with the disappearance of nine Atlanta children, six of them having turned up murdered. As he spoke, the commissioner was flanked by Atlanta police chief George Napper, FBI SAC for Atlanta John Glover, Fulton County police chief Clinton Chafin, DeKalb and Rockdale County district attorney Bob Wilson, and Fulton County district attorney Lewis Slaton. Behind them were twenty-four officials who had worked on the special police task force—including the task force's commander, Atlanta deputy chief Morris Redding, and GBI inspector Robbie Hamrick, the task force's investigative coordinator.

The reason for this impressive gathering—on the same stage—of top-flight city, county, state, and federal law enforcement officials was more than mere self-congratulation. Primarily it was to show that, despite myriad criticisms, an unheralded level of unity and cooperation had been achieved by law enforcement working across several jurisdictions to end Atlanta's nightmare.

Of the task force's seven remaining unsolved cases (i.e., six deaths and one disappearance), Brown said they would be turned over to local police departments. The unsolved deaths were of fourteen-year-old Edward Smith, fourteen-year-old Milton Harvey, eleven-year-old Jefferey Mathis, sixteen-year-old Patrick "Pat Man" Rogers, twelve-year-old Angel Lenair, and seven-year-old Latonya Wilson. The unsolved disappearance was of eleven-year-old Darron Glass.

Off the record, Atlanta police believed, however, that Wayne Williams was responsible for the deaths of Smith, Harvey, Mathis, and Rogers—a conclusion they reached based on the similarities between these deaths and the officially cleared twenty-three (see table 4). Investigators did not believe Williams was responsible for the deaths of Angel Lenair or Latonya Wilson. Sources said investigators had suspects, other than Williams, for both cases. But apparently not enough evidence had been gathered against any of the suspects to make an arrest.

Thus ended, as far as the authorities were concerned, the case of Atlanta's missing and murdered youngsters. Atlanta's tragedy had come to a logical end. The mystery was solved.

The *Atlanta Constitution* circumspectly observed the following in its lead editorial:

> The conviction of Wayne Williams for the murder of two young men left many questions unanswered about Atlanta's long night of terror that saw 29 black young people mysteriously slain. [But] a jury deliberated a minimum amount of time before pronouncing Williams guilty. Even before the jury was out, a careful review of the evidence by any unbiased person left little room for doubt. Wayne Williams was guilty. The evidence, albeit circumstantial, pointed to him. The jury concluded that, and so did nearly every seasoned courtroom observer who sat through the trial. (*AC* 1982)

Epilogue

Within the predominantly black sides of Atlanta, reaction to Williams's guilty verdict was mixed, if not muddled. Folks were willing to concede that, true enough, no killings resembling those on the Atlanta special police task force list had occurred during the six months that Wayne Williams had been confined or while he was on trial. Still, as the *Atlanta Voice*'s Harvey Gates (1982) put it, Williams's guilty verdict left local blacks in a "quandary."

The problem that many poor and working-class black Atlantans had with the verdict was not so much disbelief in the defendant's guilt—nor indeed that "one of their own" had committed the terrible crimes. It was the unconventional and, for them, the ultimately unconvincing way that Williams's guilt was "proved."

The city and state, folks in the "hood" were saying, wanted to get back to business as usual. With the business of Atlanta being so highly dependent on favorable impressions of race in the political and cultural workings of the city, ruling elites badly needed a quick and finite closure to the tragedy. And what better way to accomplish this than to "pile" the string of slayings of black Atlanta youngsters on the shoulders of an also relatively poor young black man, "who will get," as Harvey Gates so shrewdly put it, "no more punishment" for killing twenty-three of the Atlanta victims "than for killing two."

Folks in the street were willing to accept the possibility that Wayne Williams was indeed Atlanta's "mad-dog" serial killer, as the prosecution wanted them to believe. The proposition that he was a vicious murderer was not one that folks flat out rejected. But they wanted strong conventional proof. According to Gates, if Williams had "confessed, we would all accept it. If someone had seen him choking a victim, we would all accept it. If someone had witnessed him throwing a body in the river, we would all accept it. But no such evidence exists or if it does, we have not been told" (Gates 1982).

But overwhelming *physical* evidence indicating that Wayne Williams was guilty did indeed exist, despite a slew of persistent, strident voices to the contrary.[1] An approach to the evaluation and analysis of that evidence—one used for at least a hundred years to condemn as well as to set free suspects—pointed to Williams's involvement in the murder of at least twenty-three of the listed twenty-nine Atlanta victims.

True, no one saw him kill anybody. But then, few successful homicide prosecutions have involved an eyewitness to the actual murder—except, perhaps, in cases of fatal shootouts with the police or of a gun holdup gone awry.

Even more infrequent have been convictions based on the defendant's admission of the crime. Yet neither has caused any large-scale public disbelief in jury convictions of murder suspects.

Most homicide convictions have resulted from the state's convincingly piecing together the various corroborative material elements in the execution of the crime. These have generally included the following:

- opportunity on the part of the defendant to commit the crime
- ballistic evidence relating to either the firing or flight of an ammunition in effecting the crime
- conventional forensic evidence that places the defendant's fingerprints at the scene of the crime or on the murder weapon
- more technologically advanced forensic evidence that places the defendant's blood, hair, or semen (or all three) at the scene of the crime
- an explicit or implicit motive on the part of the defendant for committing the crime

Williams had the opportunity to murder the Atlanta victims. His primary activity, such as there was, involved random contacts with wandering young men and boys. And for at least one of the homicides for which he was indicted, that of Nathaniel Cater, Williams was unable to give a coherent, verifiable account of his whereabouts during the approximate time of the murder.

Several eyewitnesses saw, and others knew firsthand of, several victims interacting—if but fleetingly—with Williams. He associated with the youths under the pretext that he would make them musical "stars."

Only one Atlanta victim, Edward Smith, had died of gunshot wounds. However, investigators apparently did not seek to develop any significant ballistic evidence surrounding his death.

FBI records indicated that Williams's fingerprints were on items in Cater's hotel room and that several victims' fingerprints matched prints found in the area of the Williams home occupied by Wayne. On the night he was stopped, Williams had in his car an item that medical examiners had previously identified as the kind of object used to strangle several victims. On the front seat of

Wayne's station wagon was a two-foot nylon cord.

In addition to the extensive fiber trail, blood and hair analysis connected Williams to victims' bodies and to a number of crime scenes.

The only not-quite-as-clear item in the case against Williams is the matter of motive. What exactly drove him to seek out and murder young black men and boys? The pattern to the Atlanta murders indicated that they were the handiwork of a serial killer. Therefore, the factors that motivated Williams to murder his victims were of the same twisted, pathological sort that have been associated with serial killers generally—from "Jack the Ripper," who murdered a string of London's East End prostitutes in 1888, to Ted Bundy, who murdered some twenty-eight women and girls as he traveled across the United States in the 1970s.

Serial killers have all been sociopaths. That is, individuals who displayed little or no regard for societal norms, had little or no conscience, and lacked remorse and a capacity for caring.

Sociopaths, according to the psychological literature (e.g., Jung 1953, 1968, 1975), are manipulative and deceitful; they totally disregard the feelings of others; they are amoral and ruthless in personal dealings; they lie incessantly; they are "voluble and verbally facile" (e.g., using technical terms or jargon to impress); and they blame others for their actions.

Criminologists (e.g., Holmes and De Burger 1988; Levin and Fox 1985) have suggested that serial killers have been primarily motivated by the act of killing. Behavioral researchers have indeed been hard-pressed to find any *extrinsic* rationale governing the structure of the serial killer's acts—for example, material or even psychological gain, or "profit," from the victim's death. Rather, they have wanted only to kill again.

Every serial killer has in some way been driven by his or her private demon: the "thing" that inevitably "pushed them over the edge." Bundy attributed his to pornography. In an interview with right-wing Christian radio broadcaster James Dobson, hours before his execution in January 1989, Bundy said he was a normal person who led a normal life, except for that small, hidden segment of his life that was "overwhelmed with this brutal urge to kill." A lifelong addiction to pornography, Bundy told Dobson, motivated him to act violently toward women.

Henry Lucas, who confessed to killing more than one hundred victims in several states between 1976 and 1982, said he harbored a "real hatred" for the women hitchhikers he had killed because they were like prostitutes. "As a child, Lucas remembered having to watch his prostitute mother having sex with men and how poorly he was treated by her" (Hickey 1991: 186).

What was Wayne Williams's particular demon? We probably will never know. He has steadfastly insisted on his innocence in the Atlanta murders. Coincidentally, in doing so he has not been unlike another well-known convicted serial killer, John Wayne Gacey, who was executed by the state of Illinois for murdering some thirty-three young males in the Chicago area in the late 1970s. Gacey denied any involvement in the murders and suggested that someone else must have placed the bodies of twenty-seven victims in the crawl space of his home while he was at work.

Williams's selection of children—or men with visible childlike characteristics—as his victims demonstrated a need to control and to have power over them. Sexual violation of the victims seemed not to have been part of his pattern, unlike Dean Corll and Elmer Wayne Henley (and Gacey), who sexually tortured, before killing, the seventeen boys they had picked up off Houston area streets between 1970 and 1973.

None of the listed Atlanta victims, including the two girls whose murders were not linked to Williams, appeared to investigators to have been sexually abused. Experts advised, however, that even though the bodies of the Atlanta victims showed no visible signs of sexual trauma, this ought not to have ruled out a sexual demon in the killer's psyche. Many sexually driven serial killers have found sexual fulfillment, or release, in the act of killing—as did the "Hillside Stranglers," Kenneth Bianchi and Angelo Buono, who systematically abducted and then sexually tortured nine Los Angeles area women and girls before slaying them.

One youthful witness in Williams's trial did in fact testify that the defendant had picked him up and tried to fondle him in his car.

But Williams's principal demon, the one that kept him driving around Atlanta in search of victims, sometimes for hundreds of miles in a single day, was his hatred of poor black male children—whom he saw as street kids. In gratuitous conversations with whites whose approbation he courted, and with "important" blacks like record producers, Williams often used the terms "leechers" and "prostitutes" to describe black Atlanta youngsters. He saw himself fulfilling a mission to rid Atlanta streets of blacks who "reminded him of his own standing" (Hickey 1991: 64).

Unlike Harvey Gates and other skeptics, several mothers of victims whose murders were not included in the "true bill" indictment of Williams agreed with the Atlanta authorities that he had killed their sons. Toward the end of the trial, the *Atlanta Constitution*'s Bob Dart (1982) overheard Helen Pue, mother of Terry

Pue, tell Camille Bell outside Judge Clarence Cooper's courtroom, "I believe he killed my boy. I sure do." And Willie Mae Mathis stood outside the courtroom one day and proclaimed that Williams had also killed her son, Jefferey.

In the end, the story of the Atlanta tragedy was of youngsters whose perilous rites of passage and awful circumstance, in a city of great abundance and seemingly perpetual wealth, brought them into dreadful collision with the living, terrifying face of evil—and to an awful end.

Appendixes

Notes

Bibliography

Index

Appendix A

Special Police Task Force List of Atlanta's Missing and Murdered

Victim	Characteristics	Last Seen	Cause of Death
Edward Smith	14 yrs. old 5'4" 125 lbs.	Saturday July 21, 1979 12 A.M.	.22 gunshot wound
Alfred Evans	13 yrs. old 5'4" 87 lbs.	Wednesday July 25, 1979 3–4 P.M.	Probable asphyxiation by strangulation
Milton Harvey	14 yrs. old 5' 95 lbs.	Tuesday Sept. 4, 1979 10:30 A.M.	Undetermined
Yusef Bell	9 yrs. old 4'7" 65 lbs.	Sunday Oct. 21, 1979 5:30 P.M.	Asphyxiation by manual strangulation

Appendix A

Victim	Characteristics	Last Seen	Cause of Death
Angel Lenair 	12 yrs. old 5'4" 90 lbs.	Tuesday Mar. 4, 1980 7:30 P.M.	Asphyxiation by ligature strangulation
Jefferey Mathis 	11 yrs. old 4'8" 71 lbs.	Tuesday Mar. 11, 1980 7 P.M.	Undetermined
Eric Middlebrooks 	14 yrs. old 4'10" 88 lbs.	Sunday May 18, 1980 10:30 P.M.	Blunt trauma to head
Christopher Richardson	12 yrs. old 5' 85 lbs.	Monday June 9, 1980 1:30 P.M.	Undetermined

List of Atlanta's Missing and Murdered

Victim	Characteristics	Last Seen	Cause of Death
Latonya Wilson 	7 yrs. old 4' 60 lbs.	Sunday June 22, 1980 early morning	Undetermined
Aaron Wyche 	10 yrs. old 4'10" 55 lbs.	Monday June 23, 1980 6 P.M.	Asphyxiation from broken neck, from fall
Anthony Carter 	9 yrs. old 4'5" 73 lbs.	Sunday July 6, 1980 1:30 A.M.	Multiple stab wounds
Earl Terrell 	10 yrs. old 4'7" 80 lbs.	Wednesday July 30, 1980 3:30 P.M.	Undetermined

Appendix A

Victim	Characteristics	Last Seen	Cause of Death
Clifford Jones 	12 yrs. old 4'11" 87 lbs.	Wednesday Aug. 20, 1980 8:00 P.M.	Asphyxiation by ligature strangulation
Darron Glass 	11 yrs. old 4'9" 75 lbs.	Sunday Sept. 14, 1980 5:30 P.M.	Still missing
Charles Stephens 	10 yrs. old 5' 120 lbs.	Thursday Oct. 9, 1980 4:30 P.M.	Asphyxiation, manner undetermined
Aaron Jackson	9 yrs. old 4'8" 84 lbs.	Saturday Nov. 1, 1980 7 A.M.	Asphyxiation by suffocation

Victim	Characteristics	Last Seen	Cause of Death

Patrick Rogers

| | 16 yrs. old
145 lbs. | Monday
Nov. 10, 1980
7:30 A.M. | Blunt trauma to head |

Lubie Geter

| | 14 yrs. old
130 lbs. | Saturday
Jan. 3, 1981
2:30 P.M. | Asphyxiation by manual
strangulation |

Terry Pue

| | 15 yrs. old
5'5"
105 lbs. | Thursday
Jan. 22, 1981
2 P.M. | Asphyxiation by ligature
strangulation |

Patrick Baltazar

| | 12 yrs. old
125 lbs. | Friday
Feb. 6, 1981
5:30 P.M. | Asphyxiation by ligature
strangulation |

Appendix A

Victim	Characteristics	Last Seen	Cause of Death
Curtis Walker 	13 yrs. old 5' 75 lbs.	Thursday Feb. 19, 1981 4:00 P.M.	Asphyxiation by strangulation
Joseph Bell 	15 yrs. old 5'2" 100 lbs.	Monday Mar. 2, 1981	Asphyxiation, manner undetermined
Timothy Hill 	13 yrs. old 5'3" 95 lbs.	Sunday Mar. 15, 1981 afternoon	Asphyxiation, manner undetermined
Eddie Duncan	21 yrs. old 5'9" 140 lbs.	Friday Mar. 20, 1981	Undetermined

Victim	Characteristics	Last Seen	Cause of Death

Larry Rogers

20 yrs. old
5'1"
110 lbs.

Monday
Mar. 30, 1981
afternoon

Asphyxiation by
strangulation

Michael McIntosh

23 yrs. old
5'3"
116 lbs.

About Apr. 1,
1981

Asphyxiation, manner
undetermined

Jimmy Payne

21 yrs. old
5'1"
137 lbs.

Wednesday
Apr. 22, 1981
10:30 A.M.

Asphyxiation, manner
undetermined

William Barrett

17 yrs. old
5'4"
124 lbs.

Monday
May 11, 1981
6:00 P.M.

Asphyxiation by
strangulation

Victim	Characteristics	Last Seen	Cause of Death
Nathaniel Cater	27 yrs. old 5'10" 146 lbs.	Thursday May 21, 1981 morning	Asphyxiation, manner undetermined
John Porter*	28 yrs. old	Early April 1981	Multiple stab wounds

*Added at trial of Wayne Williams.

Appendix B

Special Atlanta Police Task Force Guidelines

Because of the multijurisdictional involvement in the cases of the missing and murdered children, law enforcement agencies in the [Atlanta] metropolitan area have held meetings to develop guidelines designed to ensure maximum cooperation and coordination. At a meeting held March 10, 1981, the following were agreed upon:

1. Organizationally, the Task Force shall remain under the control and command of the Atlanta Department of Public Safety, subject to all rules, regulations, procedures, and directives that govern that department.

2. The commander of the Task Force shall be appointed by and report to the Atlanta Commissioner of Public Safety.

3. All personnel assigned to the Task Force shall be under the supervision of the commander of the Task Force.

4. The commander of the Task Force shall have the responsibility of coordinating all aspects of the investigation of cases assigned to the Task Force, regardless of the law enforcement jurisdiction in which the body or evidence is located.

5. Members of the Task Force, by this agreement, are authorized to cross and work in different law enforcement and judicial jurisdictions for the purpose of collecting and coordinating evidence in (including crime scenes) and conducting investigations of the cases assigned to the Task Force.

6. The specific assignment of personnel to the Task Force from another jurisdiction shall be the result of an agreement reached by the Atlanta Public Safety Commissioner and the head of the respective agency involved.

7. All personnel assigned to the Task Force shall work under the direction of the Task Force managers and supervisors.

8. All personnel assigned to the Task Force shall be detached from their respective jurisdictions and shall be assigned on a full-time basis. They shall be utilized as deemed appropriate by the Task Force commander.

Issued by Atlanta Department of Public Safety, March 11, 1981

9. The Task Force commander shall have the authority to remove any person from the Task Force if and when he determines that such removal is in the best interest of the operation of the Task Force. Upon removal, the person shall return to his agency of employment.

10. All agencies agree that no one will make public statements or statements to the news media about any evidence related to the ongoing investigations. The Atlanta Public Safety Commissioner shall be responsible for handling all media matters on behalf of the Task Force.

11. If the body of a Black child under the age of 17 is discovered and evidence suggests that the case is related to the cases under investigation by the Task Force, regardless of jurisdiction, the responsible law enforcement agency shall both immediately secure the crime scene and notify the Task Force commander.

12. The Task Force commander shall have the opportunity for investigating the crime scene in cases defined in 11 above. He shall see that all evidence that is gathered is turned over to an evidence custodian who, in turn, shall immediately transport all evidence to the Georgia State Crime Laboratory.

13. Participating Task Force agencies agree to provide personnel on a temporary basis to assist the Task Force commander in the initial investigation and area search if and when a body is discovered.

14. The Task Force shall coordinate the investigations of all homicides of Black children under the age of 17 if the characteristics of the homicide are similar to the characteristics of the homicides now being investigated by the Task Force and if mutually agreed upon by the Atlanta Public Safety Commissioner and the head of the agency which has jurisdiction over the case.

15. It shall be the responsibility of the Task Force commander to maintain a master file on all cases assigned to the Task Force. He shall make information available to participating agencies when requested by agency coordinator.

16. Each participating agency shall supply the Task Force with all information it has that relates to any case being investigated by the Task Force. To insure that there is no duplication of effort, an agency conducting an independent investigation or investigative activity of such a case will notify the Task Force commander.

17. Participating agencies agree that all medical records, reports from the Georgia State Crime Laboratory, and reports of the medical examiner shall first be sent to the Task Force and that the Task Force shall supply copies to the appropriate agency.

18. The Task Force shall maintain liaison with the respective district attorneys and shall be provided necessary legal advice by the district attorney's office who is responsible for prosecuting a case assigned to the Task Force that rests in his given judicial district.

19. The Atlanta Commissioner of Public Safety shall convene meetings of the agency heads participating in the Task Force. Such meetings shall be designed to keep all members updated on the investigation and to ensure coordination and cooperation. Such meetings shall be confidential.

Presently, the following agencies have assigned investigators to the Special Task Force on Missing and Murdered Children: (1) Atlanta Bureau of Police Services, (2) Clayton County Police Department, (3) Cobb County Police Department, (4) DeKalb County Police Department, (5) East Point Police Department, (6) Fulton County District Attorney's Office, (7) Fulton County Police Department, and (8) Georgia Bureau of Investigation.

All agencies are working toward achieving the single objective of solving the unsolved cases of the missing and murdered children.

Notes

Prologue

1. The white media's generally unsympathetic interpretation of the term hustling would become a hotly contested item in the discourse surrounding the tragedy. As many in Atlanta's poor black community saw it, several of the Atlanta victims were at the time of their disappearance doing nothing terribly different from what many middle-class youngsters, black and white, would have been doing for income.

2. Toni Cade Bambara (1982) gave a whimsical summary of the multiple racialized "theories" purporting to explain the Atlanta youth murders:

> White cops taking licence in Black neighbourhoods again?
>
> The Klan and other Nazi thugs on the rampage again?
>
> Diabolical scientists experimenting on Third World people again?
>
> White avengers of Dewey Baugus, a white child beaten to death in Spring 1979 by, allegedly, Black youths . . . going berserk?
>
> Demonic cultists using human sacrifices?
>
> Porno filmmakers producing "snuff flicks" for export?
>
> A band of child molesters covering their tracks?
>
> New drug forces wiping out the young?
>
> Unreconstructed peckerwoods trying to topple the Black [Atlanta] administration?

3. The public had recently learned of the Tuskegee study, begun in 1932, during which the national Public Health Service, and later the CDC, decided to observe four hundred black men with syphilis without treating them. The subjects, who were recruited from churches and clinics throughout the South, were told only that they had "bad blood." To determine the natural course of syphilis, researchers withheld from the infected men what was then the standard treatment: mercury and arsenic compounds. In 1947, when penicillin was found to be an effective treatment for syphilis, it too was withheld. The study limped along for four decades, until Peter Buxtun, a lawyer who once had been an epidemiologist for the Public Health Service in San Francisco, went public. In July 1972 the media exposed the Tuskegee study, and it was halted immediately.

4. I deliberately use the term *black* throughout this book when referring to Americans of African ancestry because I wanted to capture a key feature of the times: *black* was then the term of political-cultural choice.

5. The black heart man is a phantom figure in Jamaican folklore. He lurks in the thick darkness of placid Caribbean nights, or he hides behind a clump of bushes or creaking bamboo trees that shade deserted, sunbaked country roads on which children walk long miles to and from school. His evil eyes scan the horizon for naughty, runaway children. He snatches them, then cuts out their heart. And he eats it!

1. A City Too Busy to Hate?

1. The expositions were the World's Fair and Great International Cotton Exposition of 1881, the Piedmont States Exposition of 1887, and the Cotton States International Exposition of 1895. It was at the latter, where "Negroes had a building," that Booker T. Washington gave his (in)famous "Atlanta Compromise" speech.

2. The railroads accounted for much of Atlanta's pre–Civil War growth. In the 1840s, three railroads terminated in the dingy northwest Georgia town known as Terminus. Atlanta's founding was therefore a good example of the coming of the industrial revolution to a primarily agricultural region, making it possible for merchants in rapidly developing market towns to trade directly with the North for the first time (Foner 1990; Garret 1974, 1988).

3. C. Wright Mills's (1956) *The Power Elite* was among the most authoritative critiques of elite domination in the American political economy. Yet the disproportionate political-economic power wielded by a mostly East Coast military-industrial elite that Mills examined could not match the absolute domination that Atlanta's business and commercial elite exercised over the city in the years following the end of the First World War through most of the 1960s.

4. Hartsfield was first elected mayor in 1937. He lost a primary battle for reelection in 1941 but regained the mayor's office the following year in a special election. He governed virtually unchallenged until his retirement from active politics in 1961.

5. Allen was arguably more in touch with black issues than Hartsfield was. In his memoirs (1971), as well as in personal conversation, Allen pointed with pride to his participation, as mayor, in a student sit-in at the Atlanta city hall cafeteria, and he noted that he was the only southern mayor to testify before Congress in favor of the 1964 civil rights bill. He regretted authorizing construction of a wall in Atlanta that was meant to restrain "hasty" racial integration.

6. In the last weeks of the campaign, Massell reportedly tried to exploit white fears around the possibility of "radical" civil rights leader Hosea Williams being elected city council president. Massell linked Maynard Jackson with Hosea Williams. His campaign advertisements ran along these lines: "The thought of a Maynard Jackson-Hosea Williams administration is scaring some Atlantans to death. . . . If such a team attempts to lead this city, many blacks and whites alike fear a new trend of flight from Atlanta. They fear an end to progress, an end to opportunity, an end to faith" (Powledge 1973, 29; see also Jamieson 1976).

7. The quotation is from *Atlanta Constitution* columnist Hal Gulliver's retelling of events at a testimonial dinner given in December 1981 in honor of the outgoing mayor and Robert W. Woodruff, "the fellow who built Coca-Cola." When Jackson walked over to Woodruff's table to greet Woodruff and the seated power structure gathering, only the aged Woodruff—who "struggled to his feet with some difficulty"—stood "out of respect to greet the mayor."

8. Power structure members had, in fact, made a calculated decision to stay in the city back when they lost to Massell. "It was as if they had all agreed with a comment made right after the election by an official of the [Atlanta] Chamber of Commerce: 'Let's don't all sit around pouting. I say the economic power structure of this town got the hell beat out of it. Let's go from there'" (Powledge 1973, 29–30).

9. In his study of "racial transition" in Atlanta, Eisinger (1980, 81) quoted one prominent white businessman as saying the following about Jackson's first few months in office: "I'm sure he's being pressured from all sides and he probably feels he's got to relieve the problems of poor blacks. . . . He also wants to consolidate power in the hands of blacks who are running the city. OK, I understand that, but it's scaring the whites."

10. Author Stanley Crouch (1981, 19) quoted a former Jackson official as saying that Eaves had "transferred cops with bad brutality records into jobs like guarding airplane runways and fire stations and made strong efforts to get the community to see the police as public servants, not trigger-happy parts of an occupying force."

2. Two Deaths Against the Backdrop of Racial Troubles

1. The allegation was that Eaves had given the answers to a screening examination to black applicants he wanted to hire.

2. In churches and at rallies, Eaves often would begin speeches with such phrases as "Though my skin is dark and my lips are thick."

3. According to a special series in the *Atlanta Constitution* (1981u), whenever available entry-level jobs were accessible by public transportation, they usually opened up on late-night shifts, when bus service had ceased.

4. So alarming was the problem of "black-on-black crime" that the entire August 1979 issue of *Ebony* (the nation's premier magazine for and about blacks in America) ran a series of articles examining its national implications. See also Headley 1984; Jenkins 1994; and Richie Mann 1993.

3. Where Have All the Children Gone?

1. One of the better-known critics of the official list was ex-Atlanta police officer Chet Dettlinger, who investigated the killings and disappearances independently. In his uneven account of what happened in Atlanta, he attacked the list for (1) the abil-

ity of more activist mothers to get the names of their murdered or missing youngsters on it whereas less visible relatives of other murdered or missing youngsters could not, and (2) imprecise age criteria for victims that allowed names of adult victims to be added without convincing rationale (see Dettlinger and Prugh 1983).

2. Police investigators were not sure that this second body was Evans. "The clothing was similar to that worn by Alfred Evans when he was reported missing, although there was a belt that Lois Evans would later say was not Alfred's. The approximate age, height, and weight were right for Alfred Evans." But when dental charts were compared, there were no similarities, according to Dettlinger and Prugh (1983, 54).

3. In FBI transcriptions, names of FBI agents, witnesses, and suspects other than the person ultimately charged with the Atlanta crimes were systematically blacked out, or "redacted," to use the government's term of art.

4. A Summer of Death

1. Eaves had a regular column in the *Atlanta Voice*. In one column he argued that to combat the climate of "great despair" surrounding the murders, residents should build "organizational strength" and "orchestrate" an "effective campaign" (Eaves 1980).

2. The ex-officers were Mike Edwards, former deputy director of the Atlanta Bureau of Police Services and former commander of its criminal investigation division; Chet Dettlinger, who at one time served as assistant to Atlanta police chiefs John Inman and Reginald Eaves; and W. K. "Jack" Perry, who headed the ABPS's homicide unit before he was suspended from the police force on charges that he had conspired to operate an illegal lottery. The private security analyst was Richard Arena.

3. One of the investigators, Mike Edwards, told writer Steve Oney that the Atlanta police investigations into the murders and disappearances had been sloppy. "We canvassed the neighborhood and discovered that they hadn't even talked to half the people. . . . Then we got a copy of their file on the Mathis case and it was unbelievable. It would say things like, 'We searched the vacant building over on such and such street,' and it wouldn't give the address or any of the specifics" (Oney 1981, 20).

4. STOP's launch pamphlet further stated:
The belief of the committee is that (1) children have a right to the love and concern of every adult in our community; (2) all children deserve an opportunity to grow and develop morally straight and as emotionally stable as possible; (3) all children are our children and therefore, we are responsible for the safety of each of them. With this in mind, we will do our best to create a child-conscious society that shelters, protects, and educates our children, because our children are our future.

5. The Pain of Finding Nothing at All

1. The number of people reported for this first rally varied considerably. The white Atlanta press reported the number at just over two hundred; the local black press held that it was over eight hundred.

2. Commissioner Lee Brown was openly contemptuous of Dettlinger, and he disparaged his idea of a geographic pattern to the abductions and killings. "Anyone can draw a map," Brown said on one occasion.

3. Langford was indicted in 1979 on charges of extortion. He was acquitted on a retrial of all charges, but he stayed out of the limelight until the Saturday searches.

4. West Hunter Street Baptist Church's pastor was the Reverend Ralph Abernathy, a longtime associate of Martin Luther King Jr.

6. Select Outsiders Only

1. In his extensive examination of the FBI's secret file on black American leaders from 1960 to 1970, historian Kenneth O'Reilly (1989) pointed out that the FBI followed black leaders not to protect them but to spy on them.

2. I found puzzling the statement about "political pressure" being attributed to SAC John Glover. Weeks after the tragedy was officially ended, Glover told me that he and other black FBI agents (such as there were) had "badly wanted" the bureau to get involved in the Atlanta cases. They wanted the world, and black Americans in particular, to see that the FBI was a "changed agency," that it was "vastly different from the bad old J. Edgar Hoover days," that it could be "trusted," and that it was interested in bringing relief from things—such as murders—that seemed willfully directed at blacks.

7. "We've Got to End This"

1. Fifteen-year-old Lee Emanuel Gooch was reported missing around the same time, but his case was never assigned to the special task force, as authorities insisted he did not fit the pattern they had detected. He was soon found living with relatives in Florida.

8. Multiple Suspects

1. The group assembled on the city hall steps included city councilwoman Carolyn Long Banks and state representatives Tyrone Brooks, Bob Holmes, John White, Billy McKinney, Lorenzo Benn, and David Scott.

9. The Politics of Federal Aid

1. Letters to the editor from suburban addresses in that same edition of the *Post* took the same position against Barry. One letter stated, "As a Jew . . . , I was hurt and angered by the mayor's hostile comments. Beyond that, I am confused as to why the mayor finds it constructive to address grievances of blacks by offending and instilling resentment of Jews."

2. The bat patrols enjoyed a type of community legitimacy not given other indigenous but uninvited anticrime groups—such as New York's Guardian Angels, a divi-

sion of which arrived in Atlanta saying they had come to protect inner-city neighborhoods from the Atlanta killer.

14. The Media Blitzkrieg and Developing Evidence

1. As expected, the appearance of the FBI having its own list caused a furor in investigative circles, eliciting in the end a disclaimer from SAC John Glover: "Our list
is consistent with the task force list, so we have no list other than the task force list"
(*AC* 1981m).

2. Many prosecutors *and* defense attorneys (particularly in sexual assault cases) have
held that scientific circumstantial evidence is in many instances better than direct evidence, since the former does not rely on one set of eyes. A case in point was an Illinois appellate judge's reversal in 1995 of a 1983 jury conviction of two indigent men,
Rolando Cruz and Alejandro Hernandez, for the rape and murder of Jeanine Nicarico,
a white ten-year-old who had lived in a Chicago suburb. The two men were awaiting
execution at the time of the reversal. The judge agreed with the defendants' attorneys
(and a supportive activist community) that the state had *no physical or circumstantial evidence* linking either man to the crime.

15. The D.A. Makes a Highly Political Arrest

1. Seeking the death penalty tended to give prosecutors a better chance of finding
a jury favorable to conviction, because the state could automatically disqualify potential jurors who opposed capital punishment. On the other hand, Fulton County
prosecutors knew that if they were to seek the death penalty for Williams, the defense
likely would stall a trial date and ask the higher courts to rule on whether the death
penalty was applicable in the case.

16. Pretrial Activity

1. U.S. authorities also were investigating to determine whether a local publisher's
advertising solicitations on behalf of STOP were fraudulent.

2. Less than a year prior to taking on Williams's case, Mary Welcome had run unsuccessfully for the post of city council president.

3. In an Atlanta Bar Association poll of members, conducted just before the judicial
elections, Cooper came in dead last of the four candidates in contention for the superior court seat.

4. Specifically, Williams said to FBI agent Gregg Gilliland, "This must be about those
boys."

5. The gambit of asking for two separate trials could have put Williams's life at risk,
because in Georgia law a conviction in one homicide case automatically permitted
punishment by death for a second.

6. A surreptitiously earned $2,000 for an interview that Williams gave *US* magazine from inside his jail cell did manage to help out a bit—but only a small bit—with his legal expenses.

17. The Trial No One Wanted to Miss

1. The prosecution said that Williams often left victims' clothing lying around in his house (including the items one eyewitness reportedly saw in his bathroom) or in his car before discarding them.

2. Throughout the Atlanta investigations and trial of Wayne Williams, Lois Evans held that the state had erroneously identified a set of remains as her son's.

Epilogue

1. Eight years after Williams's conviction, a team of celebrity trial lawyers—including William Kunstler and Alan Dershowitz—demanded that Williams be given a new trial. They had some "newly uncovered documents" consisting of "revealing" police notes taken during the GBI-led inquiry into local Klan activities that were coterminous with the Atlanta murders. In one of the documents, an informant described a Klansman's threat to kill Lubie Geter. The informant said the Klansman was "furious" because the boy had bumped his go-cart into the Klansman's parked car. "See that little black bastard," a purported memo quoted the Klansman as saying to the informant about fourteen-year-old Lubie. "I'm going to get him. I'm gonna kill him. I'm gonna choke the black bastard to death" (quoted in *USA Today* 1985; see also Fischer 1991; Keating and Cooper 1986). The purported threat was made just before Christmas 1980. Lubie Geter disappeared on January 3, 1981; his body was found February 5, 1981. The informant also said that the Klansman boasted that the Klan was trying to create an uprising in Atlanta by killing one black child a month "until things blew up." These were important items that a jury sitting in judgment of Wayne Williams should have heard, his star-studded crew of defense lawyers in waiting contended.

Bibliography

The following abbreviations are used in parenthetical citations in text for works in the bibliography.

AC   *Atlanta Constitution*
AJ   *Atlanta Journal*
AJ&C   *Atlanta Journal and Constitution* (combined Sunday edition)
AV   *Atlanta Voice*
FBI   Federal Bureau of Investigation
NYT   *New York Times*
RCP   Revolutionary Communist Party
STOP   Committee to Stop Children's Murders
UYAC   United Youth Adult Conference
WP   *Washington Post*
WSJ   *Wall Street Journal*

Adair Mortgage Company. 1976. "Amazing Atlanta." Atlanta.
Adler, Patricia A., and Peter Adler. 1987. *Membership Roles in Field Research*. Newbury Park, Calif.: Sage.
Allen, Frederick. 1981a. "A Complicated Man, He's Too Easy to Mock." *AC*, April 28.
———. 1981b. "Aroma of Politics in Williams' Arrest." *AJ&C*, June 28, 11-C.
Allen, Ivan, Jr. 1971. *Mayor: Notes on the Sixties*. New York: Simon and Schuster.
Associated Press. 1981. "Killing of Atlanta's Black Children Is Racist Violence, Kremlin Charges." March 15.
Atlanta. 1977. "Viewing 'Porn' and Politics and the Mayor's Tough Mary." May.
Atlanta Chamber of Commerce. 1981. "Forward Atlanta." March.
———. 1984. "Atlanta Operations: Fortune 500 Industrial and Service Firms." August.
Atlanta City Government. 1981. "Mayor's Action Conference on Poverty/Action Plan to Combat Poverty in Atlanta." Report of Mayor's Poverty Task Force. Department of Budget and Planning. Atlanta.
Atlanta Constitution. 1979. "Stranger Kills Secretary on Peachtree Street." October 18.
———. 1980a. "Police Draw Flak in City's String of Child Killings." August 24.

———. 1980b. "Psychic Will Try to Solve Child Slayings." September 22.

———. 1980c. "Psychic Help." September 23.

———. 1980d. "Child-Safety Program Is Underway." October 14.

———. 1980e. "Psychic Coming to Seek Slayer." October 15.

———. 1980f. "Remains Are Identified as Those of Wilson Girl." October 20.

———. 1980g. "For Team No. 5, Finding a Body Is as Painful as Finding Nothing." October 20.

———. 1980h. "Whites, Blacks Uniting in Search for Children." October 20.

———. 1980i. "Psychic Sees Respite in Children Slayings." October 22.

———. 1980j. "GBI Probing Activities of Georgia Klan." October 31.

———. 1980k. "Clearing the Air." Editorial, December 5.

———. 1981a. "Where Are the Children?" Editorial, January 27.

———. 1981b. "Eaves Comments on Slayings 'Not Helpful.'" January 30.

———. 1981c. "Thurmond Asks Federal Funds to Aid Child-Deaths Probe." February 25.

———. 1981d. "Federal Funds Needed." Editorial, February 26.

———. 1981e. "Many Atlantans Wonder: Why Here?" March 15.

———. 1981f. "Black Politicians Launch Attack on 'Profiteers.'" March 26.

———. 1981g. "CORE Claims to Know Killer." April 23.

———. 1981h. "Black Man's Body Found in River." May 25.

———. 1981i. "Atlanta Police Assign Two More Cases to Task Force." May 26.

———. 1981j. "'Arrest Is Not Imminent,' Slaton Reports." June 9.

———. 1981k. "Williams Asks Court to Limit Publicity." June 13.

———. 1981l. "Kids' Summer Program Gets $1.16 Million Grant." June 16.

———. 1981m. "Decision Is Delayed on Williams and Police." June 17.

———. 1981n. "For the Defense." June 20.

———. 1981o. "Williams Spent Life on Fringes." June 22.

———. 1981p. "Kin of Slaying Victims Express Hope about Arrest." June 22.

———. 1981q. "Thanks for the Help." Editorial, June 22.

———. 1981r. "Williams: Man Hunting for Limelight." June 28.

———. 1981s. "City's Grace under Stress Laid to Black Power Base." July 15.

———. 1981t. "Suspect Proves an Enigma to Friends and Enemies Alike." July 31.

———. 1981u. "Black and Poor in Atlanta." Editorial, October 19.

———. 1982. "'Case of the Century.'" Editorial, March 1.

Atlanta Daily World. 1981. "Committee to Stop Children Murders Reports $40,000." July 3.

Atlanta Journal. 1979a. "Crime Up 26 Percent in Last Six Months." July 19.

———. 1979b. "'Summit' Focuses on Police." July 19.

———. 1980. "GBI Joins Probe of Ku Klux Klan's Activity in Dixie." October 31.

———. 1982. "Williams Jurors Prayed, Cried When Verdicts Were Reached." March 2.

Atlanta Journal and Constitution. 1965. "What Atlanta's Prosperity Means to You." Supplement, October 17.

———. 1979. "Soaring Homicide Rate Puzzles Officials." June 30.

———. 1980a. "Atlanta Police, Firemen Get PR Consultant." March 9.

———. 1980b. "3,000 Searchers Join in Child Slayings Hunt." October 26.

———. 1981. "Atlanta's Tragedy: An Update." June 28.

Atlanta Voice. 1979. "Black Community Distressed over Death of Yusef Bell." November 17.

———. 1980a. "We Endorse Clarence Cooper for Superior Court Judge." July 2.

———. 1980b. "Try to Make Your Child Safe." July 19.

———. 1980c. "Marchers Rally in 'The Save the Children' Pilgrimage." October 11–17.

———. 1981. "Who Determines Public Accountability?" Editorial, February 21–27.

Baldwin, James. 1985. *The Evidence of Things Not Seen*. New York: Holt, Rinehart and Winston.

Bambara, Toni Cade. 1982. "What's Happening in Atlanta?" *Race and Class* 24 (2): 111–24.

Baylor, Ronald H. 1996. *Race and the Shaping of Twentieth-Century Atlanta*. Chapel Hill: University of North Carolina Press.

Best, Joel. 1987. "Rhetoric in Claims-Making: Constructing the Missing Children Problem." *Social Problems* 34 (2): 101–21.

Bisbing, Richard E. 1985. "Human Hair in a Forensic Perspective." Proceedings of the International Symposium on Forensic Hair Comparisons. Quantico, Va.

Black Enterprise. 1981. "Welcome for the Defense." November.

Brookes, Warren T. 1982. *The Economy in Mind*. New York: Universe Books.

Burman, Stephen. 1979. "The Illusion of Progress: Race and Politics in Atlanta, Georgia." *Ethnic and Racial Studies* 2 (October): 441–54.

Crouch, Stanley. 1981. "Atlanta Reconstructed." *Village Voice*, April 29–May 5.

Dart, Bob. 1982. "Circus of Humanity Surrounded Williams Trial." *AC*, March 1.

Deadman, Harold A. 1984a. "Fiber Evidence and the Wayne Williams Trial (Part 1)." *FBI Law Enforcement Bulletin*, March, 13–20.

———. 1984b. "Fiber Evidence and the Wayne Williams Trial (Conclusion)." *FBI Law Enforcement Bulletin*, May, 10–19.

Dettlinger, Chet, and Jeff Prugh. 1983. *The List*. Atlanta: Philmay.

Driskell, Curtis. 1964. "The Force of 'Forward Atlanta.'" *Atlanta Magazine*, August.

Eaves, A. Reginald. 1980. "We Must Develop Community-Based Organizational Strength." *AV*, September 6.

———. 1981. "Focusing In on Criticism during Atlanta's Tragedy." *AV*, April 11.

Eisinger, Peter. 1980. *The Politics of Displacement*. New York: Academic Press.

Emmons, Nancy J. 1980. "Crimes Against Children Affect Others." *AC*, December 12.

Epstein, Gail. 1981a. "Payne's Certificate of Death Changed." *AC*, August 8.

————. 1981b. "Cooper to Review Files on 28 Slayings." *AC*, September 25.

Federal Bureau of Investigation. N.d. Prosecutive Report of Investigation Concerning Wayne Bertram Williams, ATKID, Major Case Number 30, File #7-18251. Washington, D.C.

Ferrell, Jeff. 1997. "Criminological *Verstehen:* Inside the Immediacy of Crime." *Justice Quarterly* 14 (March): 3–23.

Fischer, Mary A. 1991. "Was Wayne Williams Framed?" *GQ*, April.

Foner, Eric. 1990. *A Short History of Reconstruction.* New York: Harper and Row.

Frazier, E. Franklin. 1957. *Black Bourgeoisie.* Glencoe, Ill.: Free Press.

Garret, Franklin M. 1974. *Yesterday's Atlanta.* Miami: E. A. Seamann.

————. 1988. *Atlanta and Environs,* vol. 1. Athens: University of Georgia Press.

Gates, Harvey. 1979a. "Who Are the Niskey Road Two?" *AV*, August 4.

————. 1979b. "Who Are the Niskey Lake Two?" *AV*, August 18.

————. 1982. "The Voice of Justice Speaks." *AV*, March 13.

Georgia Department of Labor. 1980. "Market Trends." Labor Information Systems. Atlanta.

Glover, John D., and Donald C. Witham. 1989. "The Atlanta Serial Murders." *Policing* 5 (spring): 2–16.

Gossett, Thomas F. 1965. *Race.* New York: Schocken.

Gramsci, Antonio. 1977. *Selections from Political Writings (1910–1920).* Edited by Q. Hoare. Translated by J. Mathews. New York: International.

Grizzard, Lewis. 1979. "Atlanta's Going to Hell—Does Anybody Care?" *AC*, October 18.

Guardian. 1981. "5,000 Rally in D.C. to Defend Atlanta's Children." June 3.

Gulliver, Hal. 1980. "The Murdering of Children." *AC*, October 12.

————. 1981. "Tale of Two Prominent Citizens." *AC*, December 16.

Hall, Stuart, C. Critcher, T. Jefferson, J. Clarke, and B. Roberts. 1978. *Policing the Crisis.* London: Macmillan.

Harris, Art. 1981. "Unsolved Murders May Be the Key to Mayor's Contest in Atlanta." *WP*, April 20.

Headley, Bernard. 1981. "Class and Race in Atlanta: A Note on the Missing and Murdered Children." *Race and Class* 23 (summer): 81–86.

————. 1984. "Black on Black Crime: The Myth and the Reality." *Crime and Social Justice,* no. 20: 50–62.

————. 1986. "Ideological Constructions of Race and the Atlanta Tragedy." *Contemporary Crises* 10 (spring): 181–200.

Hickey, Eric. 1991. *Serial Murderers and Their Victims.* Belmont, Calif.: Brooks/Cole.

Hobson, Fred. 1981. "A South Too Busy to Hate?" In *Why the South Will Survive,* ed. Clyde N. Wilson, 45–54. Athens: University of Georgia Press.

Holmes, Ronald M., and James De Burger. 1988. *Serial Murder.* Beverly Hills: Sage.

Hunter, Floyd. 1953. *Community Power Structure*. Chapel Hill: University of North Carolina Press.

———. 1980. *Community Power Succession*. Chapel Hill: University of North Carolina Press.

Ingle, Bob. 1981. "All Right Voters: Sock It to the Bums." *AC*, October 6.

Jamieson, Duncan R. 1976. "Maynard Jackson's 1973 Election as Mayor of Atlanta." *Midwest Quarterly* 18 (1): 7–26.

Jenkins, Herbert. 1970. *Keeping the Peace*. New York: Harper and Row.

Jenkins, Philip. 1994. *Using Murder*. New York: Aldine De Gruyter.

Jennings, M. Kent. 1964. *Community Influentials: The Elites of Atlanta*. Glencoe, Ill.: Free Press.

Jones, Mack H. 1978. "Black Political Empowerment in Atlanta: Myth and Reality." *Annals*, no. 439 (September): 90–117.

Jung, Carl Gustav. 1953. *The Collected Works of C. G. Jung*. Edited by Herbert Read, Michael Fordham, and Gerhard Adler. New York: Pantheon.

———. 1968. *Analytical Psychology: Its Theory and Practice. The Tavistock Lectures*. New York: Pantheon.

———. 1975. *Critique of Psychoanalysis*. Translated by R. F. C. Hull. Princeton: Princeton University Press.

Keating, Robert, and Barry Michael Cooper. 1986. "A Question of Justice." *Spin*, September.

Leinberger, Christopher B., and Charles Lockwood. 1986. "How Business Is Reshaping America." *Atlantic*, October.

Levin, Jack, and James Alan Fox. 1985. *Mass Murder*. New York: Plenum.

Locard, Edmond. 1930. "The Analysis of Dust Traces" (in three parts). *American Journal of Police Science* 1 (3–5): 276–98, 401–18, 496–514.

Marriner, Brian. 1991. *On Death's Bloody Trail*. New York: St. Martin's Press.

Mathias, William J., and Stuart Anderson. 1973. *Horse to Helicopter: First Century of the Atlanta Police Department*. Atlanta: Georgia State University, Community Life Publications.

Mays, Benjamin E. 1979. "Mayor Not to Blame for Crime Spurt." Letter, *AJ*, July 18.

McMillan, George. 1961. "Atlanta's Peaceful Blow for Justice." *Life*, September 15.

Mills, C. Wright. 1956. *The Power Elite*. New York: Oxford University Press.

Mitchell, E. J., and D. Holland. 1979. "An Unusual Case of Identification of Transferred Fibres." *Journal of the Forensic Science Society* 19 (23): 23–26.

Montgomery, Bill. 1981. "Penelope Street Media Stakeout and Event with a Touch of Slapstick." *AJ&C*, June 7.

National Geographic. 1969. "Atlanta, Pacesetter City of the South." February.

Newsweek. 1980a. "The Mood of Ghetto America." June 2.

———. 1980b. "Worry Time for Blacks." December 1.

New York Times. 1981a. "Tests Due on Two Skeletons Found in Atlanta's Search for Children." January 10.

————. 1981b. "Two Skeletons in Atlanta Linked to Missing Youths." January 11.

————. 1981c. "Reagan Agrees to Meeting on Child Slayings in Atlanta." January 30.

————. 1981d. "Investigators Feel Many Killers, Separately, Slew Atlanta Children." March 15.

————. 1981e. "Tension over Atlanta Killings Tests Racial Harmony." March 24.

————. 1981f. "Four Deaths in Atlanta Called Solved." April 13.

Omi, Michael, and Howard Winant. 1986. *Racial Formation in the United States.* New York: Routledge and Kegan Paul.

Oney, Steve. 1981. "A City Robbed of Light." *Atlanta Weekly,* April 19.

O'Reilly, Kenneth. 1989. *Racial Matters.* New York: Free Press.

Orfield, Gary, and Carole Ashkinaze. 1991. *The Closing Door.* Chicago: University of Chicago Press.

Outhwaite, William. 1976. *Understanding Social Life: The Method Called Verstehen.* New York: Holmes and Meier.

Patterson, Pat. 1974. "Atlanta." *Black Enterprise,* February.

Powledge, Fred. 1973. "A New Politics in Atlanta." *New Yorker,* December 31.

Raspberry, William. 1981. "Atlanta: Doing Something—Anything." *WP,* May 29.

Reed, Adolph Jr. 1981. "Narcissistic Politics in Atlanta." *Telos,* no. 48 (summer): 98–105.

Revolutionary Communist Party (RCP). N.d. "The Atlanta Youth Murders—Portent of the Future." Flyer. Atlanta.

Rice, Bradley R. 1983. "If Dixie Were Atlanta." In *Sunbelt Cities,* ed. Richard M. Bernard and Bradley R. Rice, 31–57. Austin: University of Texas Press.

Richie Mann, Cora Mae. 1993. *Unequal Justice.* Bloomington: Indiana University Press.

Roberts, Paul, and Chris Willmore. 1993. *The Royal Commission on Criminal Justice: The Role of Forensic Science Evidence in Criminal Proceedings.* London: HMSO Publications.

Rodrigue, George. 1981. "The Murdered Children's Case Now Jackson's Primary Goal." *AC,* February 8.

Rowan, Carl. 1981. "Blacks Have to 'Cool It' over Deaths." *WP,* March 4.

Sack, Kevin. 1982. "Prosecutor Mallard Has Records as Crafty, Professional Examiner." *AC,* February 24.

Schlefer, Jonathan. 1982. "A Tale of Two Cities." *Progressive,* October.

Schwendinger, Herman, and Julia Siegel Schwendinger. 1985. *Adolescent Subcultures and Delinquency.* New York: Praeger.

Shipp, Bill. 1981a. "Atlanta: A City Too Busy to Care?" *AC,* October 27.

————. 1981b. "Changes in the Hunt for Child Slayers." *AC,* February 13.

————. 1981c. "On Assailing the FBI's Director." *AC,* April 17.

Stone, Clarence N. 1976. *Economic Growth and Neighborhood Discontent.* Chapel Hill: University of North Carolina Press.

STOP (Committee to Stop Children's Murders). N.d.[a] "Join Us!" Pamphlet. Atlanta.

———. N.d.[b] "Save Our Children." Brochure. Atlanta.

Thiel, Paul. 1991. "Jesse Hill's Dilemma." *Georgia Trend*, March.

Tierney, John. 1981. "Common Threads from Atlanta." *Science* 2 (September): 18.

Time. 1980. "Terror on Atlanta's South Side." November 3.

———. 1981a. "The 27th Victim." May 25.

———. 1981b. "At Last, at Least a Suspect." June 15.

———. 1982. "A Web of Fiber and Fact." March 8.

Truzzi, Marcello. 1974. *Verstehen: Subjective Understanding in the Social Sciences*. Reading, Mass.: Addison-Wesley.

Turner, Patricia. 1993. *I Heard It Through the Grapevine: Rumor in African-American Culture*. Berkeley: University of California Press.

United Youth Adult Conference. N.d. "The United Youth Adult Conference: Bridging the Gap Between Yesterday, Today, and Tomorrow." Booklet. Atlanta.

USA Today. 1985. "Williams Defense Claims Klan Document Withheld." November 1.

U.S. Department of Commerce. 1980a. "State, County, and Selected City Employment and Unemployment." June. Washington, D.C.: Government Printing Office.

———. 1980b. *Average Household Income by Census Tracts, Atlanta SMSA*. September 1980. Bureau of the Census. Washington, D.C.: Government Printing Office.

———. 1980c. *Atlanta, Georgia, Census of Population and Housing*. September 1980. Bureau of the Census. Washington, D.C.: Government Printing Office.

U.S. Department of Labor. 1980. "Moving to the Sun: Regional Job Growth, 1968 to 1978." *Monthly Labor Review*, March. Bureau of Labor Statistics. Washington, D.C.: Government Printing Office.

WABE (Atlanta Public Radio). 1981. "Southwinds." February 23. Atlanta.

Wall Street Journal. 1978. "Atlanta's Airport Feels Growth Pains in Surge of Cut-Rate Travelers." October 23.

———. 1979a. "Pressure to Choose More Black Bankers Mounts in Atlanta." March 6.

———. 1979b. "Crime Wave in Atlanta Threatens Bid to Lure Business, Conventions." August 8.

———. 1980. "Bustling Atlanta Seems Built More for Outsiders than Its Own." September 23.

———. 1981. "Atlanta's Boosters, Businesses Agonize over Child Murders." June 2.

Washington Post. 1981a. "Baffled Police Seek Another Missing Child in Atlanta." January 8.

————. 1981b. "Fearful City Counts Dead—and Waits." January 13.

————. 1981c. "Police in Atlanta Question Suspect in Kidnap Attempt." January 17.

————. 1981d. "Atlanta Gets More Aid from Justice Department in Probing Murders." February 8.

————. 1981e. "Barry on Atlanta." March 19.

————. 1981f. "How Not to Help Atlanta." Editorial, March 20.

————. 1981g. "City 'Too Busy to Hate' May Be Set to Crack." March 23.

————. 1981h. "Police Identify 22d Victim in Atlanta Killings." April 1.

————. 1981i. "Atlanta Toll Hits 25 as Another Corpse Is Found in River." April 22.

————. 1981j. "CORE Chief Says Innis Acts on Own." April 24.

————. 1981k. "Hawkers Turn Rally for Atlanta Children into a Market." May 26.

Watts, Eugene. 1973. "The Police in Atlanta: 1890–1905." *Journal of Southern History* 39 (May): 165–82.

WGST News Radio 92. 1980a. Editorial no. 143. October 27. Atlanta.

————. 1980b. Editorial no. 144. October 28. Atlanta.

White, Dana F. 1982. "The Black Sides of Atlanta: A Geography of Expansion and Containment, 1870–1970." *Atlanta Historical Journal* 26 (summer/fall): 199–225.

White, Dana F., and Timothy J. Crimmins. 1978. "How Atlanta Grew: Cool Heads, Hot Air, and Hard Work." *Atlanta Economic Review* 28 (January): 7–15.

Williams, Juan. 1981. "Atlanta on Trial: Still No Solution." *WP*, March 12.

Williamson, Joel. 1984. *The Crucible of Race.* New York: Oxford University Press.

Willis, Ken. 1982. "Williams Deluded Himself, Friend Says." *AJ*, February 5.

Wilson, William J. 1978. *The Declining Significance of Race.* Chicago: University of Chicago Press.

Index

Index

Bernard Headley has been a professor of criminology and criminal justice at Northeastern Illinois University, Chicago, since 1983. Before that—and during the time of the events described in this book—he was a principal research investigator at the Criminal Justice Institute at Atlanta University (now Clark Atlanta University). He has written widely on issues relating to race, crime, and criminal justice in the United States and in his native Jamaica, including, most recently, *The Jamaican Crime Scene: A Perspective.*